enVision® Mathematics

Volume 1 Topics 1–7

Authors

Randall I. Charles
Professor Emeritus
Department of Mathematics
San Jose State University
San Jose, California

Jennifer Bay-Williams
Professor of Mathematics
Education
College of Education and Human
Development
University of Louisville
Louisville, Kentucky

Robert Q. Berry, III
Professor of Mathematics
Education
Department of Curriculum,
Instruction and Special Education
University of Virginia
Charlottesville, Virginia

Janet H. Caldwell
Professor Emerita
Department of Mathematics
Rowan University
Glassboro, New Jersey

Zachary Champagne
Assistant in Research
Florida Center for Research in
Science, Technology, Engineering,
and Mathematics (FCR-STEM)
Jacksonville, Florida

Juanita Copley
Professor Emerita
College of Education
University of Houston
Houston, Texas

Warren Crown
Professor Emeritus of Mathematics
Education
Graduate School of Education
Rutgers University
New Brunswick, New Jersey

Francis (Skip) Fennell
Professor Emeritus of
Education and Graduate and
Professional Studies
McDaniel College
Westminster, Maryland

Karen Karp
Professor of Mathematics Education
School of Education
Johns Hopkins University
Baltimore, Maryland

Stuart J. Murphy
Visual Learning Specialist
Boston, Massachusetts

Jane F. Schielack
Professor Emerita
Department of Mathematics
Texas A&M University
College Station, Texas

Jennifer M. Suh
Associate Professor for
Mathematics Education
George Mason University
Fairfax, Virginia

Jonathan A. Wray
Mathematics Supervisor
Howard County Public Schools
Ellicott City, Maryland

SAVVAS
LEARNING COMPANY

Mathematicians

Roger Howe
Professor of Mathematics
Yale University
New Haven, Connecticut

Gary Lippman
Professor of Mathematics and
Computer Science
California State University, East Bay
Hayward, California

ELL Consultants

Janice R. Corona
Independent Education Consultant
Dallas, Texas

Jim Cummins
Professor
The University of Toronto
Toronto, Canada

Reviewers

Katina Arnold
Teacher
Liberty Public School District
Kansas City, Missouri

Christy Bennett
Elementary Math and Science
Specialist
DeSoto County Schools
Hernando, Mississippi

Shauna Bostick
Elementary Math Specialist
Lee County School District
Tupelo, Mississippi

Samantha Brant
Teacher
Platte County School District
Platte City, Missouri

Jamie Clark
Elementary Math Coach
Allegany County Public Schools
Cumberland, Maryland

Shauna Gardner
Math and Science Instructional Coach
DeSoto County Schools
Hernando, Mississippi

Kathy Graham
Educational Consultant
Twin Falls, Idaho

Andrea Hamilton
K-5 Math Specialist
Lake Forest School District
Felton, Delaware

Susan Hankins
Instructional Coach
Tupelo Public School District
Tupelo, Mississippi

Barb Jamison
Teacher
Excelsior Springs School District
Excelsior Springs, Missouri

Pam Jones
Elementary Math Coach
Lake Region School District
Bridgton, Maine

Sherri Kane
Secondary Mathematics
Curriculum Specialist
Lee's Summit R7 School District
Lee's Summit, Missouri

Jessica Leonard
ESOL Teacher
Volusia County Schools
DeLand, Florida

Jill K. Milton
Elementary Math Coordinator
Norwood Public Schools
Norwood, Massachusetts

Jamie Pickett
Teacher
Platte County School District
Kansas City, Missouri

Mandy Schall
Math Coach
Allegany County Public Schools
Cumberland, Maryland

Marjorie Stevens
Math Consultant
Utica Community Schools
Shelby Township, Michigan

Shyree Stevenson
ELL Teacher
Penns Grove-Carneys Point
Regional School District
Penns Grove, New Jersey

Kayla Stone
Teacher
Excelsior Springs School District
Excelsior Springs, Missouri

Sara Sultan
PD Academic Trainer, Math
Tucson Unified School District
Tucson, Arizona

Angela Waltrup
Elementary Math Content Specialist
Washington County Public Schools
Hagerstown, Maryland

ISBN-13:   978-0-13-495368-7
ISBN-10:   0-13-495368-1
14 2022

Digital Resources

You'll be using these digital resources throughout the year!

Go to SavvasRealize.com

 Interactive Student Edition

Access online or offline.

 Visual Learning

Interact with visual learning animations.

 Interactive Additional Practice Workbook

Access online or offline.

 Activity

Solve a problem and share your thinking.

 Videos

Watch Math Practices Animations, Another Look Videos, and clips to support 3-Act Math.

 Practice Buddy

Do interactive practice online.

 Math Tools

Explore math with digital tools.

 Games

Play math games to help you learn.

 Glossary

Read and listen in English and Spanish.

 Assessment

Show what you've learned.

SAVVAS **realize**™ Everything you need for math anytime, anywhere

Contents

Digital Resources at SavvasRealize.com

And remember your Interactive Student Edition is available at SavvasRealize.com!

TOPICS

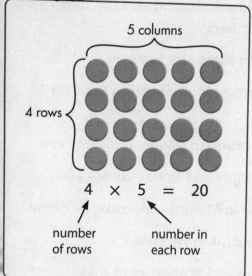

You can represent multiplication as an array with equal rows and columns.

5 columns

4 rows

$4 \times 5 = 20$

number of rows

number in each row

TOPIC 1 Understand Multiplication and Division of Whole Numbers

You can use patterns to help remember multiplication facts.

DATA

9s Facts

$0 \times 9 = 0$

$1 \times 9 = 9$

$2 \times 9 = 18$

$3 \times 9 = 27$

$4 \times 9 = 36$

$5 \times 9 = 45$

$6 \times 9 = 54$

$7 \times 9 =$

$8 \times 9 =$

$9 \times 9 =$

TOPIC 2 Multiplication Facts: Use Patterns

Properties can help you use known facts to find unknown facts.

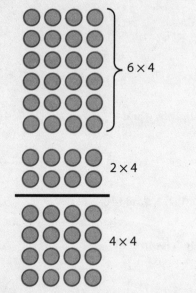

6×4

2×4

4×4

TOPIC 3 Apply Properties: Multiplication Facts for 3, 4, 6, 7, 8

Multiplication facts can help you learn division facts.

Multiplication
3 rows of 10 drums
$3 \times 10 = 30$
30 drums

Division
30 drums in 3 equal rows
$30 \div 3 = 10$
10 drums in each row

TOPIC 4 Use Multiplication to Divide: Division Facts

You can use a multiplication table to find missing factors.

$3 \times 5 = 15$ $15 \div 3 = 5$

×	0	1	2	3	4	5
0	0	0	0	0	0	0
1	0	1	2	3	4	5
2	0	2	4	6	8	10
3	0	3	6	9	12	15

TOPIC 5 Fluently Multiply and Divide within 100

You can find the area of a shape by counting the number of unit squares needed to cover it.

TOPIC 6 Connect Area to Multiplication and Addition

You can use a scaled bar graph to help compare data.

Amount Greg Saved Each Month

TOPIC 7 Represent and Interpret Data

TOPIC 8 in Volume 2
Use Strategies and Properties to Add and Subtract

TOPIC 9 in Volume 2
Fluently Add and Subtract within 1,000

TOPIC 10 in Volume 2
Multiply by Multiples of 10

TOPIC 11 in Volume 2
Use Operations with Whole Numbers to Solve Problems

TOPIC 12 in volume 2
Understand Fractions as Numbers

TOPIC 13 in volume 2
Fraction Equivalence and Comparison

TOPIC 16 in Volume 2
Solve Perimeter Problems

Math Practices and
Problem Solving Handbook

The **Math Practices and Problem Solving Handbook** is available at SavvasRealize.com.

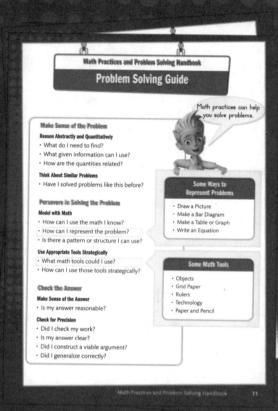

Math Practices

Problem Solving Guide
Problem Solving Recording Sheet
Bar Diagrams

Understand Multiplication and Division of Whole Numbers

Essential Question: How can thinking about equal groups help you understand the connection between multiplication and division?

Some animals form groups.

Being in a group can help birds survive.

That's teamwork! Here's a project on animals using multiplication and division.

enVision STEM Project: Forming Groups

Do Research Many types of animals form groups. Use the Internet or other sources to discover which animals form groups. Why do they do this? What are the benefits for these animals of being in a group?

Journal: Write a Report Include what you found. Also in your report:

- Draw representations of animals in equal groups. Give a reason why those animals formed groups.

- Use a multiplication equation to show the total number of animals. Use a division equation to show the number of animals in each group.

Name_____

Review What You Know

A-Z Vocabulary

Choose the best term from the box.
Write it on the blank.

| • add | • subtract |
| • skip count | • ones |

1. If you combine different sized groups to find how many in all, you

_____.

2. _____ are groups of single objects.

3. When you say the numbers 5, 10, 15, 20, you _____.

Adding

Find each sum.

4. $5 + 5 + 5 = ?$

5. $7 + 7 = ?$

6. $3 + 3 + 3 = ?$

7. $2 + 2 + 2 + 2 = ?$

8. $6 + 6 + 6 = ?$

9. $9 + 9 + 9 = ?$

Subtracting

Find each difference.

10. $21 - 7 = ?$
$14 - 7 = ?$
$7 - 7 = ?$

11. $15 - 5 = ?$
$10 - 5 = ?$
$5 - 5 = ?$

12. $27 - 9 = ?$
$18 - 9 = ?$
$9 - 9 = ?$

Skip Counting on the Number Line

13. If you continue skip counting using the same pattern, what will be the next number?

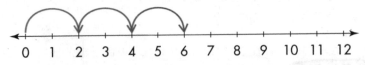

Ⓐ 8

Ⓑ 10

Ⓒ 12

Ⓓ 14

PROJECT 1A

What is the tallest building in Florida?

Project: Construct a Tall Building

PROJECT 1B

Would you like to travel to another planet?

Project: Build a Space Probe

PROJECT 1C

What are some places where you would like to live?

Project: Draw a Neighborhood

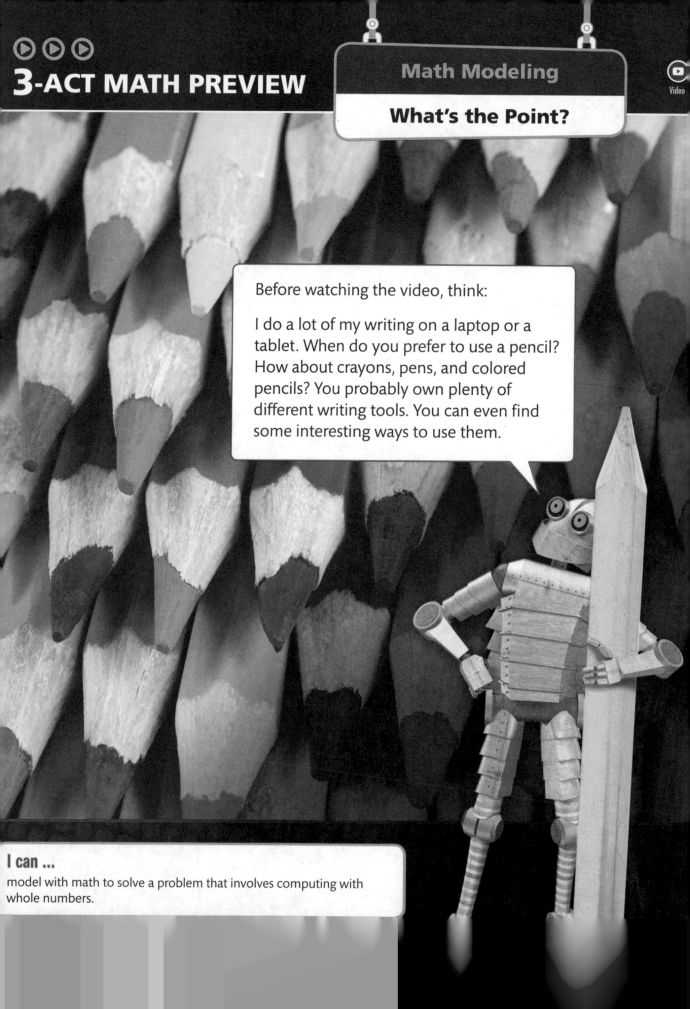

Math Modeling

What's the Point?

▶ Video

Before watching the video, think:

I do a lot of my writing on a laptop or a tablet. When do you prefer to use a pencil? How about crayons, pens, and colored pencils? You probably own plenty of different writing tools. You can even find some interesting ways to use them.

I can ...
model with math to solve a problem that involves computing with whole numbers.

Name _____

Solve & Share

Ms. Witt bought 4 boxes of paint with
5 jars of paint in each box. Ms. Karp bought 3 boxes
of paint with 6 jars in each box. Who bought more
jars of paint? How many more?

I can ...
use addition or multiplication
to join equal groups.

I can also make sense of problems.

ms.Witt
4

$5 \times 4 = 20$

| 5 | 5 | 5 | 5 | = 20

2 more than
Ms.Karp

Ms.Karp
3

You can use
counters, bar diagrams,
drawings, or equations to
make sense and persevere
in solving the problem.

| 6 | 6 | 6 | = 18

$6 \times 3 = 18$

Look Back! How can you use counters and addition
equations to help solve the problems?

A

Jessie used 3 bags to bring home the goldfish she won at the Fun Fair. She put the same number of goldfish in each bag. How many goldfish did she win?

I can use counters to show the groups.

8 goldfish in each bag

B The counters show 3 groups of 8 goldfish.

You can use addition to join **equal groups**.

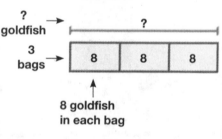

? goldfish

3 bags

8 goldfish in each bag

$8 + 8 + 8 = 24$

C **Multiplication** is an operation that gives the total number when you join equal groups.

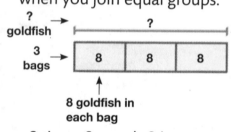

? goldfish

3 bags

8 | 8 | 8

8 goldfish in each bag

3 times 8 equals 24

$$3 \times 8 = 24$$

factor factor product

Factors are the numbers that are being multiplied. The **product** is the answer to a multiplication problem.

D You can write **equations**.

An **unknown** is a symbol that stands for a number in an equation.

Addition equation:
$8 + 8 + 8 = ?$
$8 + 8 + 8 = 24$

Multiplication equation:
$3 \times 8 = ?$
$3 \times 8 = 24$

Jessie won 24 goldfish.

Convince Me! **Model with Math** Suppose Jessie won 5 bags of 8 goldfish. Use math you know to represent the problem and find the number of goldfish Jessie won.

$5 \times 8 = 40$

$8 + 8 + 8 + 8 + 8 = 40$

Guided Practice

Do You Understand?

1. Can you write $5 + 5 + 5 + 5 = 20$ as a multiplication equation? Explain.

$5 \times 4 = 20$
yes they are equal groups

2. Can you write $3 + 4 + 7 = 14$ as a multiplication equation? Explain.

$3+4+7=14.$
No, There is no equal groups
Found $7 \times 2 = 14$

3. Jessie buys 4 packages of stones. There are 6 stones in each package. How many stones does Jessie buy?

$6+6+6+6=24$

Use counters to represent the problem. Then write an addition equation and a multiplication equation to solve.

Do You Know How?

Complete **4** and **5**. Use the pictures to help.

4.

2 groups of 4

$4 + 4 = 8$

$2 \times 4 = 8$

5.

3 groups of 6

$6 + 6 + 6 = 18$

$3 \times 6 = 18$

Independent Practice

Leveled Practice Complete **6** and **7**. Use the pictures to help.

6.

2 groups of 5

$5 + 5 = 10$

$2 \times 5 = 10$

7.

5 groups of 4

$4 + 4 + 4 + 4 + 4 = 20$

$5 \times 4 = 20$

In **8–11**, complete each equation. Use counters or draw a picture to help.

8. $8 + 8 + 8 + 8 = 4 \times 8$

9. $7 + 7 + 7 = 3 \times 7$

10. $9 + 9 + 9 = 3 \times 9$

11. $6 + 6 + 6 + 6 + 6 = 5 \times 6$

Problem Solving

12. Debra draws this shape on the back of her notebook.

What is the name of the shape Debra draws? How do you know?

13. Model with Math Salvatore gets 50 trading cards for his birthday. He gives 22 cards to Madison, and Madison gives 18 cards to Salvatore. Then Salvatore's sister gives him 14 cards. How many trading cards does Salvatore have now? Use math to represent the problem.

$50 - 22 = 18 + 14 =$

14. Higher Order Thinking Luke says you can always add and you can always multiply to join groups. Is he correct? Explain why or why not.

15. Lois says any addition equation where the addends are all the same can be written as a multiplication equation. Is Lois correct? Explain why or why not.

☑ Assessment Practice

16. Tom has 12 ears of field corn to make table decorations. He arranges them in equal groups. Which sentences could Tom use to describe his groups? Select all that are correct.

- ☐ Tom arranged 2 groups of 4 ears.
- ☐ Tom arranged 4 groups of 2 ears.
- ☐ Tom arranged 6 groups of 2 ears.
- ☐ Tom arranged 3 groups of 4 ears.
- ☐ Tom arranged 1 group of 10 ears.

17. Jenna has 24 flowers. She arranges them in vases with an equal number of flowers in each vase. Which sentences could Jenna use to describe her flowers? Select all that are correct.

- ☐ Jenna arranged 4 flowers in each of 6 vases.
- ☐ Jenna arranged 3 flowers in each of 9 vases.
- ☐ Jenna arranged 5 flowers in each of 5 vases.
- ☐ Jenna arranged 6 flowers in each of 3 vases.
- ☐ Jenna arranged 8 flowers in each of 3 vases.

Name_____

Solve & Share

Harvey the Hop Toad starts at 0 and jumps 7 times in the same direction. Each time he jumps 3 inches farther. How can you show how far Harvey goes on a number line?

I can ...
use a number line to represent and solve multiplication facts.

I can also model with math.

Model with math. A number line can be used to record and count equal groups.

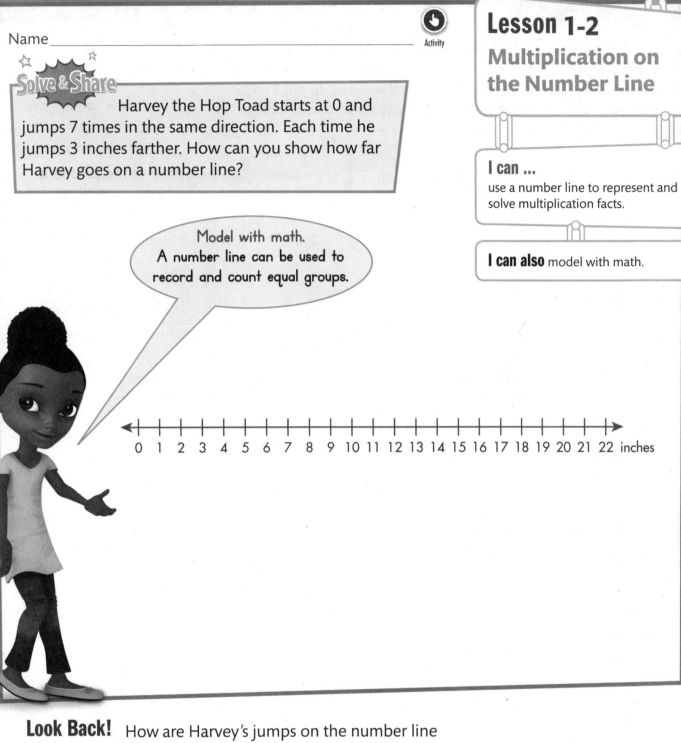

0 1 2 3 4 5 6 7 8 9 10 11 12 13 14 15 16 17 18 19 20 21 22 inches

Look Back! How are Harvey's jumps on the number line like repeated addition? How are they like skip counting?

How Can You Use a Number Line to Show Multiplication?

A

Clara is making gift bags for her 5 friends. She wants to put 3 glitter pens in each gift bag. How many glitter pens does Clara need?

You can use a number line and skip counting to show multiplication.

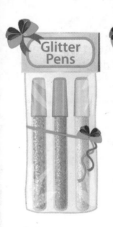     

B

Draw arrows on the number line to show the number of glitter pens for each gift bag.

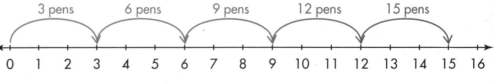

Skip counting: 3, 6, 9, 12, 15

Multiplication: $5 \times 3 = 15$

Clara needs 15 glitter pens.

 Convince Me! **Reasoning** What would skip counting by 6 look like on the number line?

Practice Tools Assessmen

☆ Guided Practice

Do You Understand?

1. On the previous page, why do you skip count by 3s on the number line?

Each jump represents the number of girrfty pens in each gift bag.

2. On the previous page, why do you make five jumps on the number line?

I skiped count by five to reprsent the amout of gift bag.

3. How would the jumps on the number line look different if there were 4 pens in each gift bag? There would be five jump of four.

Do You Know How?

In **4**, complete the arrows on the number line to show the jumps and fill in the blanks.

4. Jim ran 3 miles a day for 4 days in a row. How many miles did he run?

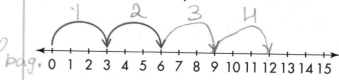

Number of jumps: __4__

I skip counted by __3__.

Jim ran __12__ miles.

$$\underline{3} \times \underline{4} = \underline{12}$$

Independent Practice ☆

In **5**, show how you found the solution using the number line.

5. Judy has 6 fruit baskets. She wants to put 2 apples into each basket. How many apples will she need? Draw the remaining jumps on the number line with arrows to show how many apples Judy will need.

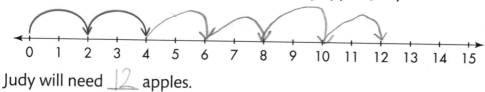

Judy will need __12__ apples.

In **6** and **7**, show the multiplication fact with arrows on the number line. Write the product.

6. $7 \times 2 = \underline{14}$

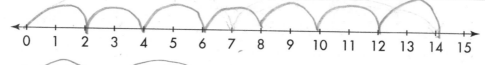

7. $3 \times 3 = \underline{9}$

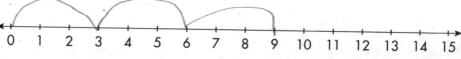

Problem Solving

8. Nikki wants to use 3 glass beads in each necklace she is making. She wants to make 6 necklaces. How many glass beads will Nikki need? Use skip counting and write a multiplication equation to solve.

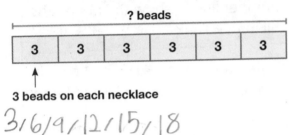

? beads

| 3 | 3 | 3 | 3 | 3 | 3 |

3 beads on each necklace

3/6/9/12/15/18

6×3=18

9. enVision® STEM Guinea pigs in the wild usually live in groups of between 5 and 10. The group members can warn each other of danger. If there are 2 groups of 7 guinea pigs, how many guinea pigs are there in all? Use the number line to solve.

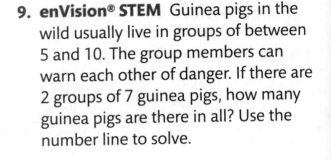

---

10. Make Sense and Persevere Tim drew this number line to show the multiplication fact $4 \times 2 = 8$.

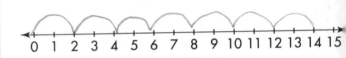

Which parts of the number line represent the factors? Which part shows the product?

11. Higher Order Thinking Draw a number line to compare skip counting by 3s four times and skip counting by 4s three times. How are they different? How are they alike?

---

12. Which of the following contexts does the number line and the expression 5×2 represent?

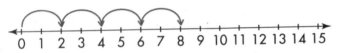

- Ⓐ 5 groups with 5 pens in each
- Ⓑ 5 groups with 2 pens in each
- Ⓒ 2 groups with 2 pens in each
- Ⓓ 2 groups with 5 pens in each

13. Which of the following contexts does the number line and the expression 5×3 represent?

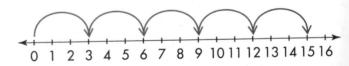

- Ⓐ 5 shelves with 5 books on each
- Ⓑ 3 shelves with 5 books on each
- Ⓒ 5 shelves with 3 books on each
- Ⓓ 3 shelves with 3 books on each

Name_____

★ ☆ ★
Solve & Share

Mark has 12 sports cards. He arranges the cards with an equal number in each row. Find ways Mark can arrange his cards.

I can ...
use arrays and multiply factors in any order to solve multiplication problems.

I can also choose and use a math tool to help solve problems.

You can use appropriate tools. Sometimes using counters or objects can help you solve a problem.

Number of Rows of Cards	Number of Cards in Each Row	Total Number of Cards

Look Back! What do you notice about the number of rows of cards, the number of cards in each row, and the total number of cards? Explain.

Essential Question

How Does an Array Show Multiplication?

A

Dana keeps her swimming medal collection in a display on the wall.

The display has 4 rows. Each row has 5 medals. How many medals are in Dana's collection?

The medals are in an array. An array shows objects in equal rows and columns.

B

The counters show 4 rows and 5 columns.

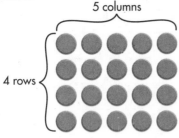

5 columns

4 rows

Each row is a group. You can use addition or skip counting to find the total.

Addition: $5 + 5 + 5 + 5 = 20$
Skip counting: 5, 10, 15, 20

C

Multiplication can also be used to find the total in an array.

You say, "4 times 5 equals 20."

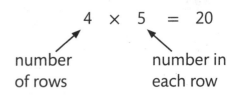

$$4 \times 5 = 20$$

number of rows   number in each row

There are 20 medals in Dana's collection.

Convince Me! **Construct Arguments** Jason also has a swimming medal collection. His display has 5 rows with 5 medals in each row. Draw an array for Jason's medals. Use skip counting to find the total number of medals. Then write a multiplication equation for your array. Who has more medals, Jason or Dana?

Jason has more medils then dana. Beacuse 25 is more than 20.

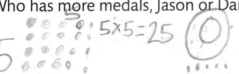

5   5×5=25 ⓞ   20

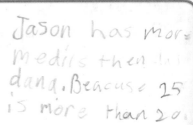

14   Topic 1 | Lesson 1-3

Another Example!

Dana rearranged her swimming medal collection.
The arrays have the same number of medals.

The Commutative (Order) Property of Multiplication says you can multiply numbers in any order and the product is the same. So, 4 × 5 = 5 × 4.

Original Array

$4 \times 5 = 20$

New Array

$5 \times 4 = 20$

☆ Guided Practice

Do You Understand?

1. Mia puts muffins in 4 rows with 7 muffins in each row. Draw an array to find the total number of muffins.

$4 \times 7 = 28$

$7 \times 4 = 28$

2. Complete the following statement.

$4 \times 7 = 28$, so $7 \times 4 =$ _____.

Do You Know How?

In **3**, write and solve a multiplication equation for the array.

3.

Independent Practice ☆

In **4** and **5**, fill in the blanks to show skip counting and multiplication for each array.

4.

2, 4, _6_, _8_

$4 \times \underline{2} = 8$

4, _2_

$2 \times \underline{2} = 8$

5.   [array of dots]

3, 6, _9_, _12_

$4 \times \underline{3} = 12$

4, _6_, _8_

$3 \times \underline{4} = 12$

Problem Solving

6. Liza draws these two arrays. How are the arrays alike? How are they different?

The first one is a colume and the second one is a row and the same is that they both have 15.

7. Use Structure Chen arranged 16 berries in the array shown below. Use counters to help complete the table to show other arrays Chen can make with the same number of berries.

Number of Rows of Berries		Number of Berries in Each Row		Total Number of Berries
4	×	4	=	16
8	×	2	=	16
2	×	8	=	16
16	×	1	=	16
1	×	16	=	16

8. Higher Order Thinking Ramón says he can use the Commutative Property of Multiplication to show the product of 4 × 6 is the same as the product of 3 × 8. Is he correct? Why or why not?

4×6=24   3×8=24
yes because the numbers are just diffrent numbers so it is the same.

9. Delbert put 5 nickels in each of his 3 empty piggy banks. How many nickels did Delbert put in the banks? Write a multiplication equation to show how you solved the problem.

3×5=15

? nickels

3 piggy banks →

5	5	5

5 nickels in each bank

Assessment Practice

10. An equation is shown.

$8 \times 5 = 5 \times \square$

Use the Commutative Property of Multiplication to find the missing factor.

Ⓐ 5

Ⓑ 8

Ⓒ 40

Ⓓ 85

11. Using the Commutative Property of Multiplication, which of the following expressions is equivalent to 5 × 4?

Ⓐ 5 + 5

Ⓑ 4 × 5

Ⓒ 5 + 4

Ⓓ 5 − 4

Name_____

Activity

☆ ☆
Solve & Share

Six friends picked 48 grapefruits. They want to share them equally. How many grapefruits should each friend get?

I can ...
use objects or pictures to show how objects can be divided into equal groups.

I can also model with math.

$16 + 16 + 16 = 48$

$8 + 8 + 8 + 8 + 8 + 8$

$6 = 8 = 42$

$48 \div 8 = 48$

+ / + addition

x / (– – subtraction

(x – multiplication) ÷

÷ division

Model with math. Using objects or drawing a picture that represents the problem can help you solve it.

Look Back! How can you use counters to help solve this problem? Explain.

Three friends have 12 toys to share equally. How many toys will each friend get?

Think of arranging 12 toys into 3 equal groups.

Division is an operation that is used to find how many equal groups there are or how many are in each group.

What You Think
Put one toy at a time in each group.

12 toys

4 toys for each friend

When all the toys are grouped, there will be 4 in each group.

C What You Write
You can write a division equation to find the number in each group.

$$12 \div 3 = 4$$

Total — Number of equal groups — Number in each group

Each friend will get 4 toys.

Convince Me! **Be Precise** What would happen if 3 friends wanted to share 13 toys equally? The thercten is not a eaqeal and I left over

Name _____

☆ Guided Practice

Do You Understand?

1. Eighteen eggs are divided into 3 rows. How many eggs are in each row? Use the bar diagram to solve.

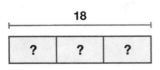

18 ÷ 3 = __6__ eggs

2. Can 12 grapes be shared equally among 5 children with no grapes remaining? Explain. NO because there is not that much.

Do You Know How?

In **3** and **4**, draw a picture to solve.

3. Fifteen bananas are shared equally by 3 monkeys. How many bananas does each monkey get?

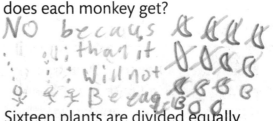

NO becaus that it Will not Be eag

4. Sixteen plants are divided equally into 4 pots. How many plants are in each pot?

☆ Independent Practice ☆

In **5** and **6**, draw a picture to solve.

5. Eighteen marbles are divided equally into 6 sacks. How many marbles are in each sack?

Yes

6. Sixteen crayons are shared equally by 2 people. How many crayons does each person have?

In **7–10**, complete each equation.

7. $12 \div 2 = \boxed{6}$

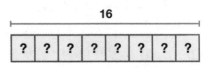

8. $16 \div 8 = \boxed{2}$

16							
?	?	?	?	?	?	?	?

9. $9 \div 3 = \underline{5}$

10. $14 \div 7 = \underline{2}$

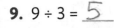

Problem Solving

11. Jim is putting 18 pens into equal groups. He says if he puts them into 2 equal groups he will have more pens in each group than if he puts them into 3 equal groups. Is Jim correct? Explain.

12. Make Sense and Persevere Ms. Terry's class is hosting a fundraising challenge. The students in her class are divided into 4 teams. Each team has an equal number of students. Do you have enough information to find how many students are on each team? Explain.

13. Erika draws a hexagon. Maria draws a pentagon. Who draws the shape with more sides? How many more sides does that shape have?

14. The flag bearers in a parade march in 9 rows with 5 flags in each row. Write an equation to show how many flags there are.

15. Number Sense Jenn and some friends share 40 jellybeans equally. Is the number that each friend gets greater than 40 or less than 40? Explain.

16. Higher Order Thinking Joy has 12 shells. She gives 2 shells to her mom. Then she and her sister share the rest of the shells equally. How many shells does Joy get? How many shells does her sister get? How do you know?

✓ **Assessment Practice**

17. Which of the following contexts does the expression $14 \div 2$ represent?

- Ⓐ 14 pens arranged in 14 equal groups
- Ⓑ 2 pens arranged in 14 equal groups
- Ⓒ 14 pens arranged in 2 equal groups
- Ⓓ 2 pens arranged in 2 equal groups

18. Which of the following contexts does the expression $12 \div 3$ represent?

- Ⓐ 12 books arranged equally on 3 shelves
- Ⓑ 12 books arranged equally on 12 shelves
- Ⓒ 3 books arranged equally on 12 shelves
- Ⓓ 3 books arranged equally on 3 shelves

Name _____

★ ☆ ★ ☆
Solve & Share

Li made 12 tacos. He wants to give some of his friends 2 tacos each. If Li does not get any of the tacos, how many of his friends will get tacos?

I can ...
use repeated subtraction to understand and solve division problems.

I can also reason about math.

You can use reasoning. How can what you know about sharing help you solve the problem?

Look Back! How can counters or other objects help you show your work?

Essential Question

How Can You Divide Using Repeated Subtraction?

A

June has 10 strawberries to serve to her guests. If each guest eats 2 strawberries, how many guests can June serve?

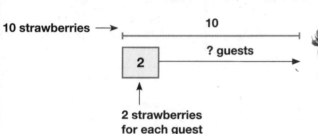

10 strawberries →

10

? guests

2

2 strawberries for each guest

B

You can use repeated subtraction to find how many groups of 2 are in 10.

$10 - 2 = 8$
$8 - 2 = 6$
$6 - 2 = 4$
$4 - 2 = 2$
$2 - 2 = 0$

You can subtract 2 five times. There are five groups of 2 in 10.

There are no strawberries left.

June can serve 5 guests.

C

You can write a division equation to find the number of groups.

Write: $10 \div 2 = ?$

Read: Ten divided by 2 equals what number?

Solve: $10 \div 2 = 5$

June can serve 5 guests.

Convince Me! **Model with Math** In the example above, what if each guest ate 5 strawberries? Use math you know to represent the problem and find how many guests June could serve.

Name_____

☆ Guided Practice

Do You Understand?

1. There are 3 boxes with 2 toys in each box. The total number of toys can be expressed as $3 \times 2 = 6$. What is meant by $6 \div 3 = 2$? What is meant by $6 \div 2 = 3$?

Do You Know How?

In **2** and **3**, use counters or draw a picture to solve.

2. The lost and found box has 16 gloves. There are 2 gloves in each pair. How many pairs of gloves are there?

6 pairs

3. Ruth gives her dogs 15 treats. Each dog gets 3 treats. How many dogs does Ruth have?

5 dogs

Independent Practice ☆

Leveled Practice In **4** and **5**, complete the equations.

4. Rosa picks 14 apples. She places 7 apples in each bag. How many bags does Rosa have?

$14 - 7 = \underline{7}$
$\underline{14} - 7 = \underline{7}$

$\underline{7} \div 7 = \underline{14}$
Rosa has $\underline{7}$ bags.

5. The wagons on the farm have 4 wheels each. There are 12 wheels. How many wagons are on the farm?

$12 - 4 = \underline{8}$
$\underline{12} - 4 = \underline{8}$
$\underline{12} - \underline{4} = \underline{8}$

$\underline{8} \div \underline{4} = \underline{12}$
There are $\underline{8}$ wagons.

In **6** and **7**, use counters or draw a picture to solve.

6. Maria bought 30 markers that came in packages of 5 markers each. How many packages did Maria buy?

$30 + 5 = 35$ Maria has only 2 packages.

7. Marcus has 18 pencils. He places 2 pencils on each desk. How many desks are there?

Problem Solving

8. Generalize The chart shows the number of pennies each of three friends has in her pocket. Each friend divides her money into groups of 3 coins. Write division equations to show how many equal groups each friend can make. Explain what repeats in the equations.

Money in Pockets

Claudia	18 cents
Zoe	12 cents
Jenna	15 cents

9. If Zoe has 6 pennies in each row, how many rows does she make?

---

10. Bella has $52. She spends $21, and then finds $12. How much money does she have now? Use equations to represent the problem.

11. Higher Order Thinking An ice cream store plans to make 8 new flavors each year. How many years will it take for the store to make 80 flavors? Write and solve an equation.

Assessment Practice

12. Eric writes $20 \div 5$. Which problem could Eric's expression represent?

- Ⓐ There are 20 apples. Each guest gets 10 apples. How many guests are there?
- Ⓑ There are 20 pencils. Each student gets 2 pencils. How many students are there?
- Ⓒ There are 5 pens. Each student gets 1 pen. How many students are there?
- Ⓓ There are $20. Each child gets $5. How many children are there?

13. Jacqui writes $24 \div 8$. Which problem could Jacqui's expression represent?

- Ⓐ There are 24 bows. Each child gets 8 bows. How many children are there?
- Ⓑ There are 24 chicks. Each box holds 2 chicks. How many boxes are there?
- Ⓒ There are 24 horses. Each arena has 12 horses. How many arenas are there?
- Ⓓ There are 24 coins. Each pile has 24 coins. How many piles are there?

Name _____

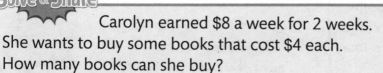

☆ ☆
Solve & Share

Carolyn earned $8 a week for 2 weeks.
She wants to buy some books that cost $4 each.
How many books can she buy?

Choose a tool to represent and solve the problem.
Explain why you chose that tool.

$8 \times 2 = 16$
$16 \div 4 = 4$
She could
buy 4 books.
We used division
to solve.

I can ...
think strategically to determine
which tool will be most useful.

I can also multiply and divide to
solve problems.

Thinking Habits

*Be a good thinker!
These questions can help you.*

• Which tools can I use?

• Why should I use this tool to
  help me solve the problem?

• Is there a different tool
  I could use?

• Am I using the tool
  appropriately?

Look Back! **Use Appropriate Tools** Explain how you used
the tool you chose.

How Can You Use Appropriate Tools to Represent and Solve Problems?

A hardware store has boxes of 18 light bulbs. 3 light bulbs cost $4. How much does it cost to buy a whole box of light bulbs? Choose a tool to represent and solve the problem.

$18 \div 3 = 6$ $18 - 3 =$

Sometimes you can use more than one tool to help you solve problems.

What do I need to do?

I need to choose an appropriate tool to help me find how much it costs to buy a box of 18 light bulbs.

Which tools can I use to help me solve this problem?

I can

- decide which tools are appropriate.

- use cubes and counters to solve this problem.

- use the tools correctly.

Here's my thinking...

I will use two tools. Both counters and ones cubes are easy to count and move around.

Each cube is 1 light bulb.
I will separate 18 cubes into groups of 3.

Each counter is $1.
I will put 4 counters with each group of 3 light bulbs.

There are 24 counters.
A box of light bulbs costs $24.

Convince Me! **Use Appropriate Tools** What other tools could you use to help solve this problem?

Name _____

☆ Guided Practice

Use Appropriate Tools

Three friends each have 8 books. They put their books into 4 equal piles. How many books are in each pile?

You can also use appropriate digital tools. Technology can help you solve a problem.

1. Choose a tool to represent the problem. Explain why you chose that tool.

2. Solve the problem. Explain how you used the tool you chose.

Independent Practice ☆

Use Appropriate Tools

Fifteen students are working in equal groups to make posters. There are 5 students in each group. For each group of students, there needs to be 2 adults helping. How many adults are needed?

3. Choose a tool to represent the problem. Explain why you chose that tool.

4. Solve the problem. Explain how you used the tool you chose.

5. The posters need to be 20 inches long. What tool could the students use to check that the posters are the correct size? Explain how they could use this tool.

Problem Solving

Bottle Cap Display

The soda bottle caps at the right are shared equally between Kerry and Nita. There are 4 orange bottle caps. Kerry wants to arrange her bottle caps into an array.

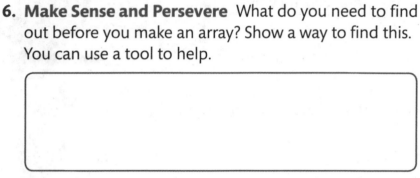

6. **Make Sense and Persevere** What do you need to find out before you make an array? Show a way to find this. You can use a tool to help.

7. **Use Appropriate Tools** Choose a tool to represent Kerry's array of soda bottle caps. Explain why you chose that tool.

8. **Model with Math** Draw a picture to show how Kerry's array might look. Then write a multiplication equation for the array.

> Think about what you need to do in the problem. Then use appropriate tools that can help you solve it.

9. **Use Structure** Write a different multiplication equation with the same two factors you used in Exercise **8**. Has the product changed? Explain.

10. **Critique Reasoning** Kerry says she can use a tens rod to represent the array. Do you agree? Explain.

Name_____

★ **Find a Match** ★

Work with a partner. Point to a clue.
Read the clue.

Look below the clues to find a match. Write the clue letter in the box next to the match.

Find a match for every clue.

I can ...
add and subtract within 20.

I can also make math argumer

Clues

A Is equal to $9 + 11 = 20$	**E** Is equal to $19 - 9 = 15$	**I** Is equal to $2 - 2 = 0$
B Is equal to $13 - 6$	**F** Is equal to $9 + 6 = 13$	**J** Is equal to $9 + 10 = 19$
C Is equal to $8 + 8 = 16$	**G** Is equal to $10 - 7 = 3$	**K** Is equal to $16 - 8 = 8$
D Is equal to $12 - 8$	**H** Is equal to $8 + 9 = 17$	**L** Is equal to $6 + 7 = 13$

G $3 + 0$	C $10 + 6$	I $9 - 9$
B $15 - 8$	L $9 + 4$	K $4 + 4$
H $10 + 7$	D $13 - 9$	A $12 + 8$
E $5 + 5$	F $8 + 7$	J $10 + 9$

Vocabulary Review

Glossary

Word List

- array
- column
- Commutative Property of Multiplication
- division
- equal groups
- equation
- factors
- multiplication
- number line
- product
- row
- unknown

Understand Vocabulary

Choose the best term from the Word List. Write it on the blank.

1. _Multiplication_ is an operation you can use to join _eaqul groups_.

2. You solve an equation by finding the value that is _unkown_.

3. You can use a(n) _Array_ to display objects in rows and columns.

4. A line marked in equal units and numbered in order is called a(n) _numberline_.

For each of these terms, give an example and a non-example.

	Example	Non-example
5. Division	$100 \div 0 = 100$	$100 + 100 = 200$
6. Equation		
7. Commutative Property of Multiplication	$2 \times 12 = 12 \times 12$	$15 \times 5 = 3$

Use Vocabulary in Writing

8. Explain how you can multiply 3×4. Use at least 2 terms from the Word List in your explanation.

You can use array to find the product of three times four.

Name **Aseel**

Set A pages 5–8

How many is 3 groups of 4?

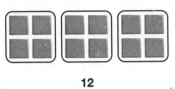

12

| 4 | 4 | 4 |

$4 + 4 + 4 = 12$
$3 \times 4 = 12$
$4 + 4 + 4 = 3 \times 4$

Remember that you can use addition or multiplication to join equal groups.

Complete each equation. Use counters or draw a picture to help.

1. $2 + 2 + 2 = 3 \times 2$

2. $2 + 2 + 2 = 3 \times 6$

3. $8 + 8 + 8 = 3 \times 8$

Set B pages 9–12

Skip count by 4s three times.

You can use a number line to find 3×4.

Number of jumps: 3
Number in each jump: 4

$3 \times 4 = 12$

Remember that you can show skip counting on a number line.

Use the number line to complete each multiplication equation.

1. $2 \times 3 = 6$

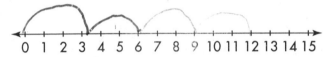

2. $4 \times 3 = 12$

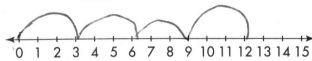

Set C pages 13–16

Find 4×6.
The array shows 4 rows of 6 counters.

Each row is an equal group. You can use skip counting or multiplication to find the total.

6, 12, 18, 24
$4 \times 6 = 24$

Remember that an array shows objects in equal rows.

Show how to use skip counting and multiplication for each array.

1.  $2 \times 4 = 8$

2.  $3 \times 6 = 18$

Set C , continued pages 13–16

This array shows 3 rows of 4.

$3 \times 4 = 12$

This array shows 4 rows of 3.

$4 \times 3 = 12$

So, $3 \times 4 = 4 \times 3$.

Remember that the Commutative Property of Multiplication says you can multiply factors in any order and the product is the same.

Draw arrays and write the products.

1. $2 \times 5 = \underline{10}$ $5 \times 2 = \underline{10}$

Set D pages 17–24

Two friends share 6 fruit snacks equally. How many fruit snacks does each friend get?

$6 \div 2 = 3$ fruit snacks

You can use repeated subtraction.

$6 - 2 = 4$ You subtract 2 from 6 three
$4 - 2 = 2$ times to reach zero.
$2 - 2 = 0$

$6 \div 2 = 3$

Remember that division is an operation to find the number of equal groups or the number in each equal group.

1. Nine raisin boxes are shared by 3 children. Each child gets $\boxed{3}$ raisin boxes.

2. $12 \div 2 = \underline{6}$ 3. $10 \div 5 = \underline{2}$

4. $25 \div 5 = \underline{5}$ 5. $16 \div 4 = \underline{4}$

6. $12 \div 3 = \underline{4}$ 7. $24 \div 6 = \underline{4}$

Set E pages 25–28

Think about these questions to help you **use appropriate tools strategically**.

Thinking Habits

Which tools can I use?

Why should I use this tool to help me solve the problem?

Is there a different tool I could use?

Am I using the tool appropriately?

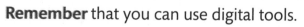

Remember that you can use digital tools.

Sam makes enough muffins to give 8 of her friends 3 muffins each. Each tray holds 6 muffins. How many trays does she need?

$8 \times 3 = 24$ $24 \div 6 = 4$

1. Choose a tool to represent the problem. Explain why you chose that tool.

$8 \times 3 = 24$ $24 \div 6 = 4$

2. Solve. Explain how the tool helped.

I used My Brain and a number line

Name_____

1. Jace drew a picture. Which multiplication expression represents the total number of circles?

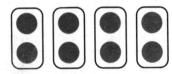

Ⓐ 4×3

Ⓑ 4×1

Ⓒ 4×2

Ⓓ 4×8

---

2. Aidan has 2 turtles in each of 4 aquariums.

A. Write an equation that represents how many turtles Aidan has in all.

$4 \times 2 = 8$

B. How many turtles does Aidan have in all?

8 turtles

---

3. Noah's watering can holds enough water for watering 4 plants. How many plants can Noah water if he fills his watering can 3 times?

12 plants

$4 \times 3 = 12$

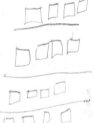

---

4. Megan organized her photos in this array. What is the multiplication equation for the array? Draw a different array that has the same factors.

$4 \times 3 = 12$

---

5. Josiah kicked six 3-point field goals in his football game. Which multiplication equation represents the number of points that Josiah scored?

Ⓐ $6 \times 3 = 18$

Ⓑ $6 \times 1 = 6$

Ⓒ $3 \times 3 = 9$

Ⓓ $6 \times 6 = 36$

---

6. Teresa is growing 2 rows of tomato plants, with 4 plants in each row. Write an expression that represents the total number of plants. Find the total number of plants.

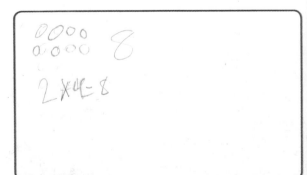

$2 \times 4 = 8$

7. Ann has 24 tennis balls. She separates them equally into 3 different baskets.

A. Write a division equation that shows the number of tennis balls in each basket.

$24 \div 3 = 8$ ✓

B. How many tennis balls are in each basket?

8 tennis balls

8. Mikael gave 3 pencils each to 7 of his friends. Which equation represents the number of pencils Mikael gave away?

Ⓐ $3 \times 1 = 3$

Ⓑ $7 \times 1 = 7$

Ⓒ $7 \times 3 = 21$ ✓

Ⓓ $3 \times 3 = 9$

9. Al needs to put 9 hats in each box. He has 45 hats. Write and solve an equation that shows how many boxes Al can fill.

$45 \div 9 = 5$ 5 boxes ✓

10. There are 48 students in a class. The teacher puts them into 8 equal groups. How many students are in each group?

6 students ✓

11. Saima makes 14 muffins to give to her friends. She wants to give 2 muffins to each friend at her party. How many friends can Saima invite to her party?

Explain how Saima can figure out how many friends to invite.

Saima could only invite 7 friends to her party

$14 \div 2 = 7$

12. Which of the following contexts does the expression $15 \div 3$ represent?

Ⓐ 15 books arranged equally on 3 shelves

Ⓑ 15 books arranged equally on 15 shelves

Ⓒ 3 books arranged equally on 15 shelves

Ⓓ 3 books arranged equally on 3 shelves

Name _____

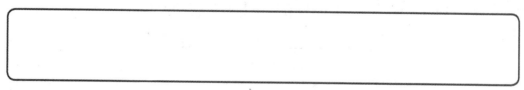

TOPIC

1

☑ Performanc
Task

Sticker Collection
Jamie saved money to buy a sticker album.
The money he has saved each week is shown in the table.

Sticker Prices
- Green sticker albums cost $6.
- Blue sticker albums cost $9.
- Yellow sticker albums cost $12.
- Stickers cost $1 for 3 stickers.

Use the **Money Saved Each Week** table to answer
Exercise **1**.

Money Saved Each Week	
Week	**Dollars Saved per Week**
1	$3
2	$3
3	$3
4	$3

1. How much money has Jamie saved after 4 weeks?
   Write a multiplication equation to solve.

   $12 \div 5 = 4$

   $12 \$$

2. Jamie divides his money into two equal parts. Jamie spends 1 part on a sticker album. Which of the albums can Jamie buy?

   Jamie can only buy the green olbume so he can have a $ left.

Use the **Sticker Prices** list to answer Exercises **2-4**.

3. Jamie spends the other part of his money on stickers. How many stickers can Jamie buy?

4. After spending his money, Jamie decides that he wants a second album. He plans to save $3 per week until he can also buy a blue sticker album. How many weeks does Jamie need to save money?

   3 1 veek 11.4 week   It will, take 4 weeks.
   6 2 week   to get it.
   8 3 week

Use the **Sticker Arrays** table to answer Exercise **5**.

5. Jamie wants to organize his stickers into arrays on a page of the album. Jamie started to make a table to show three ways he could do this.

Sticker Arrays		
Array	**Number of Rows**	**Stickers in Each Row**
Way 1	6	3
Way 2	2	9
Way 3	_____	_____

Part A

Draw arrays to show the two ways Jamie planned to organize his stickers.

Way 1

Way 2

Part B

Draw an array to show another way Jamie could organize his stickers. Complete the **Sticker Arrays** table for Way 3.

Way 3

6. Write multiplication equations for each array to check that Jamie uses all of his stickers in each plan. Are there two ways that show the same factors? Explain.

Multiplication Facts: Use Patterns

Essential Question: How can I use what I know about equal groups to help multiply numbers?

Digital Resources

Interactive Student Edition Activity Visual Learning Video Prac

Assessment Games Tools Glossary

Force makes objects move.

You can use patterns to predict how objects will move!

Let's move some numbers! Here's a project on motion and patterns.

enVision STEM Project: Motion Patterns

Do Research Swings, seesaws, and some other playground objects move with force. Use the Internet or other sources to see what happens when these objects move. Record the number of times that someone pushes or pulls to make the object move. Record the number of times that the object moves.

Journal: Write a Report Include what you found. Also in your report:

- Explain any patterns you found. Tell how you can use your patterns to predict how the objects will move in the future.

- Write an equation for one of the patterns.

- Explain what the numbers in your equation represent.

Review What You Know

Vocabulary

Choose the best term from the box.
Write it on the blank.

- multiplication
- array
- factors
- product

1. The _____ is the answer to a multiplication problem.

2. Numbers that are being multiplied are _____.

3. An operation that gives the total when you join equal groups is _____.

Multiplication as Repeated Addition

Complete each equation.

4. $2 + 2 + 2 + 2 = 4 \times$ ___

5. $9 +$ ___ $+$ ___ $=$ ___ $\times 9$

6. ___ $+$ ___ $+$ ___ $+ 5 =$ ___ $\times 5$

7. $2 \times 6 =$ ___ $+$ ___

Multiplication on the Number Line

8. Marty drew this number line.

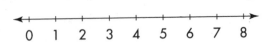

Which multiplication fact does the number line show?

Ⓐ $3 \times 5 = 15$ Ⓑ $3 \times 4 = 12$ Ⓒ $3 \times 3 = 9$ Ⓓ $3 \times 6 = 18$

9. Show the multiplication fact on the number line. Write the product.

$3 \times 2 =$ ___

The Commutative Property

10. How do the arrays represent the Commutative Property of Multiplication?

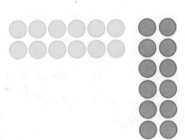

PROJECT
2A

How can you make a unique clock tower?

Project: Design a Clock Tower

PROJECT
2B

Who won the College World Series?

Project: Make a Sports Poster and Write a Report

How many are in your crew?

Project: Plan Your Own Race

How many can you sell?

Project: Create a Fundraiser

Name_____

☆ ☆
Solve & Share

Each chicken has 2 legs. How many legs are there in a group of 9 chickens? Show how you decided.

I can ...
use patterns to multiply by 2 and 5

I can also make sense of problems

You can make sense and persevere in solving the problem by using a number line or a table to record and analyze information.

Number of Chickens									
Number of Legs									

Look Back! Explain another way you could solve this problem.

How Can You Use Patterns to Multiply by 2 and 5?

How many socks are in 7 pairs of socks?
How many fingers are on 7 gloves?

You can use doubling to find the number of socks in 7 pairs, 7 + 7 = 14, or you can skip count: 2, 4, 6, 8, 10, 12, 14.

Find 7 × 2.

1 pair	2 pairs	3 pairs	4 pairs	5 pairs	6 pairs	7 pairs
1 × 2	2 × 2	3 × 2	4 × 2	5 × 2	6 × 2	7 × 2
2	4	6	8	10	12	14

There are 14 socks in 7 pairs.

Find 7 × 5.

$1 \times 5 = 5$
$2 \times 5 = 10$
$3 \times 5 = 15$
$4 \times 5 = 20$
$5 \times 5 = 25$
$6 \times 5 = 30$
$7 \times 5 = 35$

You can use skip counting to find the number of fingers on 7 gloves: 5, 10, 15, 20, 25, 30, 35.

You can also use patterns to find the number of fingers on 7 gloves.

There are 35 fingers on 7 gloves.

Convince Me! **Use Structure** Use doubling, skip counting, or patterns to answer these questions:

How many socks are in 9 pairs? 10 pairs?

How many fingers are on 9 gloves? 10 gloves?

Another Example!

Multiples are the products of a number and other whole numbers.
Multiples of 2 and 5 have patterns in their products.

2s Facts	
$0 \times 2 = 0$	$5 \times 2 = 10$
$1 \times 2 = 2$	$6 \times 2 = 12$
$2 \times 2 = 4$	$7 \times 2 = 14$
$3 \times 2 = 6$	$8 \times 2 = 16$
$4 \times 2 = 8$	$9 \times 2 = 18$

DATA

5s Facts	
$0 \times 5 = 0$	$5 \times 5 = 25$
$1 \times 5 = 5$	$6 \times 5 = 30$
$2 \times 5 = 10$	$7 \times 5 = 35$
$3 \times 5 = 15$	$8 \times 5 = 40$
$4 \times 5 = 20$	$9 \times 5 = 45$

DATA

The products for the 2s facts are multiples of 2.
Multiples of 2 end in 0, 2, 4, 6, or 8.

The products for the 5s facts are multiples of 5.
Multiples of 5 end in 0 or 5.

☆ Guided Practice

Do You Understand?

1. Explain how you can use doubling to find 2×8.

2. Bert says 2×9 is 19. How can you use patterns to show that Bert's answer is wrong?

Do You Know How?

In **3–5**, find each product.

3. $2 \times 4 = $ _____

$2 \times 1 = 2$
$2 \times 2 = 4$
$2 \times 3 = $ _____
$2 \times 4 = $ _____

4.   8
     $\times\ 2$
     _____

5.   5
     $\times\ 8$
     _____

☆ Independent Practice ☆

In **6–12**, find the missing product or factor.

6. $2 \times 2 = $ _____

7. $3 \times$ _____ $= 15$

8. _____ $\times 2 = 14$

9.   6
     $\times\ 5$
     _____

10.   4
      $\times\ 2$
      _____

11.   9
      $\times\ 2$
      _____

12.   5
      $\times\ 7$
      _____

Problem Solving

13. Eric has some nickels. He says they are worth exactly 34 cents. Can you tell if Eric is correct or not? Why or why not?

14. Critique Reasoning Brian said $78 + 92 + 85$ is equal to 300 because each addend is close to 100, and three 100s is the same as 300. Explain why Brian's reasoning is not reasonable.

15. Shannon traded 6 nickels for dimes. How many dimes did Shannon receive?

16. enVision® STEM Mike watches how the pendulum swings in his clock. He notices that it swings 1 time every 2 seconds. How long will it take to swing 5 times?

17. April has the coins shown below.

April counted the value of her coins in cents. List the numbers April would have named.

18. Higher Order Thinking Jake went bowling. On his first turn, he knocked down 2 pins. On his second turn, he knocked down twice as many pins. So far, how many pins has Jake knocked down? How do you know?

19. Mary Beth drew 4 pentagons. How many sides are on all 4 of Mary Beth's pentagons?

Ⓐ 10
Ⓑ 15
Ⓒ 20
Ⓓ 25

20. Carmen has 6 pairs of shoes. How many individual shoes does Carmen have?

Ⓐ 6
Ⓑ 8
Ⓒ 10
Ⓓ 12

Name_____

☆ ☆
Solve & Share

Maria bought 4 packages of bottled water. There are 9 bottles in each package. How many bottles did Maria buy? Explain how you solved this problem.

I can ...
use patterns to multiply by 9.

I can also make math arguments.

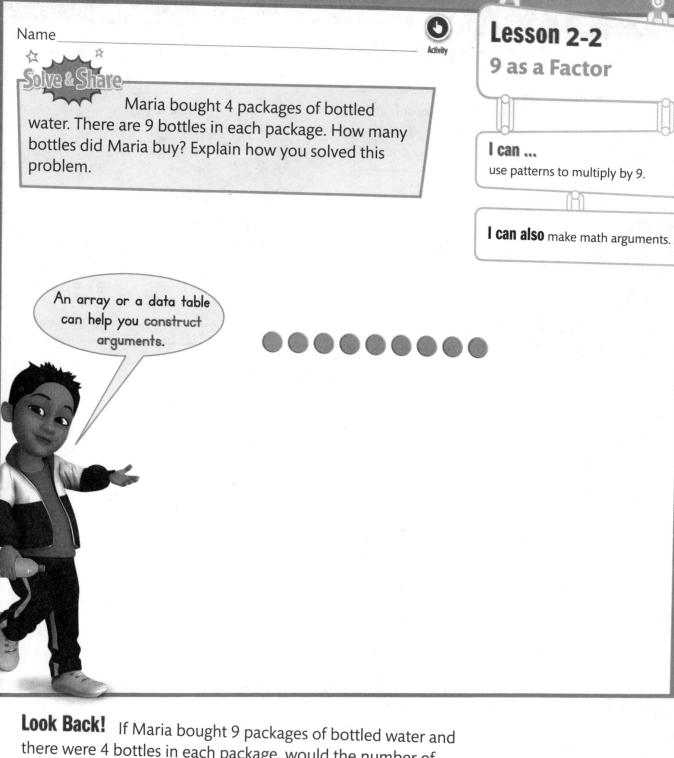

An array or a data table can help you construct arguments.

Look Back! If Maria bought 9 packages of bottled water and there were 4 bottles in each package, would the number of bottles she bought be the same or different? Explain.

How Can Patterns Be Used to Find 9s Facts?

Nine roses were put in each package for sale at the Florida Botanical Garden's annual gift and plant sale. How many roses are in 8 packages?

To find the next multiple of 9 in the table, you can add ten and then subtract 1.

DATA

9s Facts

$0 \times 9 = 0$
$1 \times 9 = 9$
$2 \times 9 = 18$
$3 \times 9 = 27$
$4 \times 9 = 36$
$5 \times 9 = 45$
$6 \times 9 = 54$
$7 \times 9 = 63$
$8 \times 9 = $ ▨
$9 \times 9 = $ ▨

B One Way

Start with $1 \times 9 = 9$.

When you add ten:
Increase the tens place by 1.

When you subtract 1:
Decrease the ones place by 1.

$2 \times 9 = 18$
$3 \times 9 = 27$
$4 \times 9 = 36$
$5 \times 9 = 45$
$6 \times 9 = 54$
$7 \times 9 = 63$
$8 \times 9 = 72$

C Another Way

Start with 0.

For each group of 9:
Add 1 ten and subtract 1 one.

For 8 groups of 9:
Add 8 tens and subtract 8 ones.

$8 \times 9 = 8 \text{ tens} - 8 \text{ ones}$
$8 \times 9 = 80 - 8$
$8 \times 9 = 72$

There are 72 roses in 8 packages.

Convince Me! **Use Structure** Use the patterns above to find 9×9.
Explain how you found the product.

Name_____

☆ Guided Practice

Do You Understand?

1. Paul thinks 3×9 is 24. Use a 9s pattern to show Paul is wrong.

2. Look at the table of 9s facts on the previous page. Describe a number pattern in the multiples of 9.

Do You Know How?

In **3–10**, find each product.

3. $9 \times 2 =$ _____

4. _____ $= 5 \times 9$

5. $7 \times 9 =$ _____

6. _____ $= 4 \times 9$

7. $2 \times 9 =$ _____

8. _____ $= 6 \times 9$

9. $\begin{array}{r} 3 \\ \times\ 9 \\ \hline \end{array}$ **10.** $\begin{array}{r} 8 \\ \times\ 9 \\ \hline \end{array}$

You can use patterns to solve multiplication facts with 9s.

Independent Practice ☆

In **11–22**, find the missing product or factor.

11. $9 \times 0 =$ _____ **12.** $2 \times$ _____ $= 18$ **13.** _____ $\times 9 = 72$ **14.** $9 \times 9 =$ _____

15. $\begin{array}{r} 4 \\ \times\ 9 \\ \hline \end{array}$ **16.** $\begin{array}{r} 9 \\ \times\ 5 \\ \hline \end{array}$ **17.** $\begin{array}{r} 9 \\ \times\ 7 \\ \hline \end{array}$ **18.** $\begin{array}{r} 9 \\ \times\ 1 \\ \hline \end{array}$

19. What is 9×3? _____

20. What is 9×6? _____

21. What is 0×9? _____

22. What is 9×8? _____

Problem Solving

In **23-25**, use the table to the right.

23. Reasoning The library is having a used book sale. How much do 4 hardcover books cost? Draw a number line to show the answer.

Library Book Sale

DATA		
Paperback Books	:	$5
Hardcover Books	:	$9
Magazines	:	$2

24. Higher Order Thinking How much more would Chico spend if he bought 3 hardcover books rather than 3 paperback books? Show how you found the answer.

25. Maggie bought only magazines. The clerk told her she owed $15. How does Maggie know the clerk made a mistake?

26. The owner of a flower shop put 9 sunflowers in each of 6 vases. Then he counted the flowers by 9s. List the numbers he named.

27. Number Sense Chris and Jerome played a video game. Chris scored 437 points. Jerome scored 398 points. Who scored more points? Explain your answer using >, <, or =.

✓ Assessment Practice

28. Sarah planted 2 groups of 9 sabal palm trees. How many palm trees did Sarah plant?

- Ⓐ 9
- Ⓑ 18
- Ⓒ 27
- Ⓓ 36

29. Corky breaks her route from Orlando to Tampa into 9 lengths of 9 miles each. How many miles is it from Orlando to Tampa?

- Ⓐ 9
- Ⓑ 27
- Ⓒ 72
- Ⓓ 81

Name _____

☆ ☆
Solve & Share

Carlos said that 6 times 0 equals 6. Do you agree? Explain your thinking.

6X5 is no 6 because
6X5 equals 30 and if
you count 6 5 times it
will take you to 30.
100X0=0
5X0=0

I can ...
use patterns and properties to multiply by 0 and 1.

I can also be precise in my work.

Be precise. What does it mean to multiply something by zero?

Look Back! Draw a picture to show $5 \times 0 = 0$.

What Are the Patterns in Multiples of 1 and 0?

A

Kira has 8 plates with 1 orange on each plate. How many oranges does Kira have?

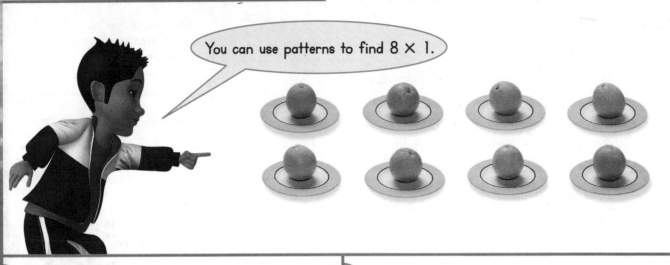

You can use patterns to find 8 × 1.

B 8 groups with 1 in each group equals 8 in all.

$$8 \times 1 = 8$$

Kira has 8 oranges.

1 plate with 8 oranges also equals 8 oranges.

$$1 \times 8 = 8$$

The Identity (One) Property of Multiplication: When you multiply a number by 1, the product is that number.

C If Kira has 4 plates with 0 oranges on each plate, she has 0 oranges.

$$4 \times 0 = 0$$

If $4 \times 0 = 0$, then $0 \times 4 = 0$.

The Zero Property of Multiplication: When you multiply a number by 0, the product is 0.

Convince Me! **Use Appropriate Tools** How would you use counters to show 7 × 1? How many counters would you have in all?

I would have 7 counters or 7 groups of 1.

Name_____

☆ Guided Practice

Do You Understand?

1. Draw a number line to show $8 \times 1 = 8$.

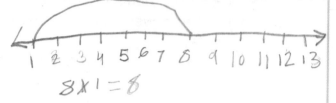
1 2 3 4 5 6 7 8 9 10 11 12 13
$8 \times 1 = 8$

2. Chad has 6 plates. Each plate has 1 apple and 0 grapes. How many apples are there? How many grapes are there?

0 grapes
6 apples

$6 \times 1 = 6$
$6 \times 0 = 0$

Do You Know How?

In **3–8**, find each product.

3.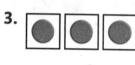

$3 \times 1 = \underline{3}$

4.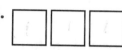

$3 \times 0 = \underline{0}$

5. $1 \times 7 = \underline{7}$

6. $\underline{0} = 5 \times 0$

7. $\begin{array}{r} 4 \\ \times\ 0 \\ \hline 0 \end{array}$

8. $\begin{array}{r} 2 \\ \times\ 1 \\ \hline 2 \end{array}$

> You can use the Identity and Zero Properties of Multiplication to find these products.

Independent Practice

In **9–15**, find each product.

9. $0 \times 4 = \underline{0}$

10. $\underline{6} = 1 \times 6$

11. $4 \times 1 = \underline{4}$

12. $\begin{array}{r} 9 \\ \times\ 1 \\ \hline 9 \end{array}$

13. $\begin{array}{r} 0 \\ \times\ 2 \\ \hline 0 \end{array}$

14. $\begin{array}{r} 1 \\ \times\ 1 \\ \hline 1 \end{array}$

15. $\begin{array}{r} 6 \\ \times\ 0 \\ \hline 0 \end{array}$

In **16–21**, write <, >, or = in each ◯ to compare.

16. $1 \times 6 \;(>)\; 8 \times 0$

17. $0 \times 6 \;(=)\; 6 \times 0$

18. $0 \times 7 \;(<)\; 5 \times 1$

19. $0 \times 0 \;(=)\; 0 \times 9$

20. $1 \times 7 \;(>)\; 5 \times 1$

21. $1 \times 4 \;(=)\; 4 \times 1$

Problem Solving

22. Brent drew this model to show that 5 groups of 1 is the same as 1 group of 5. Is Brent correct? Explain how you know.

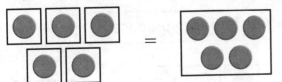

23. Make Sense and Persevere A unicycle relay team has 4 riders. Each rider has one unicycle. If each unicycle has 1 wheel, how many wheels does the team have? What property of multiplication can you use to find the answer?

24. Tickets for a school concert are free for students. The cost is $1 for each adult. What is the total cost of tickets for 5 students?

25. Higher Order Thinking The product of two factors is 0. One of the factors is 0. Can you tell what the other factor is? Explain your answer.

26. The children in the third-grade classes are having a bike parade. Barb's class has 18 bikes. Tim's class has some rows of bikes with 5 bikes in each row. Tim's class has more bikes than Barb's class. How many rows of bikes could Tim's class have? Explain.

27. Use the Zero Property of Multiplication and the Identity Property of Multiplication to select all the correct equations.

- ☐ $1 \times 4 = 1$
- ☐ $4 \times 4 = 0$
- ☐ $7 \times 1 = 7$
- ☐ $0 \times 9 = 9$
- ☐ $0 \times 1 = 0$

28. Use the Zero Property of Multiplication and the Identity Property of Multiplication to select all the correct equations.

- ☐ $0 \times 0 = 0$
- ☐ $1 \times 3 = 3$
- ☐ $6 \times 1 = 6$
- ☐ $0 \times 4 = 0$
- ☐ $1 \times 1 = 0$

Name _____

Solve & Share

Duke runs 10 miles each week. How many miles will he run in 6 weeks? 7 weeks? 8 weeks? Describe patterns you find.

Activity

I can ...
use place-value patterns to multiply by 10.

I can also look for patterns to solve problems.

|||| |||| | | 60

|||| |||| | | | 70

|||| |||| | | | | 80

You can generalize. What repeats in this problem?

$6 \times 10 = 60$
$7 \times 10 = 70$
$8 \times 10 = 80$

Look Back! How are the patterns when multiplying by 10 related to the patterns when multiplying by 5?

What Are the Patterns in Multiples of 10?

A

Greg wants to train for a race. He will each swim, run, and bike 10 miles per week. The chart shows his training schedule. How many miles will Greg each swim, run, and bike to train for the race?

Race Training Schedule	
Activity	**Weeks**
Swimming	4
Running	10
Biking	9

DATA

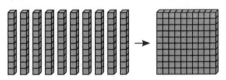 You can use place value to find multiples of 10.

B **Use place-value blocks.**

Find 4 × 10.

 4 × 10 is 4 groups of 10, or 40.
40 is ten times greater than 4.
Greg will swim 40 miles.

Find 10 × 10.

10 × 10 is 10 groups of 10, or 100.
100 is ten times greater than 10.
Greg will run 100 miles.

C **Use place-value patterns.**

When you multiply a number by 10, the number tells you what to record in the tens place.

Find 9 × 10.

1 × 10 = 10
2 × 10 = 20
3 × 10 = 30
4 × 10 = 40
5 × 10 = 50
6 × 10 = 60
7 × 10 = 70
8 × 10 = 80
9 × 10 = 90

 9 × 10 is 9 groups of 10, or 90. Greg will bike 90 miles.

Convince Me! **Use Structure** Greg also walks 10 miles per week for 5 weeks. How many miles did Greg walk while training? Write an equation, and explain how to use a pattern to find the product.

Another Example!

You can use a number line to find 3×10.

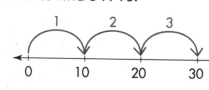

30 is 3 groups of 10.
30 is ten times greater than 3.

$3 \times 10 = 30$

☆ Guided Practice

Do You Understand?

1. How can you use place value to find 9×10?

2. If you multiply any one-digit number by 10, what do you write in the tens digit of the product?

Do You Know How?

In **3–6**, find each product.

3. $2 \times 10 = \underline{2}0$

4. $6 \times 10 = \underline{6}0$

5. $8 \times 10 = \underline{80}$

6. $9 \times 10 = \underline{90}$

Independent Practice ☆

In **7** and **8**, use the number lines to help find the product.

7. $1 \times 10 = \underline{0}$

8. $5 \times 10 = \underline{50}$

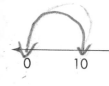

 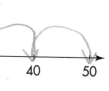

In **9–14**, find the missing product or factor.

9. $10 \times 2 = \underline{2}0$

10. $9 \times 10 = \underline{9}0$

11. $7 \times 10 = \underline{7}0$

12. $3 \times 10 = \underline{30}$

13. $5 \times \underline{10} = 50$

14. $80 = 10 \times \underline{8}$

Problem Solving

15. Reasoning Eddie borrowed $65 from his dad. Every month, he pays back $12. Complete the table to find how much money Eddie still owes his dad after 4 months.

Month	Amount Eddie Owes
April	$65 – $12 = _____
May	_____ – $12 = _____
June	_____ – _____ = _____
July	_____ – _____ = _____

---

16. Kimmy bought 7 tickets to a concert. Each ticket costs $10. She also paid $5 to have the tickets delivered. Write equations to show how much money Kimmy spent in all.

17. Write an addition equation and a multiplication equation for the array below.

---

18. Use the table to find the total number of juice boxes bought for a school picnic.

DATA

Food Item	Number of Packages	Number in Each Package
Hot dogs	8	10
Rolls	10	9
Juice boxes	7	10

Juice boxes: _____

19. Higher Order Thinking Greg bikes 9 miles and swims 4 miles each week. He multiplied 5 × 10 to find how many more miles he biked than swam in the last 10 weeks. Does that make sense? Why or why not?

✓ Assessment Practice

20. Kinsey arranges her buttons in 4 equal groups of 10. Mara arranges her buttons in 9 equal groups of 10. Seth arranges his buttons in 3 equal groups of 10. Select numbers to complete the equations that represent the button arrangements.

| 3 | 4 | 9 | 10 | 40 | 90 |

$4 \times 10 = \boxed{}$

$\boxed{} \times 10 = 90$

$3 \times \boxed{} = 30$

21. Mark arranges his cards in 2 equal rows of 10. Jeff arranges his cards in 7 equal rows of 10. Paul arranges his cards in 10 equal rows of 10. Select numbers to complete the equations that represent the card arrays.

| 2 | 7 | 10 | 20 | 70 | 100 |

$2 \times \boxed{} = 20$

$\boxed{} \times 10 = 70$

$10 \times 10 = \boxed{}$

Name_____

☆ ☆
Solve & Share

A company sells boxes of colored pencils. Each box contains 5 pencils. How many pencils are in 5 boxes? 9 boxes? 10 boxes? Explain how you found your answers.

I can ...
use basic multiplication facts to solve problems.

I can also use a math tool to help solve problems.

Number of Boxes	1	5	9	10
Number of Colored Pencils	5	25	5	50

You can use appropriate tools to make an array to show the multiplication.

Look Back! A different company sells boxes that have 9 colored pencils in each box. How many pencils are in 5 boxes? 9 boxes? 10 boxes?

Number of Boxes	5	4	10
Number of Colored Pencils	45	81	40

$5 \times 9 = 45$
$9 \times 9 = 81$
$10 \times 9 = 90$

Essential Question

How Do You Use Multiplication Facts to Solve Problems?

A

Brendan has archery practice. The target shows the points he gets for hitting a section. How many points did Brendan get from his arrows that hit the black ring? How many points did he get from the red ring?

Section of Target	Number of Arrows
10	3
9	4
5	9
2	8
1	7

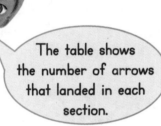

The table shows the number of arrows that landed in each section.

B **8 arrows hit the black ring.**

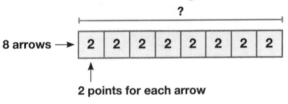

?

8 arrows → | 2 | 2 | 2 | 2 | 2 | 2 | 2 | 2 |

↑
2 points for each arrow

The bar diagram shows 8 equal groups of 2.
$8 \times 2 = 16$

Brendan got 16 points from the 8 arrows.

C **4 arrows hit the red ring.**

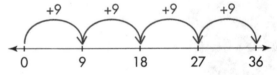

+9   +9   +9   +9

0   9   18   27   36

Skip count and record your counts.
9, 18, 27, 36
$4 \times 9 = 36$

Brendan got 36 points from the 4 arrows.

Convince Me! **Be Precise** How many points did Brendan get from the arrows that hit the yellow ring? Explain how you know.

☆ Guided Practice

Do You Understand?

1. To find 6×5, how does knowing $5 \times 6 = 30$ help you? *Because it is Just Back words and $6 \times 5 = 30$ and $5 \times 6 = 30$.*

2. How can you find $8 + 8 + 8 + 8 + 8$ without adding? *you $8 \times 5 = 40$ or $5 \times 8 = 40$.*

Do You Know How?

In **3–9**, find each product.

3. $5 \times 9 = \underline{45}$

4. $\underline{2} = 2 \times 1$

5. $\underline{0} = 0 \times 10$

6. $5 \times 4 = \underline{20}$

7. $\begin{array}{r} 1 \\ \times\ 2 \\ \hline 2 \end{array}$

8. $\begin{array}{r} 2 \\ \times\ 7 \\ \hline 14 \end{array}$

9. What is 4×9? $\underline{= 36}$

☆ Independent Practice ☆

In **10–26**, find each product.

10. $2 \times 5 = \underline{10}$

11. $\underline{0} = 9 \times 0$

12. $1 \times 4 = \underline{4}$

13. $\underline{12} = 6 \times 2$

14. $10 \times 6 = \underline{16}$

15. $\underline{7} = 7 \times 1$

16. $\begin{array}{r} 2 \\ \times\ 10 \\ \hline 20 \end{array}$

17. $\begin{array}{r} 2 \\ \times\ 1 \\ \hline 2 \end{array}$

18. $\begin{array}{r} 9 \\ \times\ 9 \\ \hline 81 \end{array}$

19. $\begin{array}{r} 7 \\ \times\ 2 \\ \hline 14 \end{array}$

20. $\begin{array}{r} 9 \\ \times\ 3 \\ \hline 27 \end{array}$

21. $\begin{array}{r} 0 \\ \times\ 7 \\ \hline 0 \end{array}$

22. $\begin{array}{r} 4 \\ \times\ 5 \\ \hline 20 \end{array}$

23. $\begin{array}{r} 5 \\ \times\ 7 \\ \hline 35 \end{array}$

24. What is 1×1? $= 1$

25. What is 10×10? $= 100$

26. What is 3×9? $= 27$

Problem Solving

27. Critique Reasoning Abdi says that 9×6 is less than 10×4 because 9 is less than 10. Do you agree with Abdi's reasoning? Explain why or why not.

28. Victoria has 5 pairs of shoes. What equation could Victoria write to find out how many shoes she has?

29. Show 7:50 on the clock.

30. Robb has 35 red counters and 39 yellow counters. He gives his sister 18 red counters. How many counters does Robb have left?

31. Kim makes an array with 4 rows and 9 columns. Rashida makes an array with 9 rows and 4 columns. Whose array has more items? Explain.

32. Higher Order Thinking Brendan shot 3 arrows in the 10-point section, 4 arrows in the 9-point section, 9 arrows in the 5-point section, 8 arrows in the 2-point section, and 7 arrows in the 1-point section. What is the total number of points Brendan scored for all his arrows?

✅ Assessment Practice

33. Craig visits a railroad museum and takes photos of engines. He arranges his photos into an array with 5 equal rows of 9 photos. How many photos are in Craig's array?

Ⓐ 5

Ⓑ 9

Ⓒ 45

Ⓓ 59

Think about the different ways you know to find and represent multiplication facts.

Name _____

☆ ☆
Solve & Share

At the pet store, Sam bought a hamster that cost $10. He also bought 5 mice at $4 each. How much did Sam spend in all? Write to explain the math you used to solve this problem.

Thinking Habits

Be a good thinker!
These questions can help you.

- How can I use math I know to help solve this problem?

- How can I use pictures, objects, or an equation to represent the problem?

- How can I use numbers, words, and symbols to solve the problem?

Look Back! **Model with Math** How would your answer above change if Sam only bought 4 mice?

How Can You Model with Math?

$2
per yard

Keisha bought 2 yards of felt to make some puppets. Tanya bought 6 yards of felt. Each yard of felt costs the same amount. How much did the girls spend on felt in all?

What math do I need to use to solve this problem?

I need to show what I know and then choose the needed operations.

B How can I model with math?

I can

- use the math I know to solve the problem.

- find and answer any hidden questions.

- use diagrams and equations to represent and solve this problem.

C

Here's my thinking...

I will use bar diagrams and equations.

The hidden question is: How many yards of felt did the girls buy?

? yards	
2 yards	6 yards

$2 + 6 = ?$
$2 + 6 = 8$. The girls bought 8 yards of felt.

So, I need to find the cost of 8 yards at $2 per yard.

? total cost							
$2	$2	$2	$2	$2	$2	$2	$2

$8 \times \$2 = ?$
$8 \times \$2 = \$16$. The girls spent $16.

Convince Me! Model with Math Use these number lines to show another way to represent the problem above.

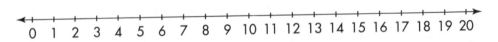

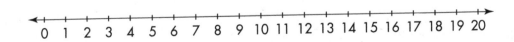

☆ Guided Practice

Model with Math

A pack of gum contains 5 pieces. Phil had
7 packs of gum before he lost 2 pieces. How
many pieces of gum does Phil have now?

> Model with math.
> You can represent and
> solve each step in a
> two-step problem.

1. What is the hidden question you need to
   answer before you can solve the problem?

2. Solve the problem. Complete
   the bar diagrams. Show the
   equations you used.

One Pack [____]

Phil's Packs [____|____|____|____|____|____|____]

? pieces of gum

_____ pieces of gum

[_____ ? _____|____]

Independent Practice ☆

Model with Math

Jen bought 4 tickets. Amber bought 5 tickets. The tickets
cost $2 each. How much did the girls spend on tickets in all?

3. What is the hidden question you need to
   answer before you can solve the problem?

4. Solve the problem. Complete the bar
   diagrams. Show the equations you used.

[_____]

5. How would your equations change if Amber
   bought only 3 tickets? Explain.

[_____]

Problem Solving

Coffee Shop

David and Jon are placing coffee orders for their friends. David orders 10 large cups of coffee. Jon orders 4 fewer large cups than David. Jon pays for his orders with a $50 bill. Jon wants to know how much he spent on coffee.

Coffee Shop Prices	
Cup	**Cost**
Small	$2
Regular	$4
Large	$5

6. **Make Sense and Persevere** What is a good plan to find the amount Jon spent on coffee?

7. **Model with Math** Find how much Jon spent on coffee. Complete the bar diagrams. Show the equations you used.

8. **Critique Reasoning** Jamie says the equation $0 \times \$2 = \$0$ shows the amount Jon spent on small cups of coffee. Is he correct? Explain.

9. **Reasoning** Would David have enough money if he paid for his order with a $20 bill? Explain.

Model with math. Think about the math you know to solve the problem.

Find a partner. Get paper and a pencil. Each partner chooses a different color: light blue or dark blue.

Partner 1 and Partner 2 each point to a black number at the same time. Both partners add those numbers.

If the answer is on your color, you get a tally mark. Work until one partner has seven tally marks.

I can ...
add within 100.

I can also make math arguments

Partner 1					Partner 2
55	80	54	94	36	**13**
23	62	25	41	57	**45**
37	76	30	100	82	**39**
12	86	50	73	68	**26**
41	49	67	38	63	**18**
	59	81	55	51	

Tally Marks for Partner 1

Tally Marks for Partner 2

Vocabulary Review

 A-Z
Glossary

Word List

- bar diagram
- factor
- Identity (One) Property of Multiplication
- multiplication
- multiples
- product
- Zero Property of Multiplication

Understand Vocabulary

Circle all correct responses.

1. Circle each number that is a *product*.

$4 \times 6 = \boxed{24}$ $7 \times 3 = \boxed{21}$ $8 \div 4 = \boxed{2}$

2. Circle each example of the *Identity Property*.

$\boxed{2 \times 2 = 4}$ $5 \times 0 = 0$ $1 \times 6 = 6$

3. Circle each example of the *Zero Property*.

$1 \times 0 = 0$ $\boxed{0 \times 9 = 0}$ $\boxed{2 \times 5 = 10}$

4. Circle each equation that shows *multiplication*.

$5 + 6 = 11$ $\boxed{4 \times 4 = 16}$ $17 - 12 = 5$ $16 \div 2 = 8$

5. Skip count by 9s. Circle each number that is a *multiple* of 9.

16   ⑨   28   ㉗   19   ㊱   ⑱   39

Write T for *true* or F for *false*.

__F__ **6.** Skip count by 4s. The number 14 is a *multiple* of 4.

__t__ **7.** The *Identity Property* says that any number times 1 equals the number itself.

__t__ **8.** A *bar diagram* can be used to show 3×6.

Use Vocabulary in Writing

9. Explain how you can find the product 4×2 and the product 8×2. Use at least 3 terms from the Word List in your explanation.

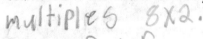

Layal multiples 8x2.
I can us a factor

Name_____

Set A pages 41–44

Find 6 × 2.

Use skip counting. Draw 6 curved arrows on a number line. Each arrow should be 2 units wide.

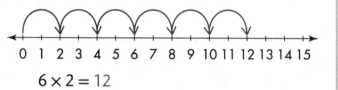

0 1 2 3 4 5 6 7 8 9 10 11 12 13 14 15

6 × 2 = 12

Find 6 × 5.

Use a pattern. Count by 5s. The 6th number in the pattern is the product.

5, 10, 15, 20, 25, 30
6 × 5 = 30

Reteaching

Remember that multiples of 2 end in 0, 2, 4, 6, or 8. Multiples of 5 end in 0 or 5.

1. 2 × 3 = _6_   **2.** 5 × 3 = _15_

3. 5 × 5 = _25_   **4.** 2 × 6 = _12_

5. 8 × 2 = _16_   **6.** 7 × 5 = _35_

7.   2
  × 2
  _4_

8.   7
  × 2
  _14_

9.   8
  × 5
  _40_

10.   9
  × 5
  _45_

Set B pages 45–48

Find 9 × 4.

List 9s facts.

9 × 1 = 9
9 × 2 = 18
9 × 3 = 27
9 × 4 = 36

Remember that there are patterns in the multiples of 9.

1. 9 × 5 = _45_   **2.** 9 × 7 = _63_

3. 6 × 9 = _54_   **4.** 8 × 9 = _69_

5. 9 × 9 = _90_   **6.** 9 × 0 = _0_

Set C pages 49–52

Find 0 × 7.

Zero Property of Multiplication: When you multiply a number by 0, the product is 0.

0 × 7 = 0

Find 1 × 7.

Identity (One) Property of Multiplication: When you multiply a number by 1, the product is that number.

1 × 7 = 7

Remember that the product of 0 and any other number is 0. When you multiply a number by 1, the product is that same number.

1. 0 × 4 = _0_   **2.** 1 × 9 = _9_

3. 0 × 9 = _0_   **4.** 1 × 6 = _6_

5. 10 × 0 = _0_   **6.** 9 × 0 = _0_

7. 3 × 1 = _3_   **8.** 8 × 1 = _8_

9. 0 × 2 = _0_   **10.** 1 × 0 = _0_

Find 6 × 10.

You can use patterns to find multiples of 10.

6 × 10 is 6 groups of 10.
6 × 10 = 60

Remember that you can use place value or number lines to find multiples of ten.

1. 10 × 7 = _70_   **2.** 10 × 10 = _100_

3. 3 × 10 = _30_   **4.** 9 × 10 = _90_

5. 10 × 0 = _0_   **6.** 1 × 10 = _10_

Find 5 × 10.

There are many patterns and properties you can use to multiply.

Use skip counting with 5s facts:
5, 10, 15, 20, 25, 30, 35, 40, 45, 50

Use a place-value pattern for 10s facts:
10 times greater than 5 is 50.

The product is the same.
5 × 10 = 50

Remember that you can use the Commutative Property of Multiplication to multiply 2 factors in any order.

1. 5 × 9 = _45_   **2.** 0 × 6 = _0_

3. 10 × 3 = _30_   **4.** 8 × 1 = _8_

5. 7 × 2 = _14_   **6.** 9 × 6 = _44_

7. 2 × 5 = _10_   **8.** 4 × 5 = _20_

Think about these questions to help you **model with math**.

Thinking Habits

- How can I use math I know to help solve the problem?

- How can I use pictures, objects, or an equation to represent the problem?

- How can I use numbers, words, and symbols to solve the problem?

Remember that representations can help you apply math that you know.

Umar has 5 dimes in his left pocket. He has 3 dimes in his right pocket. A dime is worth 10 cents. How much money does Umar have?

1. Draw a bar diagram to help answer the hidden question.

2. Draw a bar diagram to help answer the main question.

Name_____

1. A building has 9 rows of mailboxes. There are 6 mailboxes in each row. Write and solve an equation to find the total number of mailboxes.

9x6=54

54 mailboxes

2. Tickets to a juggling show cost $2 for each child. Three children go to see the show. What is the total cost of their tickets?

A. Draw a bar diagram and write an equation to solve the problem.

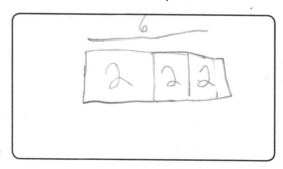

B. What is the total cost of the children's tickets?

3. Cindy got 9 questions correct on an assignment. Each question is worth 4 points. She wrote the expression 9 × 4 to represent how many points she earned in all. Which expression is equal to 9 × 4?

Ⓐ 9 × 5

Ⓒ 4 × 9

Ⓑ 5 × 4

Ⓓ 4 × 6

4. Harry told Arthur he baked 35 cookies on a rectangular pan. Which sentence could Arthur use to describe how the cookies were baked?

Ⓐ Harry baked 7 rows of 6 cookies.

Ⓑ Harry baked 5 rows of 5 cookies.

Ⓒ Harry baked 7 rows of 7 cookies.

Ⓓ Harry baked 7 rows of 5 cookies.

5. Alex has 8 dimes in his pocket. A dime is worth 10 cents. Write an expression that represents how many cents Alex has in his pocket. How much money does he have?

80¢

6. Which number completes the equation? Select all that apply.

_10_ × 0 = 0

☐ 0

☐ 9

☐ 2

☑ 10

☐ 5

7. Ben says that when any number between 1 and 9 is multiplied by 5, the product always has a 0 or 5 in the ones place. Is this reasonable? Explain.

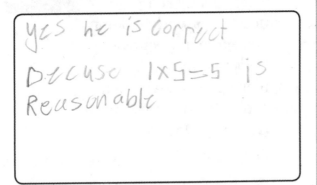

yes he is correct because 1×5=5 is Reasonable

8. Gabe has 5 birdcages. He keeps 5 birds in each cage. How many birds does Gabe have? Use a bar diagram to represent the problem.

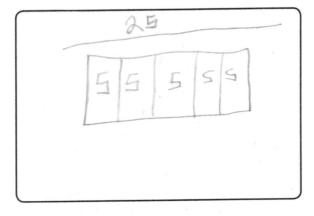

25

| 5 | 5 | 5 | 5 | 5 |

9. A set of blocks has 4 different colors that make a pattern. The pattern repeats 10 times. Write and solve an equation to find the number of blocks.

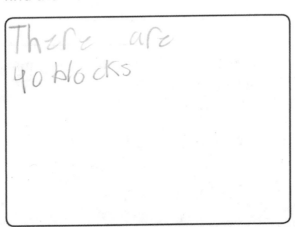

There are 40 blocks

10. Zach arranges his quarters into 6 rows and 5 columns. David arranges his quarters into 5 rows and 6 columns. Who has more quarters? Explain.

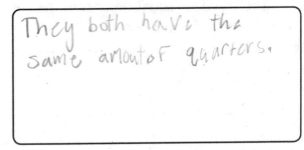

They both have the same amount of quarters.

11. Use the expression 10 × ? where ? represents a factor between 1 and 9. What is true about the digit in the ones place of each product? Explain.

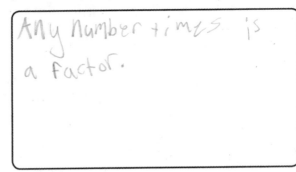

Any number times is a factor.

12. Dawn has 2 bananas. She cuts each banana into 8 slices. Write and solve an equation to find the number of banana slices that Dawn has.

2×8=16

13. Isabella has $45 to spend on shirts. All shirts in the store are on sale for $5 each. How many shirts can Isabella buy? Explain how you found your answer.

isabella could buy =9 shirts.

Name_____

Selling Cards

A soccer team is selling boxes of cards to raise money.
There are boxes of small, medium, and large cards.
The team earns a different amount for each card type.

Boxes Sold

- On Monday, Will sold 4 boxes of large cards.
- On Wednesday, Mia sold 6 boxes of small cards
  and 3 boxes of large cards.

Use the **Selling Boxes of Cards** table and **Boxes
Sold** list to answer Exercises **1** and **2**.

Selling Boxes of Cards

Card Type	Amount Earned per Box
Box of small cards	$1
Box of medium cards	$2
Box of large cards	$5

1. How much money did Will earn? Write a
   multiplication equation to solve.

   $5 \times 4 = 20$

   20 dollars

2. Complete the chart to find the amount that Mia earned
   for each card type.

Card Type	Number Sold	Amount Earned per Box	Total Earned
small	16	1	6
medium	0	0	0
large	3	5	15

Use the **Selling Boxes of Cards** table to answer Exercise **3**.

3. For 7 days, Logan sold a box of medium cards every day.
   How much did Logan earn? Create a representation for
   the problem.

   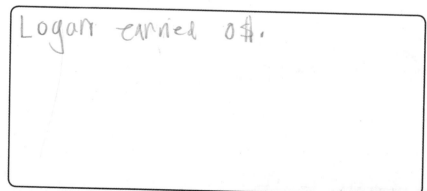

   Logan earned 0 $.

Boxes Bought
- Mrs. Carlson buys 1 box of medium cards.
- Mr. Choi buys 6 boxes of small cards.
- Mrs. Willis buys 7 boxes of medium cards and 9 boxes of large cards.

Use the **Cards in Each Box** table and **Boxes Bought** list to answer Exercises **4–6**.

4. **Part A**

   How many cards does Mr. Choi buy?

   30 cards

   Part B

   What is another way that Mr. Choi can buy the same number of cards?

   7 × 4 = 30

Cards in Each Box	
Card Type	**Number of Cards**
Box of small cards	5
Box of medium cards	9
Box of large cards	10

5. Is there another way that Mrs. Carlson can buy the same number of cards? Explain.

6. Complete the chart to find the number of cards Mrs. Willis buys of each card type.

Card Type	Number of Boxes Bought	Number of Cards in a Box	Total Cards
small			
medium	7		
large	1	10	40

Apply Properties: Multiplication Facts for 3, 4, 6, 7, 8

Essential Question: How can you use known multiplication facts to solve unknown facts?

Digital Resources

Interactive Student Edition   Activity   Visual Learning   Video   Practice

Assessment   Games   Tools   Glossary

Some roses are red and some violets are blue, but do you know why?

Flowers inherit their color. They get their color from parent plants.

My mom's roses are yellow! Here's a project on traits of organisms, multiplication, and equations.

enVision STEM Project: Inherited Traits

Do Research Some characteristics of organisms are inherited. The traits are passed from generation to generation. In flowers, one of the inherited traits is color. Use the Internet or other sources to make a list of other traits that flowers inherit from their parent plants.

Journal: Write a Report Include what you found. Also in your report:

- Compare your list of traits with lists of traits other students have made. If there is a trait you do not have, add it to your list.

- Draw flowers or animals with similar traits in an array. Show how to break apart the array and use multiplication facts to find the total number.

Name_____

Review What You Know

Choose the best term from the box. Write it on the blank.

• skip counting	• The Identity (One) Property of Multiplication
• The Commutative (Order) Property of Multiplication	• The Zero Property of Multiplication

1. The zero property of multiplication says that the product of any number and zero is zero.

2. The identify (one) property of Multicaition says that 1 times any number is that number.

3. The commutative(order) propertyof multiplactain says that you can multiply factors in any order, and the product stays the same.

Multiplying

Use multiplication to solve.

4. $10 \times 1 = $ 10

5. $2 \times 10 = $ 20

6. $0 \times 5 = $ 0

7. $9 \times 5 = $ 45

8. $2 \times 7 = $ 14

9. $1 \times 8 = $ 8

10. $5 \times 7 = ?$

    Ⓐ $7 + 5$ Ⓑ $5 + 7$ Ⓒ 7×5 Ⓓ $7 \div 5$

Adding 2-Digit Numbers

Find the sum.

11. $16 + 12 = $ 28

12. $21 + 14 = $ 35

13. $24 + 12 = $ 36

Arrays

14. How can you represent 3×6 using an array? Draw an array, and explain how to use it to find the product.

I draw an array with 3 coulms and 6 row

Name _____

PROJECT 3A

How many points can you score?

Project: Make a Basketball Data Display

PROJECT 3B

Do you like collecting seashells?

Project: Draw a Shell Array

PROJECT 3C

Would you like to run for president?

Project: Write a Presidential Report

Math Modeling

Thirsty Students

Video

Before watching the video, think:

It takes about the same amount of energy to make 20 recycled cans as it does to make 1 new can. The U.S. makes about 100 billion cans every year! No matter how many cans you use, recycling the aluminum is an important final step.

I can ...
model with math to solve a problem that involves using multiplication facts and computing.

Name _____

☆ ☆
Solve & Share

Find two ways to break the array below into two smaller arrays. What multiplication equation can you write for each array? What is the total? Tell how you decided.

I can ...
break apart unknown facts into known facts and solve multiplication problems.

I can also be precise in my work.

You can be precise. You can explain what your equations mean.

$$R \quad C$$
$$5 \times 2 = 10$$
$$R \quad C$$
$$2 \times 5 = 10$$

Look Back! Find the total number of items in both of the smaller arrays. Compare their combined total to the total number of items in the one large array. Why are the totals the same even though the arrays are different?

Essential Question

How Can You Break Up a Multiplication Fact?

A

Maria wants to set up 7 rows of 4 chairs for a meeting. She wants to know how many chairs she needs but does not know the product of 7 × 4.

You can use known facts to help find the product of unknown facts.

B What You Think

Maria thinks of **7** rows of 4 chairs as **5** rows of 4 chairs and another **2** rows of 4 chairs.

C What You Write

The Distributive Property says that a multiplication fact can be broken apart into the sum of two other multiplication facts.

Maria knows the two new facts.

$7 \times 4 = (5 \times 4) + (2 \times 4)$
$7 \times 4 = 20 + 8$
$7 \times 4 = 28$

So, $7 \times 4 = 28$.

Maria needs 28 chairs.

Convince Me! **Use Structure** What are two ways that Maria could break up the array for 7 × 4? Draw a picture of the two new arrays and write the new facts.

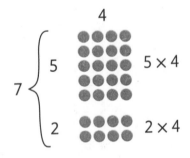

$7 \times 4 \ (3 \times 4) + (4 \times 4) \ 28$
$\qquad 12 + 16$

$7 \times 4 = (7 \times 2) + (7 \times 2) \ 28$
$\qquad 14 + 14$

Practice   Tools   Assessment

☆ Guided Practice

Do You Understand?

1. Rafael broke up an array for 6 × 3 into two new arrays. Both of his new arrays are the same. What were the two arrays?

$6 \times 3 = 18$

$(3 \times 3) + (3 \times 3) = 18$
     9   +   9

2. Ann broke up a large array into two smaller arrays. The two smaller arrays show 1 × 8 and 4 × 8. What was the large array that Ann started with?

$(1 \times 8) + (4 \times 8)$
     8   32

Do You Know How?

In **3** and **4**, use the smaller arrays and the Distributive Property to find each missing factor. You may use counters to help.

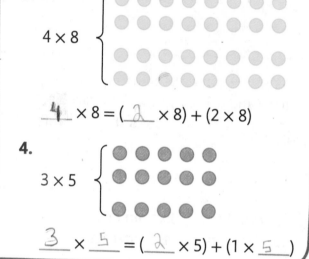

3.

4 × 8

$\underline{4} \times 8 = (\underline{2} \times 8) + (2 \times 8)$

4.

3 × 5

$\underline{3} \times \underline{5} = (\underline{2} \times 5) + (1 \times \underline{5})$

☆ Independent Practice ☆

In **5** and **6**, separate the rows in the large array into two smaller arrays. Write the new facts.

5.

$4 \times 5 = (\underline{2} \times \underline{5}) + (\underline{2} \times \underline{5})$

6.

$5 \times 6 = (\underline{6} \times \underline{2}) + (\underline{6} \times \underline{30})$

In **7–10**, use the Distributive Property to find each missing factor. Use counters and arrays to help.

7. $6 \times 8 = (4 \times \underline{2}) + (2 \times 8)$

8. $10 \times 3 = (\underline{30} \times 3) + (2 \times 3)$

9. $(\underline{} \times 7) = (3 \times 7) + (2 \times \underline{})$

10. $(8 \times \underline{8}) = (\underline{4} \times 8) + (4 \times 8)$

Problem Solving

11. Paige bakes 5 cupcakes. She puts 7 jelly beans on each cupcake. How many jelly beans does Paige need? Use the bar diagram to help write an equation.

? jelly beans

7	7	7	7	7

$7 \times 5 = 35$
35 jelly cupcakes

12. Critique Reasoning Fred wants to separate the rows of the array below into a 2 × 4 array and a 3 × 4 array. Can Fred do this? Explain.

NO because
There isn't enough

---

13. Lane uses counters to make a 4 × 7 array and a 1 × 7 array. What size array can he make using all of these counters?

$4 \times 7 = (7 \times 3) + 1 \times 7$

14. Gavin had $75 on Monday. On Tuesday, he spent $23. Then he spent $14 on Wednesday. How much money does Gavin have left?

38 $

---

15. **A-Z Vocabulary** Explain how you can use the *Distributive Property* to solve 9 × 6.

$5 \times 6 + 4 \times 6$

16. Higher Order Thinking How can you use 3 × 5 = 15 to help find 6 × 5?

$6 \times 5 = 35$

✓ Assessment Practice

17. Using the Distributive Property, which of the following expressions are equivalent to 7 × 7? Select all that apply.

- ☐ $(7 \times 7) + (7 \times 7)$
- ☑ $(5 \times 7) + (2 \times 7)$
- ☑ $(2 \times 7) + (5 \times 7)$
- ☐ $(7 \times 7) + (1 \times 7)$
- ☐ $(7 \times 7) + (2 \times 7)$

18. An equation is shown. Select all the ways you can use the Distributive Property to find the missing factors.

$7 \times 3 = (\boxed{} \times 3) + (\boxed{} \times 3)$

- ☑ $7 \times 3 = (5 \times 3) + (2 \times 3)$
- ☑ $7 \times 3 = (2 \times 3) + (5 \times 3)$
- ☐ $7 \times 3 = (7 \times 3) + (1 \times 3)$
- ☑ $7 \times 3 = (1 \times 3) + (6 \times 3)$
- ☑ $7 \times 3 = (6 \times 3) + (1 \times 3)$

Name _____

☆ ☆
Solve & Share

There are 3 rows of pictures on a wall. Each row has 7 pictures. How many pictures are on the wall?

I can ...
use tools and properties strategically to solve problems when I multiply by 3 or 4.

I can also choose and use a math tool to help solve problems.

You can use appropriate tools. You can draw arrays or make arrays with counters to help solve the problem.

Look Back! How can you use what you know about multiplication facts for 1s facts and 2s facts to solve multiplication facts for 3s facts?

Essential Question **How Can You Break Apart Arrays to Multiply with 3?**

Visual Learning Bridge

The Park District has canoes stored in 3 rows. There are 6 canoes in each row. What is the total number of canoes stored?

You can multiply to find the total for an array.

B What You Show

Find 3 × 6.

Use 1s facts and 2s facts to help you multiply with 3.

Make an array for each multiplication sentence.

$\left.\begin{array}{l}\end{array}\right\}$ 2 × 6 = 12

12 + 6 = 18

 } 1 × 6 = 6

C What You Think

3 × 6 is 3 rows of 6. That is 2 sixes plus 1 more six.

2 sixes are 12.
1 six is 6.

12 + 6 = 18

3 × 6 = 18

There are 18 canoes.

Convince Me! **Use Structure** Suppose there were 7 canoes in each of 3 rows. How can 2 × 7 = 14 help you find the total number of canoes?

Name_____

Another Example !

Find 4×7.

What You Show

Four is double 2.
4×7 is double 2×7.

$\left.\begin{array}{c}\bullet\bullet\bullet\bullet\bullet\bullet\bullet \\ \bullet\bullet\bullet\bullet\bullet\bullet\bullet\end{array}\right\}$ $2 \times 7 = 14$

$\left.\begin{array}{c}\bullet\bullet\bullet\bullet\bullet\bullet\bullet \\ \bullet\bullet\bullet\bullet\bullet\bullet\bullet\end{array}\right\}$ $2 \times 7 = 14$

What You Think

4×7 is 4 rows of 7.
That is 2 sevens plus 2 sevens.
2 sevens are 14.

$14 + 14 = 28$

So, $4 \times 7 = 28$

☆ Guided Practice

Do You Understand?

1. Besides using a 2s fact and doubling it, what is another way to break apart 4×7 using facts you already know?

$4 + 7 = (3 \times 7) + (1 \times 7)$

2. Selena arranged 3 rows of plants in her garden. She put 9 plants in each row. How many plants did Selena arrange?

9 99 27

Do You Know How?

In **3–8**, multiply. You may use counters or pictures to help.

3. $3 \times 10 = \underline{30}$

4. $\underline{20} = 5 \times 4$

5. $\underline{24} = 3 \times 8$

6. $1 \times 4 = \underline{4}$

7. $\begin{array}{r} 3 \\ \times 7 \\ \hline 21 \end{array}$

8. $\begin{array}{r} 10 \\ \times 4 \\ \hline 40 \end{array}$

☆ Independent Practice ☆

Leveled Practice In **9–13**, multiply. You may use counters or pictures to help.

9. Find $3 \times 4.$ $= 12$

$\left.\begin{array}{c}\bullet\bullet\bullet\bullet\bullet \\ \bullet\bullet\bullet\bullet\bullet\end{array}\right\}$ $2 \times 4 = \underline{8}$

$\left.\bullet\bullet\bullet\bullet\bullet\right\}$ $1 \times 4 = \underline{4}$

$8 + 4 = \underline{11}$

So, $3 \times 4 = \underline{12}$.

10. Find 4×9.

$\left.\begin{array}{c}\bullet\bullet\bullet\bullet\bullet\bullet\bullet\bullet\bullet \\ \bullet\bullet\bullet\bullet\bullet\bullet\bullet\bullet\bullet\end{array}\right\}$ $2 \times 9 = \underline{18}$

$\left.\begin{array}{c}\bullet\bullet\bullet\bullet\bullet\bullet\bullet\bullet\bullet \\ \bullet\bullet\bullet\bullet\bullet\bullet\bullet\bullet\bullet\end{array}\right\}$ $2 \times 9 = \underline{18}$

$18 + 18 = \underline{36}$

So, $4 \times 9 = \underline{36}$.

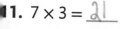**1.** $7 \times 3 = \underline{21}$

12. $\underline{12} = 4 \times 3$

13. $10 \times 3 = \underline{30}$

Problem Solving

14. Make Sense and Persevere James needs to buy supplies for his trail walk. What is the total number of cereal bars James needs to buy? Explain how you used the table to find the answer.

$4 \times 6 = 24$

ceral
bals 24

15. How many more apples than juice drinks does James need? Show how you found the answer.

apples has more

$4 \times 3 = 12$

$2 \times 8 = 16$

DATA

Trail Walk Supplies		
Item	Number of Packages Needed	Number of Items in Each Package
Apples	2	8
Cereal Bars	4	6
Juice Drinks	4	3

---

16. Allison bought 10 packages of energy bars. Each package contains 6 bars. Allison says she has a total of 65 energy bars. Is her answer reasonable? Why or why not?

No because $10 \times 6 = 60$ and not 65 so Allison has 60 bars

17. Higher Order Thinking What two multiplication facts can help you find 3×9? How could you use 3×9 to find 9×3?

$3 \times 9 = 27$

$9 \times 3 = 27$

Assessment Practice

18. Bess has 6 boxes of candles. There are 4 candles in each box. Which equation can be used to find the number of candles Bess has?

- Ⓐ $(3 \times 4) + (3 \times 4) = ?$
- Ⓑ $(6 \times 2) + (6 \times 6) = ?$
- Ⓒ $(6 \times 2) + (3 \times 2) = ?$
- Ⓓ $(2 \times 2) + (6 \times 6) = ?$

19. Which of the following shows one way to use the Distributive Property to find 9×3?

- Ⓐ $(3 \times 2) + (3 \times 1)$
- Ⓑ $(9 \times 2) + (9 \times 1)$
- Ⓒ $(9 \times 2) + (3 \times 2)$
- Ⓓ $(9 + 2) \times (9 + 1)$

Name_____

Solve & Share

Students set up 6 rows of seats for a music concert. They put 6 seats in each row. What is the total number of seats?

Activity

Lesson 3-3
Apply Properties: 6 and 7 as Factors

I can ...
make and use models to solve multiplication problems that have 6 and 7 as factors.

I can also model with math to solve problems.

You can model with math. Pictures, numbers, symbols, and words can be used to represent and solve multiplication problems.

Look Back! How can 3s facts help you solve 6s facts?

$3 \times 2 = 6$ double the 3   I can double

$6 \times 8 = (3 \overset{24}{\times} 8) + (3 \overset{24}{\times} 8)$ My 3's facts

$48 = 48$ to reach a

$+12$ 6's fact.

$12 = 24$ $12 \times 12 = 24$

Essential Question **How Can You Break Apart Arrays to Multiply?**

A

The members of the band march in 6 equal rows. There are 8 band members in each row. How many are in the band?

You can multiply to find the total for an array.

B **What You Show**

Find 6 × 8.

Use 5s facts and 1s facts.

Make an array for each multiplication sentence.

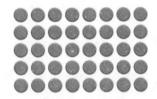
$5 \times 8 = 40$

$1 \times 8 = 8$

C **What You Think**

6 × 8 is 6 rows of 8. That is 5 eights plus 1 more eight.

5 eights are 40.
8 more is 48.
$40 + 8 = 48$

So, $6 \times 8 = 48$.

The band has 48 members.

Convince Me! **Use Structure** Use a 5s fact and a 1s fact to find 6 × 9. Draw two arrays. Explain your drawings.

$$6 \times 9 = (5 \times 9) + (1 \times 9) =$$
$$\quad\quad\quad\quad 45 \quad\quad\quad 9$$

Name_____

Another Example !

Find 7 × 8. Use 5s facts and 2s facts to help multiply by 7.

5 × 8 = 40

2 × 8 = 16

7 × 8 equals 7 rows of 8.
That is 5 eights plus 2 eights.

5 eights are 40.
2 eights are 16.

40 + 16 = 56

So, 7 × 8 = 56.

☆ Guided Practice

Do You Understand?

1. The students who are graduating are standing in 7 equal rows. There are 9 students in each row. How many students are graduating? Use a 5s fact and a 2s fact.

$$7 \times 9 = (5 \times 9) + (2 \times 9)$$

2. Chrissy bakes 3 cherry pies. She cuts each pie into 6 slices. How many slices does Chrissy have?

9 slices

Do You Know How?

In **3–8**, multiply. You may draw pictures or use counters to help.

3. 6 × 10 = __60__

4. 7 × 6 = __42__

5.
$$\begin{array}{r} 7 \\ \times 7 \\ \hline 44 \end{array}$$

6.
$$\begin{array}{r} 9 \\ \times 7 \\ \hline 58 \end{array}$$

7. Find 4 times 7. __28__

8. Multiply 6 times 5. __30__

☆ Independent Practice ☆

In **9–16**, find the product. You may draw pictures to help.

9.
$$\begin{array}{r} 5 \\ \times 7 \\ \hline 35 \end{array}$$

10.
$$\begin{array}{r} 3 \\ \times 6 \\ \hline 18 \end{array}$$

11.
$$\begin{array}{r} 7 \\ \times 8 \\ \hline 42 \end{array}$$

12.
$$\begin{array}{r} 1 \\ \times 7 \\ \hline 7 \end{array}$$

13.
$$\begin{array}{r} 10 \\ \times 6 \\ \hline 60 \end{array}$$

14.
$$\begin{array}{r} 4 \\ \times 7 \\ \hline 29 \end{array}$$

15.
$$\begin{array}{r} 7 \\ \times 3 \\ \hline 21 \end{array}$$

16.
$$\begin{array}{r} 8 \\ \times 6 \\ \hline 48 \end{array}$$

Problem Solving

17. The National Toy Train Museum has 5 exhibits for trains. In one of the exhibits, the trains are on 5 tracks. How many trains are on display at that exhibit? Write an equation to solve the problem.

$5 \times 6 = 38$

Equations can help you describe a situation.

6 trains on each track

---

18. Tracy used the flat surface of a cube to draw a plane shape. What plane shape did Tracy draw? How do you know?

The square of the airplane because then the airpane would not be so thats why i think its the cube.

19. The dance team lines up in 4 rows of 6 dancers each. How many dancers are on the dance team?

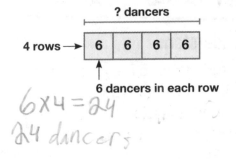

? dancers

4 rows → | 6 | 6 | 6 | 6 |

6 dancers in each row

$6 \times 4 = 24$

24 dancers

---

20. Higher Order Thinking Marge says 7×0 is equal to $7 + 0$. Is Marge correct? Why or why not?

No because in multiplication the zeros times anything eqeals zero and so
$7 + 0 = 7$ Marge is wrong.
$7 \times 0 = 0$

21. Use Structure There are 7 rows of 10 seats. How can you use the Distributive Property to find the total number of seats?

2×10

---

22. Select numbers to create a different expression that is equal to 7×8.

| 1 | 2 | 3 | 5 | 7 | 8 |

$7 \times 8 = (\boxed{3} \times 8) + (\boxed{5} \times 8)$

23. Select numbers to create a different expression that is equal to 8×6.

| 1 | 3 | 5 | 6 | 8 | 9 |

$8 \times 6 = (\boxed{3} \times 6) + (\boxed{3} \times 6)$

Name _____

Lesson 3-4
Apply Properties: 8 as a Factor

☆ ☆
Solve & Share

There are 8 rows of prizes. There are 6 prizes in each row. How many prizes are there?

I can ...
use known facts and properties to multiply by 8.

I can also make sense of problems.

8×6=48 Prizes

3×8+3×8=48

You can make sense and persevere by using known facts to solve unknown facts.

Look Back! Tell how you can use 2s, 3s, or 4s facts to solve the problem.

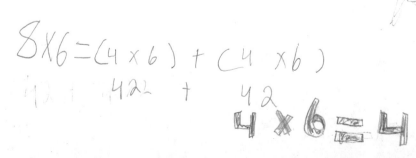

8×6=(4×6)+(4×6)

     422 + 42

4 × 6 = 4 2

Essential Question

How Can You Use Doubles to Multiply with 8?

A

At a school fun fair, students try to toss a table tennis ball into a bowl. There are 8 rows of bowls. There are 8 bowls in each row. How many bowls are there?

What 2s and 4s facts can you find in the bowl array?

B **One Way**

Use 2s facts to find 8 × 8.

8 × 8 equals 4 groups of 2 eights.

} 2 × 8 = 16

} 2 × 8 = 16

} 2 × 8 = 16

} 2 × 8 = 16

16 + 16 + 16 + 16 = 64

So, 8 × 8 = 64.

C **Another Way**

Double a 4s fact to find 8 × 8.

8 × 8 equals 4 eights plus 4 eights.

} 4 × 8 = 32

} 4 × 8 = 32

32 + 32 = 64

So, 8 × 8 = 64.

Convince Me! **Use Structure** How does knowing 5 × 8 = 40 help you find 8 × 8?

If you change 5 to it will turn

8×8=64

Name_____

Do You Understand?

1. Multiply 8 times 3. Write and solve a multiplication equation.

$8 \times 3 = 24$

2. Multiply 5 times 8. Write and solve a multiplication equation.

$5 \times 8 = 40$

3. Multiply 8 times 1. Write and solve a multiplication equation.

$8 \times 1 = 8$

Do You Know How?

In **4–9**, multiply. You may draw pictures or use counters to help.

4. $8 \times 7 = \underline{32}$

5. $\underline{32} = 8 \times 4$

6. $6 \times 8 = \underline{39}$

7. $\underline{80} = 10 \times 8$

8. $\begin{array}{r} 9 \\ \times 8 \\ \hline 48 \end{array}$ **9.** $\begin{array}{r} 8 \\ \times 3 \\ \hline 24 \end{array}$

☆ **Independent Practice** ☆

In **10–23**, find the product. You may draw pictures to help.

10. $8 \times 4 = \underline{32}$

11. $1 \times 8 = \underline{8}$

12. $\underline{16} = 2 \times 8$

13. $\underline{40} = 5 \times 8$

14. $8 \times 2 = \underline{16}$

15. $8 \times 6 = \underline{48}$

16. $\begin{array}{r} 8 \\ \times 8 \\ \hline 64 \end{array}$

17. $\begin{array}{r} 8 \\ \times 5 \\ \hline 40 \end{array}$

18. $\begin{array}{r} 0 \\ \times 8 \\ \hline 0 \end{array}$

19. $\begin{array}{r} 4 \\ \times 8 \\ \hline 32 \end{array}$

20. $\begin{array}{r} 10 \\ \times\ 8 \\ \hline 80 \end{array}$

21. $\begin{array}{r} 8 \\ \times 1 \\ \hline 8 \end{array}$

22. $\begin{array}{r} 3 \\ \times 8 \\ \hline 24 \end{array}$

23. $\begin{array}{r} 7 \\ \times 8 \\ \hline 56 \end{array}$

Problem Solving

24. Use Structure Ming bought 8 belts for gifts. How much money did Ming spend? Show how you can use a 4s fact to find the answer.

$8 \times 4 = (2 \times 4) + (6 \times 4)$

25. Willa bought a shirt and a sweater. She had $14 left. How much money did Willa start with? How do you know?

She use to Have 75$ and i know because If yo do 23+38+14=75 and then yeah

Clothing Sale	
Shirt	$23
Belt	$9
Sweater	$38
Pair of jeans	$42

26. Mr. Garner spends $52 on groceries and $24 on gas. How much does Mr. Garner spend? Write an equation and solve.

75$?	
$52	$24

$24 + 52 = 75$

27. Algebra Mischa bought 7 boxes of orange tiles. There are 8 tiles in each box. How many tiles did Mischa buy? Write an equation and solve. Use ? to represent the unknown quantity of tiles.

$8 \times 7 = 56$

$7 \times 8 = (3 \times 8) + (4 + 8)$
$24 + 32$
56

28. Aaron bought 6 packs of sports cards. There are 7 cards in each pack. How many sports cards did Aaron buy in all? Use properties to solve the problem.

$7 \times 6 = (4 \times 6) + (3 \times 6)$
$24 + 18$
42

29. Higher Order Thinking Sophie says, "To find 8×8, I can find $8 \times (4 + 4)$." Do you agree? Explain.

Assessment Practice

30. Ms. Vero has boxes of crayons. Each box has 8 crayons. Select all the correct equations that could show how many crayons Ms. Vero has.

- [ ] $8 \times 8 = 64$
- [ ] $4 \times 8 = 32$
- [ ] $2 \times 8 = 15$
- [ ] $3 \times 8 = 24$
- [ ] $6 \times 8 = 84$

31. Select all the expressions that can be used to find 8×7.

- A [ ] $(4 \times 7) + (4 \times 7)$
- [ ] $(4 \times 6) + (4 \times 1)$
- [ ] $(4 \times 5) + (4 \times 2)$
- D [ ] $(8 \times 5) + (8 \times 2)$
- E [ ] $(2 \times 7) + (2 \times 7) + (2 \times 7) + (2 \times 7)$

Name _____

Solve & Share

Jermaine has 7 coolers. Each cooler contains 8 bottles of sports drink. How many bottles of sports drink does Jermaine have in all?

I can ...
use strategies and tools to represent and solve multiplication facts.

I can also model with math to solve problems.

You can model with math. Pictures, objects, words, numbers, and symbols can be used to represent and solve the problem.

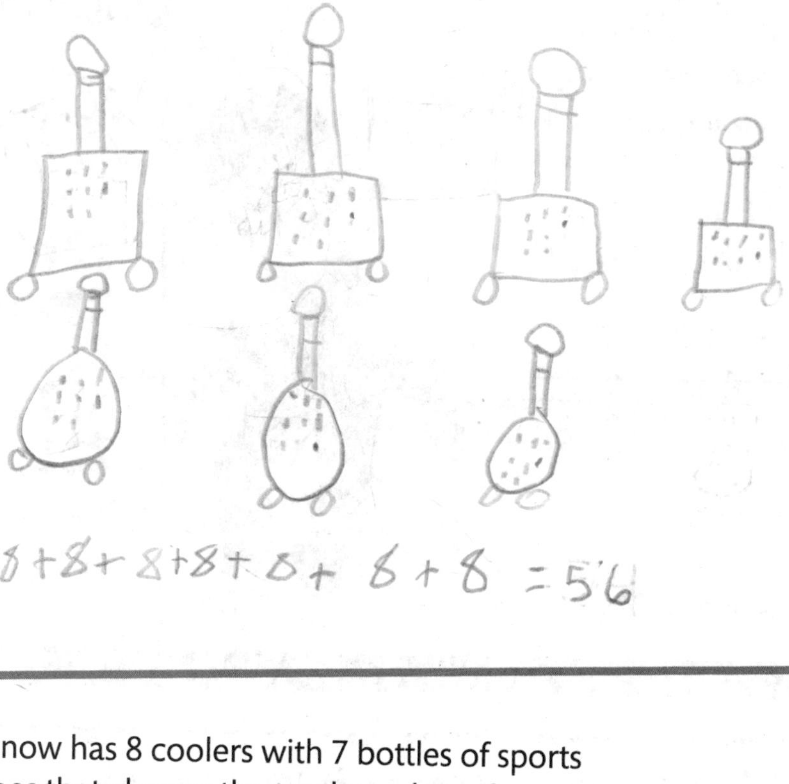

$8 + 8 + 8 + 8 + 8 + 8 + 8 + 8 = 56$

Look Back! Jermaine now has 8 coolers with 7 bottles of sports drink in each cooler. Does that change the total number of bottles of sports drink that Jermaine has? Explain why or why not.

No because 7coolers and 8 Bottles were 56 so if you do 8coolers and 7bottles you are just switching the number around

How Do You Use Strategies to Multiply?

Justin and Dolores made a dragon float for a parade. They connected 9 equal sections to make the dragon's body. What is the total length of the dragon's body in feet?

The dragon's body is made of equal sections, so you can multiply to find its length.

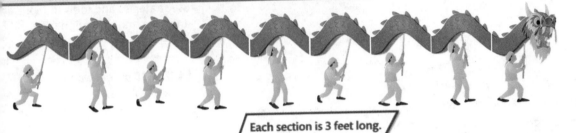

Each section is 3 feet long.

B One Way

Draw a picture to find 9 × 3.

9 × 3 means 9 groups of 3. Combine the groups to find the product.

Dragon's body length
?

3	3	3	3	3	3	3	3	3

↑
3 feet each section

9 × 3 = 27

The dragon's body is 27 feet long.

C Another Way

Use known facts to find 9 × 3.

Use 4s facts and 5s facts to help.

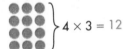 4 × 3 = 12

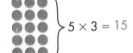 5 × 3 = 15

12 + 15 = 27

The dragon's body is 27 feet long.

Convince Me! **Make Sense and Persevere** What two other facts can you use to find 9 × 3? Explain.

Name_____

☆ Guided Practice

Do You Understand?

1. What known facts can you use to find 7 × 5? $5 \times 4 = 25$
$5 \times 6 = 30$

2. To find 8 × 6, how does knowing 6 × 6 = 36 help you?

$8 \times 6 = (1 \times 6) + (5 \times 6)$

Do You Know How?

In **3–8**, multiply.

3. $3 \times 7 = \underline{21}$ **4.** $\underline{30} = 6 \times 5$

5. $9 \times 4 = \underline{36}$ **6.** $\underline{0} = 3 \times 0$

7.
$$\begin{array}{r} 1 \\ \times 7 \\ \hline 7 \end{array}$$

8.
$$\begin{array}{r} 10 \\ \times 8 \\ \hline 80 \end{array}$$

Independent Practice ☆

In **9–25**, use known facts and strategies to find the product.

9. $7 \times 7 = \underline{49}$ **10.** $8 \times 2 = \underline{16}$ **11.** $3 \times 10 = \underline{30}$

12. $\underline{72} = 8 \times 9$ **13.** $\underline{24} = 4 \times 6$ **14.** $\underline{16} = 4 \times 4$

15.
$$\begin{array}{r} 10 \\ \times 7 \\ \hline 70 \end{array}$$

16.
$$\begin{array}{r} 2 \\ \times 6 \\ \hline 12 \end{array}$$

17.
$$\begin{array}{r} 1 \\ \times 3 \\ \hline 3 \end{array}$$

18.
$$\begin{array}{r} 2 \\ \times 7 \\ \hline 1.4 \end{array}$$

19.
$$\begin{array}{r} 8 \\ \times 0 \\ \hline 0 \end{array}$$

20.
$$\begin{array}{r} 10 \\ \times 6 \\ \hline 60 \end{array}$$

21.
$$\begin{array}{r} 4 \\ \times 7 \\ \hline 28 \end{array}$$

22.
$$\begin{array}{r} 8 \\ \times 9 \\ \hline 72 \end{array}$$

23. What is 6 × 9? $\underline{54}$ **24.** What is 7 × 2? $\underline{14}$ **25.** What is 8 × 1? $\underline{8}$

Problem Solving

26. Reasoning Mr. Ling walks 5 miles each day. How many total miles does he walk in one week? Explain.

35 miles

7X5=35

Remember, there are 7 days in a week.

27. David wants to buy new shoes and a jersey. The shoes cost $56. The jersey costs $42. How much money does David need to buy both items?

56
+42
98

98 ?	
$56	$42

---

28. Ms. Wilson drank three 8-ounce glasses of tea before lunch. Then she drank three 8-ounce glasses of water before dinner. How many ounces of liquid did she drink in all? Write an equation to help solve.

48-ounces

24+24=48

29. Higher Order Thinking Show how you can use known facts to find 4 × 11. Explain how you chose the known facts.

8X8

---

30. Mr. Evans needs to assign 32 students into 8 equal groups. He says, "I can use repeated subtraction. Because I subtract 3 times, each group has 3 students." Do you agree with Mr. Evans? Explain why or why not.

32÷8=4

32 – 16 = 16
16 – 8 = 8
8 – 8 = 0

☑ **Assessment Practice**

31. Select the possible ways to display 20 counters in equal groups.

A ☐ 2 groups of 10
B ☐ 4 groups of 5
C ☐ 5 groups of 4
☐ 4 groups of 6
☐ 10 groups of 2

32. Select the possible ways to display 24 counters in an array.

☐ 8 rows of 4
B ☐ 3 rows of 6
C ☐ 6 rows of 4
☐ 3 rows of 8
☐ 2 rows of 9

Name **Aseel**

Lesson 3-6
The Associative Property: Multiply with 3 Factors

☆ ☆
Solve & Share

Gina has 2 quilts. Each quilt has 5 rows with 3 squares in each row. How many squares are in both quilts? Solve this problem any way you choose. Then find another way to solve the problem.

I can ...
multiply 3 factors in any order to find a product.

I can also make sense of problems

 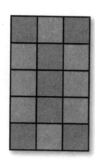

5×3=15
5×3=15
3+5=15
5+10=15
10+5=15
11+4=15
12+3=15

15 boxes

You can make sense and persevere in solving problems. You can solve this problem in more than one way.

Look Back! Did you get a different answer when you solved the problem a different way? Explain why or why not.

How Can You Multiply 3 Numbers?

A

Drew is joining 3 sections of a quilt. Each section has 2 rows with 4 squares in each row. How many squares are in these 3 sections? Find 3 × 2 × 4.

You can multiply to find the total for an array.

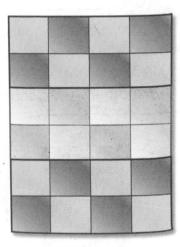

B **One Way**

Find 3 × 2 first.

(3 × 2) × 4

  ↓

  6   × 4 = 24

6 rows, 4 squares in each row

There are 24 squares in all.

C **Another Way**

Find 2 × 4 first.

3 × (2 × 4)

     ↓

3 ×   8 = 24

3 sections, 8 squares in each section

There are 24 squares in Drew's quilt.

The Associative (Grouping) Property of Multiplication says that you can change the grouping of the factors and the product will be the same.

Convince Me! **Generalize** Use the Associative Property of Multiplication to show two different ways to find 5 × 2 × 3. Did you get the same answer both ways? What can you generalize?

5x2=3=26 So yeah you can do two diffrent
2x5=3=26 eqeation So yeah.

Name _____

☆ Guided Practice

Do You Understand?

1. Sarah has 4 pages of stickers in an album. Each page has 3 rows with 2 stickers in each row. How many stickers are in Sarah's album? You may use objects to help.

$4 \times 2 \times 3 = 17$

2. Billy concludes the product of $(2 \times 3) \times 5$ is not equal to the product of $2 \times (3 \times 5)$. Is Billy correct? Explain.

Billy is incorrect because 2×(3×5), is the same as (2×3)×5.

Do You Know How?

In **3-6**, use the Associative Property of Multiplication to find the missing number. You may use objects or draw a picture to help.

3. $2 \times (4 \times 2) = (2 \times 4) \times \underline{2}$

4. $(3 \times 4) \times 3 = 3 \times (\underline{4} \times 3)$

5. $2 \times (2 \times 3) = (2 \times 2) \times \underline{3}$

6. $(3 \times 2) \times 4 = \underline{3} \times (2 \times 4)$

Independent Practice

In **7-12**, use the Associative Property of Multiplication to find the missing number. You may use objects or draw a picture to help.

7. $8 \times (3 \times 6) = (8 \times 3) \times \underline{6}$

8. $5 \times (6 \times 9) = (5 \times 6) \times \underline{1}$

9. $5 \times (7 \times 2) = (5 \times 7) \times \underline{2}$

10. $5 \times (2 \times 9) = (5 \times \underline{2}) \times 9$

11. $3 \times (2 \times 5) = (3 \times 2) \times \underline{3}$

12. $4 \times (2 \times 2) = (4 \times \underline{2}) \times 2$

In **13-18**, use the Associative Property of Multiplication to find the product. You may use objects or draw a picture to help.

13. $2 \times 3 \times 2 = \underline{12}$

14. $3 \times 6 \times 2 = \underline{36}$

15. $2 \times 6 \times 2 = \underline{24}$

16. $5 \times 2 \times 4 = \underline{40}$

17. $5 \times 2 \times 2 = \underline{20}$

18. $3 \times 3 \times 2 = \underline{18}$

Problem Solving

19. Reasoning There are 7 mockingbird nests at a park with eggs in them. What is the greatest number of eggs there could be at this park? What is the least number of eggs there could be?

$5 \times 7 = 35$ 35 eggs

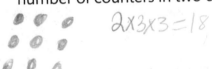

Mockingbirds lay 3 to 5 eggs.

20. At another park, there are 3 mockingbird nests with 4 eggs in each nest and 1 more nest with 3 eggs. How many eggs are there at this park?

$3 \times 4 = 15$. 15 eggs

---

21. Maria says she can find the product for $2 \times 3 \times 4$ by solving $3 \times 2 \times 4$. Is Maria correct? Explain.

yes because it is the same product so yeah.
yes because it

22. Anita has 2 arrays. Each array has 3 rows of 3 counters. Explain why Anita can use the Associative Property to find the total number of counters in two different ways.

$2 \times 3 \times 3 = 18$

---

23. Algebra Which number makes both equations true?

$4 \times (3 \times 2) = (④ \times ?) \times 2$

$3 \times (⑤ \times 2) = (? \times 5) \times 2$

24. Higher Order Thinking How do you know that $4 \times 2 \times 2$ is the same as 4×4? Explain.

Because it is the same number just changed

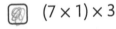

Assessment Practice

25. Use properties of operations to select all the expressions that could be used to find $7 \times 1 \times 3$.

- ☒ $(7 \times 1) \times 3$
- ☒ $7 \times (1 \times 3)$
- ☒ $(1 \times 7) \times 3$
- ☐ $7 \times 1 \times 1$
- ☒ $7 \times (3 \times 1)$

26. An expression is shown. Select all the equivalent expressions.

$4 \times 2 \times 3$

- ☒ $4 \times (2 \times 3)$
- ☐ $(4 \times 2) \times 3$
- ☐ $(2 \times 4) \times 3$
- ☐ $(4 \times 2) \times 4$
- ☐ $(3 \times 2) \times 2$

You can use properties to solve problems in different ways.

Name_____

☆ ☆
Solve & Share

You have learned that you can use known facts to find unknown facts. For each of the 4 multiplication facts below, list two multiplication facts from the box that can be added to find the given product. The first solution is completed for you.

What do you notice about the facts you used to find the products when 6 or 7 is a factor?

Activity

I can ...
use reasoning to look for and describe general strategies for finding products.

I can also apply properties of operations to multiply.

6×7

$5 \times 7 + 1 \times 7 = 42$

6×9

$\underline{5 \times 9} + \underline{1 \times 9} = 54$

7×8

$\underline{5 \times 8} + \underline{2 \times 8} = 56$

7×9

$\underline{2 \times 9} + \underline{5 \times 9} = 63$

1×9	2×8	1×7
5×8	5×9	1×8
5×7	2×7	2×9

Thinking Habits

Be a good thinker!
These questions can help you.

- Are any calculations repeated?

- Can I generalize from examples?

- What shortcuts do I notice?

Look Back! **Generalize** Use your observations from your work above to complete these facts.

$(\underline{4} \times 6) + (\underline{2} \times 6) = 36$

$(\underline{3} \times 7) + (\underline{4} \times 7) = 49$

How Can You Use Repeated Reasoning When Multiplying?

A

Ellie wrote the equations below to find the total number of squares in each of these rectangles. Look at the equations. Known facts with which factors are used repeatedly to find the products?

A $3 \times 6 = (2 \times 6) + (1 \times 6) = 12 + 6 = 18$

B $4 \times 9 = (2 \times 9) + (2 \times 9) = 18 + 18 = 36$

C $6 \times 8 = (5 \times 8) + (1 \times 8) = 40 + 8 = 48$

D $7 \times 7 = (5 \times 7) + (2 \times 7) = 35 + 14 = 49$

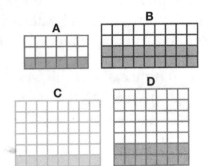

What do I need to do to complete the task?

I need to see if there are known facts that can be used repeatedly to find other facts.

B **How can I make a generalization from repeated reasoning?**

I can

- look for repeated calculations.

- make generalizations about the repeated calculations.

- test whether my generalizations work for other numbers.

C I see that the factors 1, 2, and 5 are used repeatedly. I see two generalizations.

> Here's my thinking...

I can break facts with 3 or 4 into 2s and 1s facts.
$3 \times 6 = (2 \times 6) + (1 \times 6)$
$4 \times 9 = (2 \times 9) + (2 \times 9)$

I can break facts with 6 or 7 into 5s, 2s, and 1s facts.
$6 \times 8 = (5 \times 8) + (1 \times 8)$
$7 \times 7 = (5 \times 7) + (2 \times 7)$

I can test this with other facts.
$3 \times 5 = (2 \times 5) + (1 \times 5)$
$6 \times 7 = (5 \times 7) + (1 \times 7)$

Convince Me! **Generalize** Use the generalizations above to complete each of the following. Tell how you decided.

$7 \times 5 = (\underline{7 \times 3}) + (\underline{7 \times 2})$

$7 \times 6 = (\underline{2 \times 8}) + (\underline{5 \times 6})$

Name_____

☆ Guided Practice

Generalize

Ricardo wrote the equations below.

When you generalize, you make a statement about a larger group based on examples that are true.

1. Which factors did Ricardo use repeatedly to find the products? Make a generalization.

$3 \times \textcircled{8} = (\textcircled{2} \times \textcircled{8}) + (1 \times 8) = \textcircled{2}4$

$3 \times \textcircled{7} = (\textcircled{2} \times \textcircled{7}) + (1 \times \textcircled{7}) = \textcircled{2}1$

$\textcircled{6} \times 3 = (\textcircled{6} \times \textcircled{1}) + (\textcircled{6} \times 2) = \textcircled{1}8$

2. Complete this equation to test whether your generalization is true for other facts. Explain.

$3 \times 9 = (\underline{2} \times \underline{9}) + (\underline{1} \times \underline{9}) = \underline{22}$

☆ Independent Practice ☆

Generalize

Mary wrote the equations at the right.

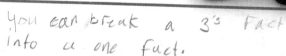
You can break a 3's fact into a one fact.

3. Which factors did Mary use repeatedly to find the products? Make a generalization.

$8 \times \textcircled{7} = (5 \times \textcircled{7}) + (3 \times \textcircled{7}) = 56$

$\textcircled{6} \times 8 = (\textcircled{6} \times 5) + (\textcircled{6} \times 3) = 48$

$8 \times \textcircled{9} = (3 \times \textcircled{9}) + (5 \times \textcircled{9}) = 72$

4. Complete this equation to test whether your generalization is true for other facts. Explain.

$8 \times 3 = (\underline{2} \times \underline{8}) + (\underline{1} \times \underline{8}) = \underline{24}$

5. What is another way you can use known facts to solve 8×3? What generalization can you make from this way?

$8 \times 3 = (6 \times 3 + 2 \times 3) = 24$

Problem Solving

✓ Performance Task

Baking Pizzas

Adam is baking 4 pizzas. Each pizza is a rectangle. It takes Adam 35 minutes to bake the pizzas. He divides each pizza into the equal-size square slices shown.

Pizza 1 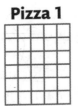 **Pizza 2**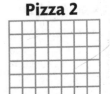

6. **Make Sense and Persevere** Adam multiplies to find the total number of square slices for each pizza. For each pizza, tell the factors Adam multiplies.

Pizza 3 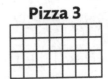 **Pizza 4**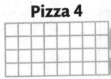

$4 \times 7 = 16$ $6 \times 7 =$ $4 \times 8 =$ $6 \times 7 =$

7. **Use Structure** Look at the facts you wrote in Exercise **6**. Break apart these facts into 1s, 2s, or 5s facts to find the total number of slices for each pizza.

Pizza 1
$(6 \times 5) = (5 \times 1) + (1 \times 5) = 30$

Pizza 2
$(8 \times 6) = (8 \times 1) + (7 \times 5) = 48$

Pizza 3
$(8 \times 4) = (4 \times 2) + (4 \times 2) = 32$

Pizza 4
$(4 \times 5) = (4 \times 4) + (4 \times 4) = 32$

8. **Generalize** Look at how you used the 1s, 2s, and 5s facts above. What generalizations can you make? Test your generalizations with another fact.

I can a break 6s fact into a 3.

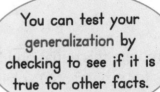
You can test your generalization by checking to see if it is true for other facts.

9. **Critique Reasoning** Look at the model for Pizza 3. Adam says he can use 2s facts to solve 4 × 7 or 7 × 4. Is he correct? Explain.

yes you can use a two Fact

101

Name_____

Follow the Path

Shade a path from **START** to **FINISH**.
Follow the differences that are correct.
You can only move up, down, right, or left.

I can ...
subtract within 100.

I can also be precise in my wor

Start				
75 − 13 62	99 − 63 36	85 − 39 46	70 − 48 32	41 − 31 11
39 − 21 12	24 − 16 10	59 − 37 22	55 − 32 67	91 − 65 47
77 − 38 45	47 − 40 87	46 − 27 19	100 − 62 58	45 − 27 17
69 − 21 47	34 − 29 15	65 − 59 6	81 − 29 52	67 − 19 48
82 − 46 58	38 − 12 23	93 − 34 69	24 − 18 9	78 − 35 43

Finish

Vocabulary Review

A-Z
Glossary

Word List

- Associative (Grouping) Property of Multiplication
- Commutative (Order) Property of Multiplication
- Distributive Property
- factor
- Identity (One) Property of Multiplication
- multiple
- product
- Zero Property of Multiplication

Understand Vocabulary

Match the example to the term.

1. $5 \times 0 = 0 \times 5$ Associative (Grouping) Property of Multiplication

2. $(3 \times 8) + (1 \times 8) = 4 \times 8$ Commutative (Order) Property of Multiplication

3. $(6 \times 2) \times 2 = 6 \times (2 \times 2)$ Distributive Property

     Identity (One) Property of Multiplication

4. $7 \times 1 = 7$

Write T for *true* or F for *false*.

_____True_____ **5.** 3 and 8 are *multiples* of 24.

_____True_____ **6.** You can multiply *factors* in any order.

_____False_____ **7.** The *product* of zero and any number is that number.

_____True_____ **8.** There are 3 *factors* in the equation $5 \times 3 \times 2 = 30$.

Use Vocabulary in Writing

9. Explain how to use $8 \times 5 = 40$ to find 8×6. Use at least 2 terms from the Word List in your explanation.

You can wouse Idintify Property

Name_____

Set A pages 77–80

You can break an array into 2 smaller arrays.

You can write an unknown fact as the sum of 2 known facts.

$4 \times 8 = (3 \times 8) + (1 \times 8)$

Remember that the Distributive Property says that a multiplication fact can be broken apart into the sum of two other multiplication facts.

In **1** and **2**, find the missing value.

1. __8__ $\times 4 = (2 \times 4) + (2 \times 4)$

2. $6 \times 5 = (4 \times 5) + (\underline{6} \times 5)$

Set B pages 81–84

Find 3×4.

You can use a 2s fact to help multiply by 3.

3×4 {
$2 \times 4 = 8$
$1 \times 4 = 4$
}

$8 + 4 = 12$

You can also find 4s facts.

$3 \times 4 = (3 \times 2) + (3 \times 2) = 6 + 6 = 12$

Remember that to find a 3s fact, add a 2s fact and a 1s fact. To find a 4s fact, double the product of a 2s fact.

1. $3 \times 7 = \underline{21}$ 2. $4 \times 9 = \underline{36}$

3. $4 \times 10 = \underline{40}$ 4. $3 \times 10 = \underline{30}$

5. $3 \times 8 = \underline{24}$ 6. $8 \times 4 = \underline{32}$

7. $9 \times 3 = \underline{27}$ 8. $10 \times 4 = \underline{40}$

Set C pages 85–88

You can use known facts to help multiply. Find 6×9.

$6 \times 9 = (5 \times 9) + (1 \times 9)$

$6 \times 9 = 45 + 9$

$6 \times 9 = 54$

Find 7×4.

$7 \times 4 = (5 \times 4) + (2 \times 4)$

$7 \times 4 = 20 + 8$

$7 \times 4 = 28$

Remember that you can break a multiplication problem into two smaller problems.

1. $6 \times 6 = \underline{36}$ 2. $7 \times 9 = \underline{63}$

3. $7 \times 7 = \underline{49}$ 4. $6 \times 8 = \underline{48}$

5.   6
   $\times 5$
   ___
   30

6.   6
   $\times 3$
   ___
   18

7.   10
   $\times 7$
   ___
   70

Set D | pages 89–96

Find 8 × 9.

You can use 2s facts.

8 × 9 = (2 × 9) + (2 × 9) + (2 × 9) + (2 × 9)

8 × 9 = 18 + 18 + 18 + 18

8 × 9 = 72

You can use skip counting.

8, 16, 24, 32, 40, 48, 56, 64, 72

Remember to use patterns, known facts, or skip counting to find products.

1. 8 × 6 = 56

2. 8 × 8 = 64

3. 8 × 7 = 64

4. 8 × 10 = 80

5. 1 × 8 = 8

6. 0 × 8 = 0

7.
$$\begin{array}{r} 8 \\ \times\ 5 \\ \hline 40 \end{array}$$

8.
$$\begin{array}{r} 8 \\ \times\ 3 \\ \hline 24 \end{array}$$

9.
$$\begin{array}{r} 8 \\ \times\ 2 \\ \hline 16 \end{array}$$

Set E | pages 97–100

You can use the Associative Property to group the factors. The product does not change.

Find 4 × 2 × 2.

One Way	Another Way
4 × (2 × 2)	(4 × 2) × 2
4 × 4 = 16	8 × 2 = 16

Remember that you can use properties to write unknown facts as known facts.

In **1–3**, find the product. Show how you grouped the factors.

1. 4 × 2 × 5 = 10 × 4 = 40

2. 3 × 3 × 7 = 9 × 3 = 63

3. 5 × 5 × 2 = ___ × ___ = ___

Set F | pages 101–104

Think about these questions to help you use **repeated reasoning**.

Thinking Habits

- Are any calculations repeated?
- Can I generalize from examples?
- What shortcuts do I notice?

Remember that patterns can help you make a generalization.

1. What is repeated in these equations? Use what you see to make a generalization.

6 × 6 = (6 × 3) + (6 × 3) = 18 + 18 = 36

7 × 6 = (7 × 3) + (7 × 3) = 21 + 21 = 42

8 × 6 = (8 × 3) + (8 × 3) = 24 + 24 = 48

2. Solve this equation to test whether your generalization is true.

10 × 6 = ?

10 × 6 = (9 × 6) + (___ × ___

= ___ + ___ = ___

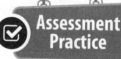

1. Krista arranged her buttons in an array. Which two expressions can be used to find the total number of buttons?

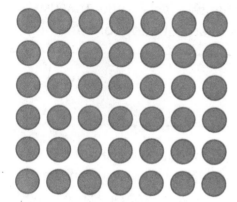

Ⓐ 6 × 7 and 6 × 1

Ⓑ 4 × 7 and 2 × 7

Ⓒ 4 × 4 and 2 × 3

Ⓓ 3 × 7 and 4 × 7

2. Choose *Yes* or *No* to tell if the Distributive Property is being used.

2a. 4 × (2 + 3) =
    4 × 2 + 4 × 3   ◉ Yes   ○ No

2b. (4 + 5) × 2 =
    4 × 2 + 5 × 2   ◉ Yes   ○ No

2c. 2 × 4 =
    2 × (3 + 1)   ○ Yes   ◉ No

2d. 7 × (5 − 2) =
    7 × 5 − 7 × 2   ◉ Yes   ○ No

3. Jeff makes the generalization that a 10s fact can be broken into two 5s facts. Write an equation to test his generalization.

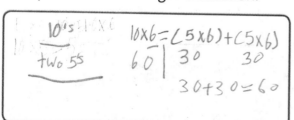

10's   10×6=(5×6)+(5×6)
two 5s   60 | 30   30
                   30+30=60

4. June broke up a large array into a 3 × 4 array and a 5 × 4 array. What was the large array? Show your work.

Assessment Practice

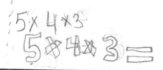

5 × 4 × 3
5 × 4 × 3 =

5. Which facts can you use to find 4 × 8? Select all that apply.

☐ 2 × 8 and 2 × 9

☑ 2 × 8 and 2 × 8

☑ 2 × 4 and 1 × 8

☑ 4 × 5 and 4 × 3

☑ 3 × 8 and 1 × 8

6. A bakery uses 3 cups of flour for each loaf of bread. There are 3 loaves of bread on a tray. There are 6 trays on a cart. How many cups of flour are used to make the bread on the cart? Show your work.

6×3×3=51

7. Find the number that makes the equation correct. Explain your reasoning.
(3 × 4) + (3 × 4) = __24__

3×4=12
3×4=12
12+12=24

8. Casey has 3 bags of baseballs. Each bag has 6 baseballs. How many baseballs does he have? Show your work.

18 baseballs

3×6= 18

9. Jonathan organizes his pictures into a 6 × 4 array. Kim organizes her pictures into a 7 × 5 array. How can Kim and Jonathan break apart their arrays? Write each pair of facts in the correct space.

6 × 4	7 × 5

5 × 5 and 2 × 5

1 × 4 and 5 × 4

4 × 5 and 3 × 5

1 × 5 and 6 × 5

3 × 4 and 3 × 4

10. A farm stand has cherries on 2 shelves. Each shelf has 4 boxes. Each box has 8 ounces of cherries. How many ounces of cherries are displayed in all? Write an expression that represents the amount.

56 ounces

8×4+2 =56

11. Amy arranged her counters into this array.

A. What two facts could Amy use to write an equation for the array?

9×3=27

B. If Amy adds one more row of 9 counters to her array, can she still use the facts you wrote in Part A to find the total number? Explain why or why not.

No

12. Tim's family rented a canoe for 6 hours on Monday and 2 hours on Tuesday. How much did they spend? Show any equations you used.

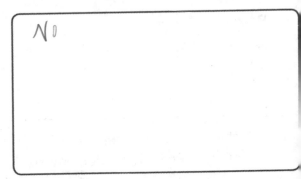

Rentals

Canoe $7 each hour

Kayak $6 each hour

56 $

Name_____

School Fair

Kay and Ben are helping to organize the School Fair.
Kay is organizing the school band.
Ben is organizing the bake sale.

The 3 × 7 array at the right shows how chairs
have been set up for the school band.
Use the array to answer Exercises **1** and **2**.

1. Kay wants to have chairs in a 6 × 7 array.
   Add to the array to show how the new array
   will look.

2. Kay needs a path between two of
   the rows, so she separates the chairs
   into two smaller arrays.

   ### Part A

   Draw a line to show one way Kay
   can separate the chairs into two
   smaller arrays.

   ### Part B

   Kay wants to know the number of chairs in each new
   array. Write a multiplication fact for each of the new
   arrays to show how she can find this.

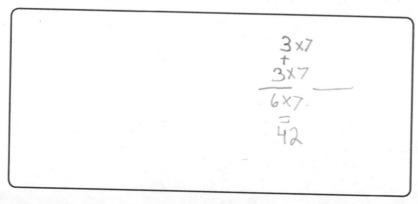

   $7 \times 3 = 21$ $3 \times 7 = 21$

   ### Part C

   Kay wants to find the total number of chairs that are
   being used. Show how to use the facts in Part B to find
   the total number of chairs.

   $$3 \times 7$$
   $$+$$
   $$3 \times 7$$
   $$\overline{6 \times 7}$$
   $$= 42$$

The **Bake Sale** table shows the baked goods Ben has for sale at the School Fair. Use the **Bake Sale** table to answer Exercises **3-5**.

Bake Sale			
Baked Goods	Number of Trays	Number on Each Tray	Cost per Tray
Blueberry Muffins	4	7	$6
Strawberry Tarts	7	8	$4
Granola Bars	8	6	$3

3. Ben sells 4 trays of granola bars in the morning and 4 trays of granola bars in the afternoon. How much money does this raise? Show your work.

4×4=16

4. Ben organizes the blueberry muffins into a 4 × 7 array.

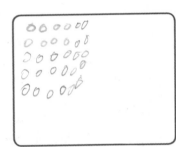

Part A

Ben breaks up the array of blueberry muffins into 2 arrays that look the same. At the right, draw the 2 arrays of blueberry muffins.

Part B

Ben wants to check the total number of blueberry muffins. He knows 2 × 7 = 14. How can he use this to find the total number of blueberry muffins?

5. Two friends each bought 3 trays of strawberry tarts. Ben says they spent more than $20 in total. Do you agree? Explain.

yes because they spent 24$.

Use Multiplication to Divide: Division Facts

Essential Questions: How can you use known multiplication facts to find unknown division facts? How are multiplication and division related?

> It takes a lot of testing to make a new car.

> To build a better car, people make models or prototypes and then test them.

> Let's see how numbers are used in testing. Here's a project on using tests to review models.

enVision STEM Project: Testing Models

Do Research Tests can be done to see if a model works or if a change makes it better. Use the Internet or other sources to find information about a model or prototype that was tested. Identify how the testing was done.

Journal: Write a Report Include what you found. Also in your report:

- Make a chart that includes the model, what changed in the test, and what stayed the same.

- Explain the results of the test.

- Write an equation to show one of the relationships in the test. Explain what the numbers represent.

Name _____ 6/7 _____

Review What You Know

Vocabulary

Choose the best term from the box.
Write it on the blank.

- division ✓
- factors ✓
- equation
- multiplication ✓

1. __factors__ are multiplied together to give a product.

2. Use __division__ to find how many equal groups or how many are in each group.

3. __multiplication__ is an operation that gives the total number when you put together equal groups.

Division

Solve each problem. You can use bar diagrams, counters, or draw a picture to help.

4. Stuart has 15 stickers to give to his 3 friends.
   How many stickers can each friend have?

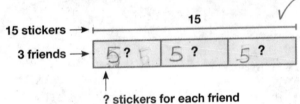

15 stickers → | 15 |
3 friends → | 5 ? | 5 ? | 5 ? |
↑
? stickers for each friend

5. There are 32 muffins. Eight people share them equally.
   How many muffins does each person get?

   32 ÷ 8 = 4 ✓

6. Suzy has 12 granola bars. There are 2 granola bars in each package.
   How many packages of granola bars are there?

   6 × 6 = 12   12 ÷ 2 = 6

Equations

7. Brian has 5 boxes. He puts 8 markers in each box. Which equation shows the total number of markers?

   Ⓐ 5 + 8 = 13   Ⓑ 5 × 8 = 40   Ⓒ 40 ÷ 5 = 8   Ⓓ 40 ÷ 8 = 5

PROJECT 4A

Who are your favorite athletes?

Project: Make a Poster of Your Favorite Athletes

PROJECT 4B

Who is on our money?

Project: Write a Report About Money

PROJECT 4C

How do you score in horseshoes?

Project: Create a Score Sheet

PROJECT 4D

What kind of game would you create?

Project: Develop a Game

Name_____

Solve & Share

Use 24 counters to make arrays with equal rows. Write multiplication and division equations to describe your arrays.

You can use appropriate tools to help see the relationship between multiplication and division.

Lesson 4-1
Relate Multiplication and Division

I can ...
use fact families to see how multiplication and division are related

I can also use a math tool to help solve problems.

$12 \times 2 = 24$
$6 \times 4 = 24$

ooo ooo|ooooo
oooooo|ooooo

Look Back! What relationships do you see between the multiplication and division equations for each of your arrays?

Essential Question

How Can Multiplication Facts Help You Divide?

A

This array can show the relationship between multiplication and division.

Multiplication
3 rows of 10 drums
$3 \times 10 = 30$
30 drums

Division
30 drums in 3 equal rows
$30 \div 3 = 10$
10 drums in each row

B A fact family shows how multiplication and division are related.

Fact family for 3, 10, and 30:

$3 \times 10 = 30 \qquad 30 \div 3 = 10$

$10 \times 3 = 30 \qquad 30 \div 10 = 3$

| dividend | divisor | quotient |

A fact family is a group of related facts using the same numbers.

C The **dividend** is the number of objects to be divided.

The **divisor** is the number by which another number is divided.

The **quotient** is the answer to a division problem.

Remember, a product is the answer to a multiplication problem.

Convince Me! **Reasoning** $4 \times 7 = 28$ is one fact in a fact family. Draw an array for this fact. Write the other three facts in the fact family.

$7 \times 4 = 28$

$28 \div 4 = 7$

$4 \times 7 = 28$

☆ Guided Practice

Do You Understand?

1. Look at the fact family for 3, 10, and 30 on the previous page. What do you notice about the products and the dividends?

$3 \times 10 = 30$

2. Is $4 \times 6 = 24$ part of the fact family for 3, 8, and 24? Explain.

NO

Do You Know How?

In **3–5**, use the relationship between multiplication and division to complete each equation.

3. $3 \times 7 = 21$

$21 \div 3 = \underline{7}$

4. $18 \div 2 = 9$

$2 \times \underline{9} = 18$

5. $2 \times 10 = 20$

$20 \div 2 = \underline{10}$

Independent Practice

In **6** and **7**, use the relationship between multiplication and division to complete each equation.

6. $2 \times \underline{8} = 16$

$16 \div 2 = \underline{8}$

7. $56 \div 8 = 7$

$8 \times \underline{7} = 56$

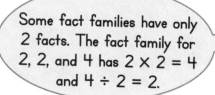
Some fact families have only 2 facts. The fact family for 2, 2, and 4 has $2 \times 2 = 4$ and $4 \div 2 = 2$.

In **8–13**, write the fact family.

8. Write the fact family for 6, 7, and 42.

$7 \times 6 = 42$ $42 \div 6 = 7$
$6 \times 7 = 42$ $42 \div 7 = 6$

9. Write the fact family for 9, 10, and 90.

$9 \times 10 = 90$ $90 \div 10 = 9$
$10 \times 9 = 90$ $90 \div 9 = 10$

10. Write the fact family for 2, 3, and 6.

$2 \times 3 = 6$ $6 \div 3 = 2$
$3 \times 2 = 6$ $6 \div 2 = 3$

11. Write the fact family for 1, 5, and 5.

$1 \times 5 = 5$ $5 \div 1 = 5$
$5 \times 1 = 5$ $5 \div 5 = 1$

12. Write the fact family for 3, 8, and 24.

$3 \times 8 = 24$ $24 \div 3 = 8$
$8 \times 3 = 24$ $24 \div 8 = 3$

13. Write the fact family for 5, 6, and 30.

$6 \times 5 = 30$ $30 \div 6 = 5$
$5 \times 6 = 30$ $30 \div 5 = 6$

Problem Solving

14. Write a multiplication equation and a division equation for the array.

$4 \times \underline{5} = 20$

$20 \div \underline{4} = 5$

15. Make Sense and Persevere
How many inches shorter is the red fabric than the green and yellow fabrics combined?

Sophia's Fabrics	
Color	**Length in Inches**
Red	72
Blue	18
Green	36
Yellow	54

DATA

16. Higher Order Thinking Anya says that with 24 counters she can make only 6 possible arrays. Todd says he can make 8 arrays. Who is correct? Explain. *Anya is correct because you put the bigger number last.*

17. Algebra Carla picked 9 apples a day for three days. Which number tells you how many apples she picked in three days and makes this equation true?

$\boxed{27} \div 3 = 9$

18. (A-Z) **Vocabulary** Can you write a *fact family* for 3, 5, and 7? Explain. *No because 3×5 does not equal 7*

19. Lisa, Bret, and Gary harvested apples. Lisa filled 3 carts with apples. Bret also filled 3 carts with apples. Gary filled another 3 carts with apples. Write a multiplication equation and a division equation for this story.
3×3×3

Assessment Practice

20. Select numbers to create a multiplication equation that could be used to solve $20 \div 5 = \boxed{4}$.

| 2 | 3 | 4 | 5 | 10 | 20 |

$\boxed{20} \times 5 = \boxed{4}$

21. Select numbers to create a multiplication equation that could be used to solve $24 \div 8 = \boxed{4}$.

| 2 | 3 | 4 | 8 | 10 | 24 |

$\boxed{24} \times 8 = \boxed{4}$

Name_____

☆ ☆
Solve & Share

Kara puts 30 toys into 5 party bags. She puts the same number of toys into each bag. How many toys are in each bag?

I can ...
divide by 2, 3, 4, and 5 by thinking about how I multiply with those numbers.

I can also look for patterns to solve problems.

You can use structure. How can a fact family that uses 30 and 5 help you solve the problem?

$6 \times 5 = 30$ $30 \div 6 = 5$

$5 \times 6 = 30$ $30 \div 5 = 6$

6 toys

Look Back! Show two pictures you might draw to represent 30 ÷ 5.

Dee has 14 noisemakers. She puts the same number on each of 2 tables. How many noisemakers are on each table?

Find $14 \div 2$.

What You Think	What You Write
2 times what number is 14? $2 \times 7 = 14$	$14 \div 2 = 7$ 7 noisemakers are on each table.

B Dee has 40 stickers. If she puts 5 stickers on each bag, how many bags can Dee decorate?

Find $40 \div 5$.

What You Think	What You Write
What number times 5 is 40? $8 \times 5 = 40$	$40 \div 5 = 8$ Dee can decorate 8 bags.

C Dee wants to put 15 cups in 3 equal stacks on the table. How many cups will Dee put in each stack?

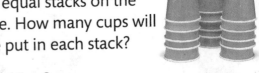

Find $15 \div 3$.

What You Think	What You Write
3 times what number is 15? $3 \times 5 = 15$	$15 \div 3 = 5$ Dee will put 5 cups in each stack.

You can use multiplication to help divide.

Multiplication and division facts form relationships.

Convince Me! **Reasoning** How can you use multiplication to help solve $20 \div 4$? Write the related multiplication fact you use to help solve the problem.

$20 \div 5 = 4$

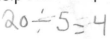

Name_____

Another Example!

Here are two ways to write a division problem.

$$24 \div 4 = 6$$

dividend   divisor   quotient

$$6 \leftarrow \text{quotient}$$
divisor $\longrightarrow 4\overline{)24} \leftarrow$ dividend

☆ Guided Practice

Do You Understand?

1. How can $5 \times 3 = 15$ help you divide 15 by 3?

Becaus it is the same as multiplacation so it is $15 \div 3 = 5$

2. Mr. Dean has 3 children. He buys 30 pencils to share equally among his children for the school year. How many pencils will each child get? Write the answer and the fact family you used. each child will get 10 penciels.

Do You Know How?

In **3** and **4**, complete each fact family.

3. $3 \times 6 = 18$ $16 \div 6 = 13$

$18 \div 3 = 6$ $6 \times 3 = 18$

4. $9 \times 4 = 36$ $36 \div 9 = 4$

$36 \div 4 = 9$ $4 \times 9 = 36$

In **5–8**, find each quotient.

5. $36 \div 4 = \underline{9}$ **6.** $\underline{3} = 15 \div 5$

7. $2\overline{)18}$ **8.** $5\overline{)50}$

☆ Independent Practice ☆

In **9–20**, find each quotient.

9. $12 \div 2 = \underline{6}$ **10.** $\underline{4} = 12 \div 3$ **11.** $16 \div 4 = \underline{4}$ **12.** $35 \div 5 = \underline{7}$

13. $14 \div 2 = \underline{7}$ **14.** $20 \div 4 = \underline{5}$ **15.** $\underline{6} = 24 \div 4$ **16.** $45 \div 5 = \underline{10}$

17. $3\overline{)27} = 9$ **18.** $4\overline{)40} = 10$ **19.** $5\overline{)40} = 8$ **20.** $3\overline{)21} = 7$

Problem Solving

In **21** and **22**, use the rectangle at the right.

21. How many individual squares are inside the rectangle? Write a division equation in which the quotient represents the number of rows.

$20 \div 5 = 4$

22. Make Sense and Persevere If Anna arranges the squares into an array with 2 columns, how many rows will there be? Thier will be 20 rows

---

23. Number Sense Joey says, "I cannot solve $8 \div 2$ by using the fact $2 \times 8 = 16$." Do you agree or disagree? Explain.

I do not agree with Joey because 8 divinded by 8 is 16

24. Miko has 8 counters to arrange in an array. Write multiplication and division equations to represent all the ways Miko might arrange her counters.

$4 \times 2 = 8$ $8 \div 2 = 4$ $8 \times 1 = 8$
$2 \times 4 = 8$ $8 \div 4 = 2$ $1 \times 8 = 8$
                                    $8 \div 1 = 8$
                                    $8 \div 8 = 1$

---

25. **A-Z Vocabulary** Write a division equation. Tell which number is the *quotient*, the *dividend*, and the *divisor*.

$30 \div 3 = 10$

26. Higher Order Thinking Chris gives 18 pretzels equally to 3 friends. Martha gives 20 pretzels equally to 4 friends. Whose friends got more pretzels? Use equations to justify your answer.

$18 \div 3 = 6$
$20 \div 5 = 4$

✓ Assessment Practice

27. Which expression can help you divide $12 \div 3$?

Ⓐ 2×3

Ⓑ 3×3

Ⓒ 4×3

Ⓓ 5×3

28. Which expression can help you divide $28 \div 4$?

Ⓐ 7×4

Ⓑ 6×4

Ⓒ 5×4

Ⓓ 4×4

Name_____

Solve & Share

There are 18 children in a ballet class. They are standing in rows of 6 for a dance recital. How many rows of children are there?

$18 \div 6 = 3$

$6 \times 18 = 3$

6

I can ...
divide by 6 and 7 by thinking about how I multiply with those numbers.

I can also model with math to solve problems.

You can use reasoning. How are the numbers in this problem related?

Look Back! Draw a bar diagram to represent the problem.

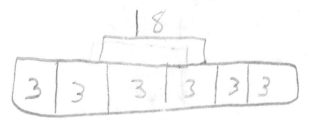

How Do You Divide with 6 and 7?

A

There are 48 dogs entered in a dog show. The judge wants 6 dogs in each group. How many groups will there be?

You can divide to find how many groups of dogs there will be.

B Find $48 \div 6$.

What You Think	What You Write
What number times 6 is 48? $8 \times 6 = 48$	$48 \div 6 = 8$ There will be 8 groups.

Use a multiplication problem to make sense of a division problem.

C Another dog was entered in the show. There will now be 7 dogs in each group. How many groups will there be?

Find $49 \div 7$.

What You Think	What You Write
What number times 7 is 49? $7 \times 7 = 49$	$49 \div 7 = 7$ There will be 7 groups.

Convince Me! **Model with Math** Draw a bar diagram using the numbers 36, 6, and 6. Write the division fact and the related multiplication fact that your bar diagram shows.

$36 \div 6 = 6$

$6 \times 6 = 36$

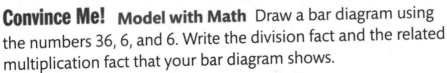

Name_____

☆ Guided Practice

Do You Understand?

1. How can you tell without dividing that $42 \div 6$ will be greater than $42 \div 7$?

Because 6 is more than 7 so thats how i know

2. How can $8 \times 6 = 48$ help you divide 48 by 6?

do Because you could 48 ÷ 6 = 8

Do You Know How?

In **3–8**, write the related multiplication fact, and then find each quotient.

3. $36 \div 6 = \underline{6}$

4. $\underline{8} = 42 \div 6$

5. $42 \div 7 = \underline{7}$

6. $\underline{\quad} = 18 \div 6$

7. $6 \overline{)24}$

8. $6 \overline{)30}$

Independent Practice ☆

Leveled Practice In **9–20**, use related multiplication and division facts to find the quotient.

9. $12 \div 6 = ?$
What number times 6 is 12?
$6 \times \boxed{2} = 12$
$12 \div 6 = \boxed{\ }$

10. $21 \div 3 = ?$
What number times 3 is 21?
$3 \times \boxed{7} = 21$
$21 \div 3 = \boxed{7}$

11. $30 \div 6 = ?$
What number times 6 is 30?
$6 \times \boxed{6} = 30$
$30 \div 6 = \boxed{6}$

12. $2 \overline{)14}$ 7

13. $7 \overline{)49}$ 7

14. $6 \overline{)60}$ 10

15. $6 \overline{)54}$ 9

16. $6 \overline{)6}$ 4

17. $7 \overline{)28}$ 4

18. Find 49 divided by 7.   7

19. Divide 54 by 6.   9

20. Find 35 divided by 7.   7

Problem Solving

21. A pizza parlor made 88 deep-dish pizzas. It made 10 more thin-crust pizzas than deep-dish pizzas. How many thin-crust pizzas did the parlor make?

98 pizzas

22. Higher Order Thinking There are 35 new tires. Each truck will get 6 tires plus 1 tire for a spare. How many trucks will get new tires?

5 trucks will get tires

23. Make Sense and Persevere Explain the mistake in the fact family below. Give the correct fact.

$$4 \times 7 = 28 \qquad 7 \times 4 = 28$$
$$7 \div 4 = 28 \qquad 28 \div 7 = 4$$

They made a mistake by doing 7÷4=28.

24. Gloria mowed 7 lawns and earned $56. She was paid the same amount for each lawn. How much money did Gloria earn for mowing each lawn? Write an equation to represent this problem.

56÷7=8

1 package of 7 red beads

1 package of 6 green beads

1 package of 5 gold beads

25. Andy bought 35 beads. He bought only one color of beads. Which beads could Andy have bought? How many packages of that color bead did he buy?

8

26. Cassidy bought 48 beads. She bought only one color of beads. Which beads could Cassidy have bought? How many packages of that color bead did she buy?

6

Assessment Practice

27. Which multiplication fact can you use to help find the value of the unknown number in the equation $42 \div 7 = \boxed{5}$?

- Ⓐ 5×7
- Ⓑ 6×7
- Ⓒ 7×7
- Ⓓ 8×7

28. Which multiplication fact can you use to help find the value of the unknown number in the equation $36 \div 6 = \boxed{6}$?

- Ⓐ 5×6
- Ⓑ 6×6
- Ⓒ 7×6
- Ⓓ 8×6

Name **aseel**

★ ☆ ★
Solve & Share

An art teacher has 72 crayons. The crayons came in boxes with 8 crayons in each box. How many boxes of crayons were there?

I can ...
divide by 8 and 9 by thinking about how I multiply with those numbers

I can also reason about math.

You can use reasoning. Which fact family uses the numbers 72 and 8 and could help you solve the problem?

$$72 \div 8 = 9$$
$$72 \div 9 = 8$$
$$9 \times 8 = 72$$
$$8 \times 9 = 72$$

Look Back! Draw a picture you could use to help solve the problem above.

72

| 8 | 8 | 8 | 8 | 8 | 8 | 8 | 8 | 8 |

Essential Question **What Multiplication Fact Can You Use?**

John has 56 straws. He needs 8 straws to make a spider. How many spiders can John make? Find 56 ÷ 8.

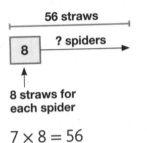

56 straws

| 8 | ? spiders → |

8 straws for each spider

$7 \times 8 = 56$

John can make 7 spiders.

What number times 8 is 56?

To make each spider, you need 8 straws.

B Luz made 9 animals. She used 54 straws. She used the same number of straws for each animal. How many straws did Luz use for each animal?

Find 54 ÷ 9.

You can divide to find the number of straws Luz used for each animal.

54 straws

| ? | ? | ? | ? | ? | ? | ? | ? | ? |

? straws for one animal

What You Think	What You Write
9 times what number is 54?	$54 \div 9 = 6$
$9 \times 6 = 54$	Luz used 6 straws for each animal.

Convince Me! **Look for Relationships** Write the related multiplication fact that can be used to complete each division fact.

Division Fact	Related Multiplication Fact
72 ÷ 8 = _9_	_8_ × _9_ = _72_
48 ÷ 8 = _6_	_6_ × _8_ = _48_
63 ÷ 9 = _7_	_7_ × _9_ = _63_

Name_____

Do You Understand?

1. What multiplication fact can you use to find $18 \div 9$?

$9 \times 2 = 18$

2. Carla and Jeff each use 72 straws. Carla makes animals with 9 legs. Jeff makes animals with 8 legs. Who makes more animals? Explain.

JEFF because he has animals with 8 legs,

Do You Know How?

In **3** and **4**, use the multiplication equation to help find each quotient.

3. $16 \div 8 = ?$
What number times 8 is 16?
$\underline{2} \times 8 = 16$
So, $16 \div 8 = \underline{2}$.

4. $64 \div 8 = ?$
What number times 8 is 64?
$\underline{8} \times 8 = 64$
So, $64 \div 8 = \underline{8}$.

Independent Practice ☆

Leveled Practice In **5–7**, use the multiplication equation to help find each quotient.

5. $24 \div 8 = ?$
What number times 8 is 24?
$\underline{3} \times 8 = 24$
$24 \div 8 = \underline{3}$

6. $45 \div 9 = ?$
What number times 9 is 45?
$\underline{5} \times 9 = 45$
$45 \div 9 = \underline{5}$

7. $27 \div 9 = ?$
What number times 9 is 27?
$\underline{3} \times 9 = 27$
$27 \div 9 = \underline{3}$

In **8–16**, find each quotient.

8. $48 \div 8 = \underline{6}$

9. $72 \div 9 = \underline{8}$

10. $\underline{1} = 8 \div 8$

11. $\underline{6} = 54 \div 9$

12. $72 \div 8 = \underline{9}$

13. $90 \div 9 = \underline{10}$

14. $8\overline{)80}$
10

15. $8\overline{)32}$
4

16. $9\overline{)9}$
1

Problem Solving

17. Callie biked 27 miles on Saturday. She biked 9 miles every hour. How many hours did Callie bike? Draw a picture to represent the problem.

Callie rode 3 hours

18. enVision® STEM Eight friends decide to test how far 40 paper airplanes with different shapes will fly. If each friend tests the same number of airplanes, how many airplanes does each friend test?

every friend will get 5 paper airplane

19. Reasoning What other equations are in the same fact family as $18 \div 9 = 2$?

$9 \times 2 = 16$ $18 \div 2 = 9$
$2 \times 9 = 16$ $18 \div 9 = 2$

20. Higher Order Thinking Jeremy had 30 gummy bears. He ate 6, and then gave the rest to 8 friends. Each friend got the same number of gummy bears. How many did each friend get?

$24 \div 8 = 3$

21. Mr. Stern spends $36 on tickets. He buys only one type of ticket.

  a. Which types of ticket could he buy?

  Childs ticket

  b. Which type of ticket could Mr. Stern **NOT** buy? Explain why not.

  youth

DATA

Playhouse Ticket Prices

Type of Ticket	Price of Ticket
Child	$4
Youth	$8
Adult	$9

✓ Assessment Practice

22. Find $32 \div 8$ by selecting numbers to complete the following equations. Numbers may be selected more than once.

2	4	6	8	16

$8 \times \boxed{4} = 32$

$32 \div 8 = \boxed{4}$

23. Find $54 \div 9$ by selecting numbers to complete the following equations. Numbers may be selected more than once.

2	3	6	9	19

$9 \times \square = 54$

$54 \div 9 = \square$

Name_____

☆ ☆
Solve & Share

Prizes for a school fair are packaged with 2 of the same prizes in each package. Which of the prizes listed below can be packaged with none left over? Tell how you decided.

Prize Type	cars	hats	balls	boats	books
Number of Prizes	6	15	23	18	36

6 cars   6 ÷ 2 = 9 and books 6×6=36
boats

I can ...
find and explain patterns for even and odd numbers.

I can also reason about math.

You can use reasoning. Think about numbers that can be separated into two equal groups.

Look Back! What do you notice about the numbers for the prizes that can be packaged in 2s with none left over? What do you notice about the numbers for the other prizes?

Essential Question

How Can You Explain Multiplication Patterns for Even and Odd Numbers?

Nita says that the product of an even number and an odd number is always even. Is she correct?

Even numbers have 0, 2, 4, 6, or 8 in the ones place.

Even numbers are whole numbers that can be divided by 2 with none left over.

Odd numbers are whole numbers that cannot be divided by 2 with none left over.

1	2	3	4	5	6	7	8	9	10
11	12	13	14	15	16	17	18	19	20
21	22	23	24	25	26	27	28	29	30
31	32	33	34	35	36	37	38	39	40

B Even numbers greater than 0 can be shown as two equal groups.

Think about 2×3 and 2×5.

2 is an even number.

2×3 means 2 equal groups of 3.
$2 \times 3 = 6$

2×5 means 2 equal groups of 5.
$2 \times 5 = 10$

There are always 2 equal groups, so the product of 2 times any number is even.

C You can **generalize**.

All even numbers are multiples of 2.

Think about 4×3.

You can think of 4 as 2 groups of 2.

Using properties you can write
$4 \times 3 = (2 \times 2) \times 3$ as
$4 \times 3 = 2 \times (2 \times 3)$.

So, $4 \times 3 = 2 \times 6$.

There are 2 equal groups of 6. So, the product will be even.

You can write any even number as 2 equal groups. So, Nita is correct: even × odd = even.

Convince Me! **Generalize** Does multiplying by 8 also always result in an even product? Explain.

Name_____

Another Example!

An odd number cannot be divided by 2 with none left over.

Think about 3×5.
3 cannot be divided by 2 with none left over.
5 cannot be divided by 2 with none left over.

$3 \times 5 = 15$

15 is odd.

Both factors are odd. Odd numbers cannot be divided into 2 equal groups with none left over. So: odd $\times$ odd = odd.

☆ Guided Practice

Do You Understand?

1. If you multiply two even numbers, will the product be even or odd? Explain with an example.

It will be even

$6 \times 6 = 36$

Do You Know How?

Write or circle to complete the sentences. Then solve.

2. $4 \times 6 = ?$

Can 4 be divided by 2? _18_ yes

Can 6 be divided by 2? _12_ yes

So 4×6 is even
                   odd .

$4 \times 6 = $ _24_

Independent Practice

In **3–5**, circle the factors that can be divided by 2.
Then write *even* or *odd* to describe the product and solve the equation.

3. $9 \times 5 = ?$

9×5 is _45_.

$9 \times 5 = $ _45_

4. $8 \times 7 = ?$

8×7 is _51_.

$8 \times 7 = $ _51_

5. $4 \times 8 = ?$

4×8 is _32_.

$4 \times 8 = $ _32_

Problem Solving

In **6–8**, use the table at the right. Look at the factors. Write *even* or *odd* to describe the product. Then solve.

6. How many miles did Joseph bicycle in 6 days?

The product is ___18___.

7. How many miles did Caitlin bicycle in 8 days?

The product is ___24___.

8. How many miles did Maria and Riaz bicycle in 3 days?

The total is ___27___.

DATA	Distances Bicycled Per Day	
	Cyclist	**Miles Bicycled per Day**
	Riaz	5
	Caitlin	6
	Joseph	3
	Maria	4

9. Critique Reasoning Ryan says that the following patterns are true:

even × **odd** = **even**

odd × **even** = **odd**

Is he correct? Explain.

10. Draw a shape with an odd number of sides. Then write the name of the shape.

Triangle
3'.

11. Higher Order Thinking The bakery had 84 muffins. Ms. Craig bought 5 packs of 6 muffins. Did she purchase an even or an odd number of muffins? Is the number of muffins left even or odd? Explain.

She orderd a even number because 84 is even.

Assessment Practice

12. Select all of the equations where you can use properties of operations to show that the product will be even.

- ☑ 7 × 9 = ?
- ☐ 1 × 6 = ?
- ☐ 9 × 2 = ?
- ☐ 7 × 5 = ?
- ☐ 5 × 3 = ?

13. Select all of the equations that do **NOT** have even products.

- ☐ 5 × 1 = ?
- ☐ 8 × 8 = ?
- ☐ 2 × 7 = ?
- ☐ 6 × 4 = ?
- ☐ 3 × 9 = ?

Name _____

Solve & Share

Find $5 \div 1$, $0 \div 5$, and $5 \div 5$. Explain how you found each quotient. You can use counters to help.

I can ...
understand the patterns of division with 0 and 1.

I can also look for patterns to solve problems.

Look for relationships. Think about the relationship between division and multiplication.

I do 10 counters

And take 5 counters.

Look Back! Use your understanding of multiplying by 0 to find $0 \div 7$, $0 \div 4$, and $0 \div 10$. Describe the patterns you see.

IF your divca is zero your aotet is zero

Visual Learning
 (A-Z) Glossary
Essential Question **How Do You Divide with 1 or 0?**

A

Neil has 3 goldfish. He puts 1 goldfish in each bowl. How many bowls did Neil use? Find 3 ÷ 1.

Any number divided by 1 is itself.

3 put into groups of 1

What number times 1 is 3?

$3 \times 1 = 3$
So, $3 \div 1 = 3$.

Neil used 3 bowls.

B **1 as a Quotient**

Find 3 ÷ 3.

3 times what number equals 3?

$3 \times 1 = 3$

So, $3 \div 3 = 1$.

Rule: Any number (except 0) divided by itself is 1.

C **Dividing 0 by a Number**

Find 0 ÷ 3.

3 times what number equals 0?

$3 \times 0 = 0$

So, $0 \div 3 = 0$.

Rule: 0 divided by any number (except 0) is 0.

D **Dividing by 0**

Find 3 ÷ 0.

0 times what number equals 3?

There is no such number. So, $3 \div 0$ can't be done.

Rule: You cannot divide any number by 0.

Convince Me! **Be Precise** Sue wrote 9 invitations.
She put 1 invitation in each mailbox on her street.
How many mailboxes got invitations? Which equation shows the problem and the solution? Explain your thinking.

$0 \div 9 = 0$ $9 \div 1 = 9$

Name_____

Do You Understand?

1. How can you tell, without dividing, that $375 \div 375 = 1$?

2. Use a representation to explain why zero divided by any number except zero is zero.

Do You Know How?

In **3** and **4**, solve the multiplication equation to find each quotient.

3. Find $8 \div 8$.

$8 \times \underline{1} = 8$

So, $8 \div 8 = \underline{1}$.

Remember, you cannot divide any number by 0.

4. Find $0 \div 9$.

$9 \times \underline{0} = 0$

So, $0 \div 9 = \underline{0}$.

☆ Independent Practice ☆

Leveled Practice In **5–7**, solve the multiplication equation to find each quotient.

5. Find $0 \div 7$.

$7 \times \underline{0} = 0$

So, $0 \div 7 = \underline{0}$.

6. Find $4 \div 4$.

$4 \times \underline{1} = 4$

So, $4 \div 4 = \underline{1}$.

7. Find $6 \div 1$.

$1 \times \underline{6} = 6$

So, $6 \div 1 = \underline{6}$.

In **8–18**, find each quotient.

8. $3 \div 3 = \underline{0}$

9. $\underline{8} = 0 \div 8$

10. $\underline{0} = 5 \div 5$

11. $7 \div 1 = \underline{7}$

12. $6\overline{)6}$ — 36

13. $1\overline{)5}$ — 5

14. $25\overline{)25}$ — 50

15. $1\overline{)13}$ — 13

16. Find 0 divided by 8.

$\underline{0}$

17. Find 9 divided by 1.

$\underline{9}$

18. Find 10 divided by 10.

$\underline{100}$

Problem Solving

In **19-22**, use the picture at the right.

19. Addie hiked 3 different trails for a total distance of 11 miles. Which trails did Addie hike?

20. Marty hikes one of the trails 4 times. In all, he hikes more than 10 miles but less than 16 miles. Which trail does Marty hike? Explain your answer.

21. Four teams are tidying the Green trail. They will each tidy an equal distance. How many miles does each team tidy?

22. Fiona hiked on Wednesday and Sunday. Each day she hiked all of the trails. How many miles did Fiona hike?

23. Model with Math Use a representation to explain why any number divided by 1 is itself.

24. Higher Order Thinking Yvonne says that $0 \div 21$ and $21 \div 0$ both have a quotient of 0. Is Yvonne correct? Explain.

25. Use division properties to match each equation to its quotient.

	0	1
$8 \div 8 = ?$	☐	☐
$0 \div 4 = ?$	☐	☐
$3 \div 3 = ?$	☐	☐

26. Use division properties to match each equation to its quotient.

	0	1
$4 \div 4 = ?$	☐	☐
$0 \div 5 = ?$	☐	☐
$0 \div 7 = ?$	☐	☐

Name_____

☆ ☆
Solve & Share

A tour bus to a national park holds 56 people. There are 7 tour guides at the park to lead equal groups of people from the bus. How many people are in each tour group? Each person in a group pays a $2 entrance fee to a tour guide. How much does 1 tour guide collect?

Lesson 4-7

Practice Multiplication and Division Facts

I can ...
use patterns and related facts to solve multiplication and division problems.

I can also model with math to solve problems.

Model with math. Use any strategies you know to solve.

$56 \div 7 = 8$

$8 \times 2 = 16$

Look Back! How can $7 \times ? = 56$ help you find $56 \div 7 = ?$

its because its the same $7 \times 8 = 56$
and $56 \div 7 = 8$.   7   8   56   are
apart of an fact family.

Essential Question # What Fact Can You Use?

Sabrina has 28 quarters in her bank. She wants to trade all of them for one-dollar bills. How many one-dollar bills will Sabrina get?

> There are 4 quarters in one dollar.

B One Way

How many groups of 4 are in 28?

> You can draw a bar diagram to help solve the problem.

28 quarters

| 4 | ? → |

↑
4 quarters in one dollar

$28 \div 4 = 7$

There are 7 groups of 4 in 28. Sabrina can trade 28 quarters for 7 one-dollar bills.

C Another Way

What number times 4 equals 28?

> You can use multiplication facts to help solve the problem.

$? \times 4 = 28$

$7 \times 4 = 28$

Sabrina can trade 28 quarters for 7 one-dollar bills.

Convince Me! **Construct Arguments** Why can both $28 \div 7 = ?$ and $? \times 7 = 28$ be used to solve the problem above?

because   4 7 28   are   in   a   fact   family

Name_____

Do You Understand?

1. Look back at the problem on the previous page. Suppose Sabrina put 8 more quarters in her bank. How many one-dollar bills can she trade for the quarters in her bank now?

$9 \times 4 = 36$

2. Calvin solves the equation $49 \div 7 = \boxed{7}$. How does this help him complete the equation $7 \times \boxed{7} = 49$?

Do You Know How?

In **3–7**, use a multiplication or a division fact to complete the equations.

3. $\underline{9} = 45 \div 5$

$45 = 5 \times \underline{9}$

4. $\underline{4} \times 7 = 21$

$21 \div \underline{4} = 7$

5. $6 \times \underline{6} = 30$

$30 \div 6 = \underline{6}$

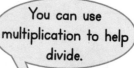
You can use multiplication to help divide.

6. $4 = 24 \div \underline{7}$

$24 = \underline{7} \times 4$

7. $6 \times \underline{2} = 12$

$12 \div 6 = \underline{2}$

☆ **Independent Practice** ☆

Leveled Practice In **8–10**, use fact families to complete the equations.

8. $42 \div 7 = \underline{6}$

$7 \times \underline{6} = 42$

9. $18 = 6 \times \underline{3}$

$\underline{3} = 18 \div 6$

10. $9 = \underline{22} \div 8$

$9 \times 8 = \underline{22}$

In **11–19**, find the product or quotient.

1. $36 \div 4 = \underline{9}$

12. $\underline{64} = 8 \times 8$

13. $15 \div 3 = \underline{5}$

4. $6\overline{)36}$ — 6

15. $9\overline{)63}$ — 7

16. $9\overline{)54}$

7. Multiply 8 times 5. $\underline{10}$

18. Divide 18 by 9. $\underline{2}$

19. Divide 27 by 3. $\underline{7}$

Problem Solving

In **20-22**, use the recipe at the right.

20. How many cups of peanuts would Eric need to make 5 batches of trail mix? Write an equation to show your thinking.

20 cups of peanuts,

Eric's Trail Mix

Makes one batch

Ingredients:
4 cups peanuts
3 cups raisins
2 cups walnuts

21. How many batches of trail mix can Eric make with 16 cups of peanuts, 15 cups of raisins, and 8 cups of walnuts?

4 batches

$16 \div 4$

22. Reasoning Eric spends $30 to buy the ingredients for 5 batches of trail mix. Find the cost of the ingredients Eric needs for one batch. How much would Eric need for 2 batches?

$30 \div 5 = 6$

23. Emilia drew lines to divide these squares into parts. What is one way to name these parts?

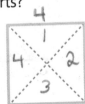

24. Higher Order Thinking Wilson is thinking of 2 one-digit numbers. When he multiplies them, the product is 27. What is the sum of the two numbers? Explain your answer.

36

Assessment Practice

25. Use the relationship between multiplication and division to find the value of each unknown.

Equation	Value of Unknown
$42 \div 7 = ?$	8
$7 \times ? = 42$	37
$9 = 36 \div ?$	4
$9 \times ? = 36$	4

26. Use properties of operations to find the value of each unknown.

Equation	Value of Unknown
$8 \div 1 = ?$	8
$? = 9 \div 9$	1
$? = 0 \div 3$	0
$6 \times 0 = ?$	0

Name_____

Lesson 4-8

Solve Multiplication and Division Equations

☆ ☆
Solve & Share

The expression 24 ÷ 4 is on the right side of the balance below. What can you write on the left side that will have the same value as the right side? Write 5 different multiplication or division problems that will keep the pans balanced.

I can ...
use multiplication and division facts to find unknown values in an equation.

I can also generalize from examples.

You can generalize to find 5 problems that keep the pans balanced. What part of the problem is repeated?

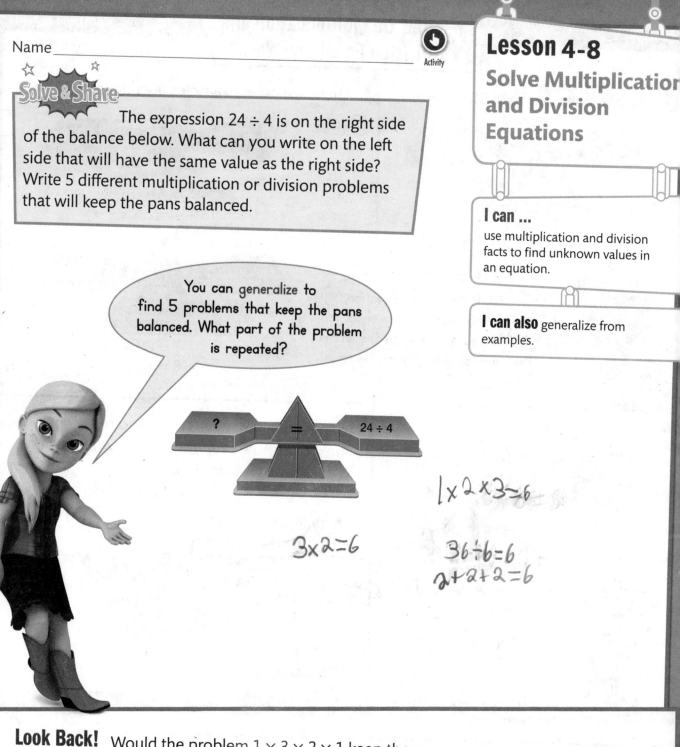

? = 24 ÷ 4

$3 \times 2 = 6$

$1 \times 2 \times 3 = 6$

$36 \div 6 = 6$
$2 + 2 + 2 = 6$

Look Back! Would the problem 1 × 3 × 2 × 1 keep the pans above balanced? Explain.

$1 \times 3 = 6$
$3 \times 2 = 6$

Essential Question

How Do Multiplication and Division Equations Work?

A The pan balance shows $35 \div 7 = 5$.

B These are other examples of equations.

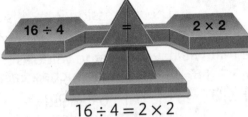

$16 \div 4 = 2 \times 2$

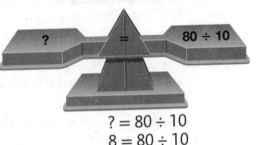

$? = 80 \div 10$
$8 = 80 \div 10$

Remember, in an equation, the symbol $=$ means "is equal to." It tells you the value on the left is the same as the value on the right.

C Frank has some tubes of tennis balls. Each tube has 4 tennis balls. Frank has 8 tennis balls in all. How many tubes of tennis balls does he have?

You can write an equation to represent the problem.

$8 = ? \times 4$

D Some equations have symbols to represent unknowns. The ? represents the number of tubes of tennis balls Frank has.

$8 = ? \times 4$

A multiplication fact that matches this is $8 = 2 \times 4$.

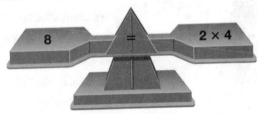

The value of ? is 2. So, $? = 2$.

Convince Me! **Reasoning** Use the value of ? in the multiplication equation to write and solve two division equations.

$7 \times 6 = 42$ $42 \div 7 = \boxed{6}$ $42 \div \boxed{6} = 7$

Name_____

Do You Understand?

1. Write an equation that represents the following problem:

Walt makes some sandwiches. Each sandwich uses 2 slices of bread. He uses 16 slices of bread. How many sandwiches does Walt make? Use ? to represent the number of sandwiches.

$16 \div 2 =$

Do You Know How?

In **2-5**, find the value for ? that makes the equation true.

2. $9 \times ? = 27$

3. $8 = 40 \div ?$

4. $32 = ? \times 8$

5. $? \div 3 = 6$

Independent Practice ☆

In **6-9**, find the value for ? that makes the equation true.

6. $? \div 4 = 7$

7. $25 = 5 \times ?$

8. $72 = ? \times 9$

9. $4 = 20 \div ?$

In **10-13**, write and solve an equation that represents the problem.

10. Sasha has 21 dimes. She puts them in stacks with the same number of dimes in each stack. In all, she has 3 stacks. How many dimes are in each stack? Use? to represent the number of dimes in each stack.

$21 \div 3 = 7$

11. There were some sheep in a barnyard. Each sheep had 4 legs. There were 24 legs in the barnyard. How many sheep were in the barnyard? Use ? to represent the number of sheep in the barnyard.

$24 \div 4 = 6$

12. A football team scored 48 points. The team only scored on touchdowns, worth 6 points each. How many touchdowns did the team score? Use ? to represent the number of touchdowns.

$48 \div 8 = 6$

13. There were 6 ladybugs on a leaf. Each ladybug had the same number of spots. There were 36 spots. How many spots were on each ladybug? Use ? to represent the number of spots on each ladybug.

$36 \div 6 = 6$

Problem Solving

14. A baker is decorating 5 cakes. He uses 9 chocolate flowers to decorate each cake. How many flowers will he need to decorate all the cakes? Write an equation to represent the problem, using ? to represent the missing information. Then solve your equation.

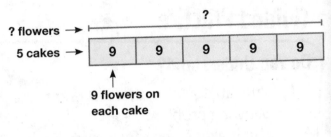

? flowers →
5 cakes →

| 9 | 9 | 9 | 9 | 9 |

↑
9 flowers on each cake

$5 \times 9 = 45$

---

15. Be Precise Hal asked 20 people to name their favorite sport. The tally chart shows how many people answered *baseball* and *swimming*. All the other people he asked said their favorite sport was *football*. Complete the tally chart to show how many people chose football.

Favorite Sport	
Baseball	///
Swimming	THH ////
Football	THH /

$20 - 12 = 8$

---

16. Higher Order Thinking A building has more than 2 stories but fewer than 10 stories. Each story of the building has the same number of windows. The building has 25 windows. Complete the sentence. Then explain how you found your answer.

The building has __5__ stories, and each story has __5__ windows.

17. Rosi and Karen are trying to solve $4 = ? \div 8$. Rosi says the value of the unknown is 32. Karen says the value of the unknown is 2. Is Rosi or Karen correct? Explain.

Rosi because $2 \div 8 = ?$
So it is rosi $4 + 2 = 8$.

---

18. What is the value of the unknown in the equation $30 \div ? = 6$?

Ⓐ 4

Ⓑ 5

Ⓒ 6

Ⓓ 7

19. What is the value of the unknown in the equation $8 \times ? = 64$?

Ⓐ 5

Ⓑ 6

Ⓒ 7

Ⓓ 8

Name _____

Solve & Share

Natalie prepared a crate of oranges for shipment. She packed the oranges in 2 layers. In each layer, she packed 6 rows with 7 oranges in each row. How many oranges did Natalie pack? Use equations to represent your work.

Problem Solving

Lesson 4-9
Make Sense and Persevere

I can ...
make sense of problems and keep working if I get stuck.

I can also solve multi-step problems.

Thinking Habits

Be a good thinker!
These questions can help you.

- What do I need to find?
- What do I know?
- What's my plan for solving the problem?
- What else can I try if I get stuck?
- How can I check that my solution makes sense?

Look Back! **Make Sense and Persevere** How did you find how many oranges Natalie packed in each layer? How did this plan help you solve the problem?

Visual Learning

 A-Z Glossary

Essential Question How Can You Make Sense of a Problem and Persevere in Solving It?

Visual Learning Bridge

A store has boxes of video games for sale. In each box, the video games are in 2 rows with 3 video games in each row.

Each video game costs the same amount.

What is the cost of each video game?

To persevere you can check your strategy and your work.

What do I need to do?

I need to make sense of the problem before I can solve it. If I get stuck, I need to persevere until I find the cost of each video game.

$54   VIDEO GAMES

B **How can I make sense of and solve this problem?**

I can

- identify what is known from the problem.

- look for and answer hidden questions in the problem.

- make a plan to solve the problem.

- check to make sure my work and answer make sense.

C

Here's my thinking...

I know a box costs $54.
There are 2 rows of 3 games in a box.

First, I need to find the total number of games in a box.

I will **multiply** the number of rows by the number of games in each row.

$2 \times 3 = 6$ 6 games are in a box.

Then I will **divide** the cost of a box by the total number of games to find the cost of each game.

$\$54 \div 6 = \$9$ Each game costs $9.

Convince Me! **Make Sense and Persevere** How can you check to make sure the work and answer given above make sense?

☆ Guided Practice

Make Sense and Persevere

Twelve friends went camping. All except 4 of them went on a hike. The hikers carried 32 water bottles. Each hiker carried the same number of water bottles. How many water bottles did each hiker carry?

1. Tell what you know. Then explain what you need to find first to solve the problem.

If you are stuck, you can persevere. Think: Does the strategy I am using make sense?

2. Tell which operations you will use. Then solve the problem.

Independent Practice ☆

Make Sense and Persevere

Four students went bowling. They bowled 2 games each. The cost was $5 per game. How much money did the students spend on bowling? Explain.

3. Tell what you know. Then explain what you need to find first to solve the problem.

4. Tell which operations you will use. Then solve the problem.

5. How can you check that your work is correct?

County Fair

The table shows costs at the county fair.
Mr. Casey spent $24 on admission tickets
for himself and the children in his group.
How many children are in his group?
Answer Exercises **6–9** to solve the problem.

County Fair		
Kind of Ticket	**Adult**	**Child**
Admission	$8	$4
Boat Rides	$2	$1

DATA

6. **Make Sense and Persevere** What do you know? What
are you asked to find?

7. **Be Precise** Why is it important to know which kind of
tickets Mr. Casey bought?

As you make sense
of a problem, you can
think about whether you
have solved a problem
like it before.

8. **Critique Reasoning** Dan says there are 6 children in
Mr. Casey's group because $24 ÷ $4 = 6. Does Dan's
reasoning make sense? Explain.

9. **Reasoning** Solve the problem. Write an equation for
each step and explain.

Name_____

★ ☆
Find a Match
☆

Work with a partner. Point to a clue.

Read the clue.

Look below the clues to find a match. Write the clue letter in the box next to the match.

Find a match for every clue.

I can ...
add and subtract within 100.

I can also make math arguments

Clues

A Is equal to $59 + 19$	**E** Is equal to $72 - 24$	**I** Is equal to $39 - 17$
B Is equal to $13 - 6$	**F** Is equal to $35 + 15$	**J** Is equal to $29 + 44$
C Is equal to $48 + 38$	**G** Is equal to $100 - 19$	**K** Is equal to $56 - 47$
D Is equal to $57 - 18$	**H** Is equal to $65 + 33$	**L** Is equal to $16 + 35$

☐ $73 - 64$	☐ $24 + 26$	☐ $19 - 12$
☐ $37 + 14$	☐ $56 - 8$	☐ $52 + 26$
☐ $47 + 39$	☐ $65 - 43$	☐ $72 + 26$
☐ $48 + 25$	☐ $92 - 11$	☐ $66 - 27$

Word List

- dividend
- divisor
- even number
- fact family
- odd number
- product
- quotient

Understand Vocabulary

1. Circle the *divisor* in each equation.

$30 \div 6 = 5$ $24 \div 3 = 8$ $14 \div 2 = 7$ $45 \div 5 = 9$

2. Circle the *dividend* in each equation.

$63 \div 7 = 9$ $4 \div 1 = 4$ $0 \div 5 = 0$ $8 \div 4 = 2$

3. Circle the *quotient* in each equation.

$21 \div 3 = 7$ $54 \div 9 = 6$ $15 \div 5 = 3$ $16 \div 8 = 2$

4. Circle the *even numbers*.

19   24   45   68

5. Circle the *odd numbers*.

21   36   13   47

6. Look at the equations below. Write **Y** if the *product* is 6. Write **N** if the *product* is NOT 6.

$4 \times 6 = 24$ ___N___ $2 \times 3 = 6$ ___Y___ $6 = 3 \times 2$ ___Y___

7. Look at the equations below. Write **Y** if the group shows a *fact family*. Write **N** if the group does NOT show a *fact family*.

$3 \times 9 = 27$ ___Y___
$27 \div 9 = 3$
$9 \times 3 = 27$
$27 \div 3 = 9$

$12 \div 6 = 2$ ___N___
$2 \times 6 = 12$
$12 \div 3 = 4$
$6 \times 2 = 12$

$56 \div 8 = 7$ ___Y___
$56 \div 7 = 8$
$8 \times 7 = 56$
$7 \times 8 = 56$

Use Vocabulary in Writing

8. Explain how to find the fact family for 2, 4, and 8. Use at least 2 terms from the Word List in your explanation.

The diveden is in the middle
The sdivesere is in the first

Name_____

Set A | pages 117–120

Monica has 24 chairs to arrange equally in 3 rows. You can use an array to find the number of chairs in each row.

This array shows the relationship between multiplication and division.

3 rows of 8   24 in 3 equal rows
$3 \times 8 = 24$ $24 \div 3 = 8$

A fact family shows how multiplication and division are related.

Fact family for 3, 8, and 24:

$3 \times 8 = 24$ $24 \div 3 = 8$
$8 \times 3 = 24$ $24 \div 8 = 3$

Remember that a fact family is a group of related facts using the same numbers.

In **1–4**, write the other three facts in the fact family.

1. $3 \times 7 = 21$
$7 \times 3 = 21$
$21 \div 3 = 7$
$21 \div 7 = 3$

2. $5 \times 3 = 15$
$3 \times 5 = 15$
$15 \div 3 = 5$
$15 \div 5 = 3$

3. $8 \times 6 = 48$
$6 \times 8 = 48$
$48 \div 8 = 6$
$48 \div 6 = 8$

4. $4 \times 5 = 20$
$5 \times 4 = 20$
$20 \div 5 = 4$
$20 \div 4 = 5$

Set B | pages 121–124

You can use multiplication to solve division problems.

Hector has 24 oranges. He puts 4 oranges in each basket. How many baskets does Hector need for all the oranges?

What number times 4 is 24?

$6 \times 4 = 24$
$24 \div 4 = 6$

Hector needs 6 baskets.

Remember that you can use multiplication to help divide.

In **1** and **2**, solve each problem. Write the multiplication fact and division fact you use to solve the problem.

1. Sally has 32 flowers. She puts 8 flowers in each vase. How many vases does Sally need for all the flowers?
$32 \div 8 = 4$
$8 \times 4 = 32$
Sally has four vases.

2. Jon has 18 peaches. He uses 3 peaches to make a peach tart. How many peach tarts does Jon make if he uses all the peaches?
$18 \div 3 = 6$
$3 \times 6 = 18$

Jon makes six tarts.

Brent is putting 42 books on shelves. He puts 6 books on each shelf. How many shelves will Brent need?

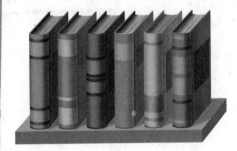

What number times 6 is 42?

$7 \times 6 = 42$
$42 \div 6 = 7$

Brent will need 7 shelves.

How many shelves would Brent need if he put 7 books on each shelf?

What number times 7 is 42?

$6 \times 7 = 42$
$42 \div 7 = 6$

Brent would need 6 shelves.

Remember that you can use multiplication facts for 6s and 7s to help you divide by 6s and 7s.

In **1–3**, solve each problem. Write the multiplication fact and division fact you use to solve the problem.

1. There are 36 runners entered in a marathon. They run in groups of 6. How many groups are there?
   Thier is $6 \times 6 = 36$.

2. Lani has 35 bird stickers. There are 5 stickers on each sheet. How many sheets of bird stickers does she have?
   Thier are 7 sheets of stickers.

3. Jake has 18 remote-controlled boats for 6 friends to share equally. How many boats will each friend get?
   $18 \div 6 = 3$
   $6 \times 3 = 18$

Lu made 9 bracelets. He used 72 beads. He used the same number of beads for each bracelet. How many beads did Lu use for each bracelet?

72 beads

| ? | ? | ? | ? | ? | ? | ? | ? | ? |

↑
**? beads for
one bracelet**

9 times what number is 72?

$9 \times 8 = 72$
$72 \div 9 = 8$

Lu used 8 beads for each bracelet.

Remember that you can use multiplication facts for 8s and 9s to help divide by 8s and 9s.

In **1–5**, write the related multiplication fact that can be used to complete each division fact. Then find the quotient.

1. $54 \div 9 = \underline{6}$ $\underline{9} \times \underline{6} = \underline{54}$

2. $64 \div 8 = \underline{8}$ $\underline{8} \times \underline{8} = \underline{64}$

3. $36 \div 9 = \underline{4}$ $\underline{9} \times \underline{4} = \underline{36}$

4. $56 \div 8 = \underline{7}$ $\underline{8} \times \underline{7} = \underline{54}$

5. $72 \div 8 = \underline{9}$ $\underline{8} \times \underline{9} = \underline{72}$

Set E pages 133–136

A whole number is **even** if it can be divided by 2 with none left over.

A whole number is **odd** if it cannot be divided by 2 with none left over.

Which product is even? Which is odd?

$3 \times 7 = $ odd $5 \times 8 = $ even
        product   product

All even numbers can be thought of as 2 equal groups.

When at least one factor is even, the product is even.

Remember that you can think about dividing by 2 to tell whether a number is even or odd.

In **1–3**, circle the factors that can be divided by 2. Then circle even or odd to describe the product.

1. ⑥ × ④ = ?   **(even)**   **odd**

2. 9 × 1 = ?   **even**   **(odd)**

3. ⑧ × 7 = ?   **(even)**   **odd**

Set F pages 137–140

Find $5 \div 1$. Five plants are divided into groups of 1.

What number times 1 is 5?

$5 \times 1 = 5$ So, $5 \div 1 = 5$.

Find $0 \div 8$.

$8 \times 0 = 0$ So, $0 \div 8 = 0$.

Remember that any number divided by 1 is itself. Any number (except 0) divided by itself is 1. Zero divided by any number (except 0) is 0.

In **1–3**, use division to solve.

1. $0 \div 16 = \underline{0}$

2. $10 \div 10 = \underline{1}$

3. Leroy had 4 oranges. He gave one orange to each of his 4 friends. How many oranges did each friend get? Write an equation to show your answer.

$4 \div 4 = 1$ each friend got 1

Set G pages 141–144

How many groups of 4 are in 24?

24

4 in each group → | 4 | ?

You can use multiplication facts.

$? \times 4 = 24$ $6 \times 4 = 24$

There are 6 groups of 4 in 24.

Remember that you can use bar diagrams or multiplication facts to help solve a division problem.

In **1** and **2**, use related multiplication and division facts to solve.

1. $21 \div 7 = \underline{3}$ 2. $5 \times \underline{9} = 45$

    $7 \times \underline{3} = 21$ $45 \div 5 = \underline{9}$

Look at the equation $3 \times ? = 15$.

The ? stands for an unknown number.

Read the equation like this:

"Multiply 3 by a number. The result is 15."
Then find the value of the unknown.
Think of a fact that uses the numbers in
the equation.

$3 \times 5 = 15$, so the unknown number is 5.

Remember that you can use multiplication
and division facts to find the value of
an unknown.

In **1–6**, find the value of the unknown.

1. $? \div 2 = 6$
12

2. $7 \times ? = 42$
6

3. $20 = 4 \times ?$
5

4. $9 = ? \div 3$
7

5. $16 \div ? = 2$
8

6. $24 \div ? = 6$
4

Think about these questions to help you
**make sense of problems and persevere
in solving them.**

Thinking Habits

- What do I need to find?

- What do I know?

- What's my plan for solving
  the problem?

- What else can I try if I get stuck?

- How can I check that my
  solution makes sense?

14
− 6
8
×3
24

Remember to use the information in each
step to solve the problem.

In **1** and **2**, answer to solve a two-step
problem.

Fourteen friends went to the county fair.
All except 6 of them bought a hot dog. Each
hot dog costs $3. How much did the friends
spend on hot dogs?

1. Tell what you know. Then explain what you
need to find first to solve the problem.

14−6=8   24÷8 =3
8×3=24
The friends spent 24$

2. Tell which operations you will use.
Then solve the problem.

I used × and −.

Name_____

1. A. Heather wrote a multiplication fact and a division fact for the array below. Select all of the equations that show a fact Heather could have written.

- ☑ $5 \times 9 = 45$
- ☐ $5 \times 5 = 25$
- ☐ $45 \div 5 = 9$
- ☐ $10 \times 5 = 50$
- ☐ $50 \div 5 = 10$

B. Look at the multiplication fact you selected in **Part A**. Which of these is a way to rewrite the product in it?

- Ⓐ $(5 \times 3) + (5 \times 4)$
- Ⓑ $(5 \times 5) + (5 \times 4)$
- Ⓒ $(5 \times 5) + (5 \times 2)$
- Ⓓ $5 \times 5 \times 4$

2. Colin wrote three equations. What number will make all of Colin's equations true?

$14 = ? \times 2$

$56 \div 8 = ?$

$? \times ? = 49$

$7 \times 2 = 14$
$8 \times 7 = 56$
$4 \times 7 = 49$

3. If a group of objects is divided into 2 equal groups, 1 object is left over. Is the total number of objects even or odd? What could the total number of objects be? Use a drawing to explain.

even because thier
is a two.

4. Mrs. Raspa wrote the expression 6×3 on the board. Which of the following expressions has the same value?

- Ⓐ $(3 \times 3) + (3 \times 1)$
- Ⓑ $(6 \times 2) + (6 \times 1)$
- Ⓒ $(6 \times 0) + (6 \times 4)$
- Ⓓ $(4 \times 3) + (5 \times 3)$

5. A. Mr. Vargas is buying used computer equipment. He buys 3 keyboards and 4 mice. He spends $42. If the items are all the same price, how much does each item cost?

$42 \div 3$

B. Mr. Vargas decides to buy more keyboards that cost another $12 in all. How many more keyboards does Mr. Vargas buy?

12$

6. Look at the counters below.

A. Draw lines around the counters to show $12 \div 6$.

B. Write a multiplication fact related to the drawing you completed in **Part A**.

$6 \times 2 = 12$

7. Match each expression on the left with an equivalent expression.

	9 ÷ 1	0 ÷ 3	1 × 6	7 ÷ 7
8 ÷ 8				
0 × 7				
24 ÷ 4				
27 ÷ 3				

8. A. Peter wrote five numbers. Which of Peter's numbers can be divided into 7 equal groups with 0 left over? Select all that apply.

☑ 56 ☐ 35 ☐ 52

☐ 27 ☑ 42

B. How can you check to make sure the numbers you chose are divisible by 7?

Ⓐ Check that each number is even.

Ⓑ Check that each number is odd.

Ⓒ Use multiplication to multiply 0 by a number to determine if it is equal to the number you chose.

Ⓓ Use multiplication to multiply 7 by a number to determine if it is equal to the number you chose.

9. Crystal drew this bar diagram to model a division problem. Write a multiplication equation Crystal could use to help solve the problem.

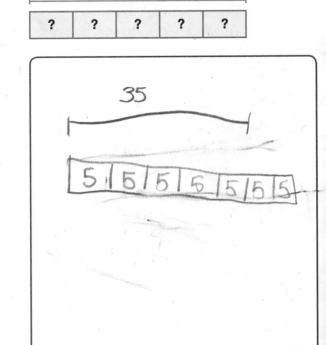

35

?	?	?	?	?

10. A. Xavier divided his action figure collection into 2 equal groups. Which describes the number of action figures Xavier has?

Ⓐ It is an even number.

Ⓑ It is an odd number.

B. Xavier finds 2 more action figures. Select all statements that are true.

☑ Including the action figures he found, Xavier has an even number of action figures.

☐ Including the action figures he found, Xavier has an odd number of action figures.

☑ Xavier can divide all of the action figures into 2 equal groups.

☑ Xavier could now have a total of 6 action figures in his collection.

☑ Xavier could now have a total of 8 action figures in his collection.

---

11. Mandy is trying to find $6 \div 0$. She says the answer is 6 because $6 \times 0 = 6$. Is Mandy correct? Explain.

No becaus $6 \times 0 = 6$ but when you add,

---

12. Luz has 36 pencil toppers. She sorts her pencil toppers into 6 equal groups.

A. Write an expression that represents how many pencil toppers are in each group.

6

B. How many are in each group?

6

---

13. Kira has 63 sheets of recycled paper. She gives the same number of sheets to each of 9 friends. How many sheets does Kira give to each friend? Use the bar diagram to help.

63 sheets

?	?	?	?	?	?	?	?	?

Ⓐ 6 Ⓒ 8

Ⓑ 7 Ⓓ 9

---

14. Jules has 4 classes. For each class, he needs 3 folders. Find how many folders he needs in all. Then write the fact family related to this situation.

$4 \times 3 = 12$

$3 \times 4 = 12$

$12 \div 4 = 3$

$12 \div 3 = 4$

15. A. Gennaro wrote 4 true statements about even and odd products. Select all of the true statements.

- ☑ An even number times an even number has an even product.

- ☑ An even number times an odd number has an even product.

- ☐ An odd number times an odd number has an odd product.

- ☑ An odd number times an even number has an odd product.

- ☑ If one factor is even, then the product is even.

B. Look at the statement you did **NOT** select in **Part A**. Give an example of why it is not true.

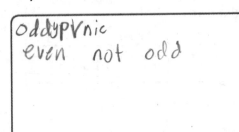
oddypvnic
even not odd

16. Which number makes both equations true?

$$18 \div 9 = ? \qquad ? \times 9 = 18$$

2

17. Anna drew the bar diagram below. Write two equations that could be used to represent the problem shown in Anna's bar diagram. Then solve the equations.

18		
?	?	?

6

18. A balloon artist wants to make 6 different kinds of balloon animals. She needs 4 balloons to make each animal. How many balloons will she need to buy?

Tell which operations you will use. Then solve the problem.

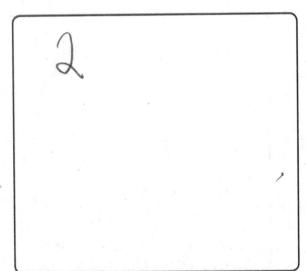
$6 \times 4 = 24$

Name_____

Relay Race

Mrs. Achilles teaches Physical Education. She is planning a relay race for her school. Each grade forms teams. Each student is on 1 team.

Race Details
- The field is 40 feet wide.
- Each runner gets 1 lane.
- Mrs. Achilles has 7 trophies.

Use the **Race Details** list to answer the following question.

1. Each lane must be an equal width. Mrs. Achilles wants to use the entire width of the field for lanes. How wide will each lane be if Mrs. Achilles sets out 10 lanes? 5 lanes? Use multiplication facts to help you.

Use the **Race Details** list and **Grade Size** table to answer the following question.

2. Each grade gets an equal number of trophies. How many trophies does each grade get? Write a division fact and a related multiplication fact you can use to solve this problem.

Use the **Grade Size** table to answer the following question.

3. Mrs. Achilles wonders whether each team can have exactly 2 people. Explain whether or not this is possible.

Grade Size	
Grade	Students
K	24
1	28
2	27
3	24
4	30
5	25
6	32

Use the **Grade Size** and **Grade 3 Possible Team Sizes** tables to answer the following question. Use related multiplication facts to help you.

4. Mrs. Achilles puts more than 2 students on each team. Each team must have an equal number of students.

Grade 3 Possible Team Sizes	
Number of Students on Team	Number of Teams
4	
3	

Part A

Complete the table to show the 4 different ways Mrs. Achilles can form teams for Grade 3.

Part B

Mrs. Achilles tries to make teams of 4 students each. She can do this for some grades but not for all. Which grades can have equal teams of 4?

Fill out the table for the grades written above. Use the same-size team for each of these grades.

Team Size			
Grade	Number of Students	Number of Students on Team	Number of Teams
K	24		
1	28		
2	27		
3	24		
4	30		
5	25		
6	32		

Part C

In the **Team Size** table, write the grades that you did **NOT** fill out in Part B.

Choose team sizes that let everyone in these grades participate. Use different sizes for each of these grades. Fill out the rest of the table.

TOPIC 5

Fluently Multiply and Divide within 100

Essential Question: What are strategies to solve multiplication and division facts?

Digital Resources

Interactive Student Edition   Activity   Visual Learning   Video   Practi

Assessment   Games   Tools   Glossary

The weather changes from day to day and from place to place.

Scientists look for patterns in the weather. These patterns help them understand different climates!

I predict that I will use math to understand the forecast! Here is a project on weather information and basic facts.

ēnVision STEM Project: Weather Information

Do Research Use the Internet or other sources to find the weather in different places on Earth. Find the weather at different times of day. Write down the temperature for each place. Also write down any conditions such as rain or snow.

Journal: Write a Report Include what you found. Also in your report:

- Tell how many places you checked.

- Tell how many times you checked the weather in one day.

- Write a multiplication or division story using your information. Then find an answer for your story.

Name _____

Review What You Know

A-Z Vocabulary

Choose the best term from the box.
Write it on the blank.

• dividend	• product
• divisor	• quotient
• factor	

1. The answer to a division problem is the _____.

2. A _____ is the answer to a multiplication problem.

3. The _____ is the number in a division problem that is divided into equal groups.

4. Multiply a factor by a _____ to solve a multiplication problem.

Multiplication

5. $6 \times 2 =$ ____

6. $5 \times 1 =$ ____

7. $4 \times 10 =$ ____

8. $7 \times 5 =$ ____

9. $4 \times 4 =$ ____

10. $9 \times 3 =$ ____

11. The oranges in a store are in 7 rows and 8 columns. How many oranges are there?

Division

12. $60 \div 6 =$ ____

13. $25 \div 5 =$ ____

14. $12 \div 3 =$ ____

15. $30 \div 6 =$ ____

16. $14 \div 2 =$ ____

17. $9 \div 3 =$ ____

18. If 28 stamps are arranged into an array with 4 columns, how many rows are there?

The Distributive Property

19. Explain how to use 2s facts to find 4×9.

Name _____

**PROJECT
5A**

How many books are in a library?

Project: Design a Library

**PROJECT
5B**

How would you use number cubes?

Project: Make a Multiplication Game

**PROJECT
5C**

Would you rather ride a bike or a "trike"?

Project: Create a Bike Chart

Before watching the video, think:

Cheese is made from milk. It takes between 6 and 10 pounds of milk to make 1 pound of cheese. A gallon of milk weighs about 8 pounds.

I can ...
model with math to solve a problem that involves multiplying and dividing with whole numbers.

Name_____

Solve & Share

Max found $6 \times 8 = 48$. He noticed that $(6 \times 4) + (6 \times 4)$ also equals 48. Use the multiplication table to find two other facts whose sum is 48. Use facts that have a 6 or 8 as a factor. What pattern do you see?

I can ...
use structure and properties to explain patterns for multiplication facts.

I can also look for patterns to solve problems.

×	0	1	2	3	4	5	6	7	8
0	0	0	0	0	0	0	0	0	0
1	0	1	2	3	4	5	6	7	8
2	0	2	4	6	8	10	12	14	16
3	0	3	6	9	12	15	18	21	24
4	0	4	8	12	16	20	24	28	32
5	0	5	10	15	20	25	30	35	40
6	0	6	12	18	24	30	36	42	48
7	0	7	14	21	28	35	42	49	56
8	0	8	16	24	32	40	48	56	64

← These are factors

These are factors

These are products

You can look for relationships. Use the multiplication table to make connections.

Look Back! How can a multiplication table help you find products that equal 48 when added together?

Essential Question

How Can You Explain Patterns in the Multiplication Chart?

Yolanda noticed that 4 × 6 is double 2 × 6. How can you explain this?

You can use a multiplication table to find patterns.

×	1	2	3	4	5	6	7	8	9
1	1	2	3	4	5	6	7	8	9
2	2	4	6	8	10	12	14	16	18
3	3	6	9	12	15	18	21	24	27
4	4	8	12	16	20	24	28	32	36
5	5	10	15	20	25	30	35	40	45
6	6	12	18	24	30	36	42	48	54

B

4 is the double of 2.

So, 4 × 6 is double 2 × 6.

You can use the Distributive Property of Multiplication to explain.

$4 \times 6 = (2 \times 6) + (2 \times 6)$
$4 \times 6 = \quad 12 \quad + \quad 12$
$4 \times 6 = \quad\quad 24$

C Look at the highlighted rows.

The product of any number multiplied by 4 will be double the product of that number multiplied by 2.

×	1	2	3	4	5	6	7	8	9
1	1	2	3	4	5	6	7	8	9
2	2	4	6	8	10	12	14	16	18
3	3	6	9	12	15	18	21	24	27
4	4	8	12	16	20	24	28	32	36
5	5	10	15	20	25	30	35	40	45
6	6	12	18	24	30	36	42	48	54

Properties can be used to understand a pattern and check if it is always true.

Convince Me! **Look for Relationships** Look at the highlighted rows of numbers multiplied by 2 or 4. What pattern do you see across the rows?

Name_____

Do You Understand?

1. How are 3 × 7 and 6 × 7 related?

2. In the table on the previous page, is the pattern that Yolanda found also true for factors that are multiplied by 3 and 6? Explain.

Do You Know How?

In **3** and **4**, use the multiplication table shown below.

3. What pattern do you see in the columns and rows that have 0 as a factor?

4. Use a property to explain why this pattern is true.

Independent Practice ☆

In **5–8**, use the multiplication table shown at the right.

5. Look at the shaded products. What pattern do you see?

6. Write the equation for each shaded product.

×	0	1	2	3	4	5	6	7	8	9
0	0	0	0	0	0	0	0	0	0	0
1	0	1	2	3	4	5	6	7	8	9
2	0	2	4	6	8	10	12	14	16	18
3	0	3	6	9	12	15	18	21	24	27
4	0	4	8	12	16	20	24	28	32	36
5	0	5	10	15	20	25	30	35	40	45
6	0	6	12	18	24	30	36	42	48	54
7	0	7	14	21	28	35	42	49	56	63
8	0	8	16	24	32	40	48	56	64	72
9	0	9	18	27	36	45	54	63	72	81

7. Look at the factors you wrote. Use a property to explain why the pattern for the products is true.

A multiplication table helps you see lots of products at the same time.

8. Shade a line in the multiplication table to show how this pattern is true for other products.

Problem Solving

9. enVision® STEM How many arms do 9 starfish have if ...

a   each starfish has 6 arms? Write a multiplication equation to solve.

b   each starfish has 7 arms? Write a multiplication equation to solve.

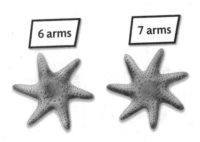

10. Higher Order Thinking Karen found a pattern on the multiplication table. What pattern did she find? Explain why it is true.

×	1	2	3	4	5	6	7	8
3	3	6	9	12	15	18	21	24
6	6	12	18	24	30	36	42	48

11. Write the fact family for each fact: 2×0, 2×1, 2×2, 2×3, 2×4, 2×5, 2×6, 2×7, 2×8, 2×9, and 2×10.

12. Be Precise Describe a pattern you see in the 9s row of the multiplication table.

13. One row and 1 column are shaded in the multiplication table below.

×	0	1	2	3	4	5	6	7	8	9
0	0	0	0	0	0	0	0	0	0	0
1	0	1	2	3	4	5	6	7	8	9
2	0	2	4	6	8	10	12	14	16	18
3	0	3	6	9	12	15	18	21	24	27
4	0	4	8	12	16	20	24	28	32	36
5	0	5	10	15	20	25	30	35	40	45
6	0	6	12	18	24	30	36	42	48	54
7	0	7	14	21	28	35	42	49	56	63
8	0	8	16	24	32	40	48	56	64	72
9	0	9	18	27	36	45	54	63	72	81

← These are factors.

↑ These are factors.

↑ These are products.

What pattern and property of operations is shown in the shaded row and column?

Ⓐ   The products are all equal to the factor that is multiplied by 1; The Identity Property of Multiplication

Ⓑ   The products in the shaded row are equivalent to the products in the shaded column; The Zero Property of Multiplication

Ⓒ   Each product is 1 greater than the product before; The Distributive Property

Ⓓ   There are no patterns or properties.

Name_____

Find 18 ÷ 3 any way you choose.

You can use reasoning. Think about how the quantities in the problem are related.

I can ...
use reasoning and the relationship between multiplication and division to find basic facts.

I can also reason about math.

×	0	1	2	3	4	5	6	7	8	9	10
0	0	0	0	0	0	0	0	0	0	0	0
1	0	1	2	3	4	5	6	7	8	9	10
2	0	2	4	6	8	10	12	14	16	18	20
3	0	3	6	9	12	15	18	21	24	27	30
4	0	4	8	12	16	20	24	28	32	36	40
5	0	5	10	15	20	25	30	35	40	45	50
6	0	6	12	18	24	30	36	42	48	54	60
7	0	7	14	21	28	35	42	49	56	63	70
8	0	8	16	24	32	40	48	56	64	72	80
9	0	9	18	27	36	45	54	63	72	81	90
10	0	10	20	30	40	50	60	70	80	90	100

Look Back! Describe another way you can find 18 ÷ 3.

Essential Question

How Can You Use a Multiplication Table to Solve Division Problems?

A

Write a missing factor equation and then use the multiplication table to find 15 ÷ 3.

×	0	1	2	3	4	5
0	0	0	0	0	0	0
1	0	1	2	3	4	5
2	0	2	4	6	8	10
3	0	3	6	9	12	15

Look at where rows and columns intersect in a multiplication table to solve a division problem.

$15 \div 3 = ?$

$3 \times ? = 15$

3 times what number equals 15?

B Step 1

You know one factor is 3. Find the 3 in the first column of this multiplication table.

×	0	1	2	3	4	5
0	0	0	0	0	0	0
1	0	1	2	3	4	5
2	0	2	4	6	8	10
3	0	3	6	9	12	15

C Step 2

You know the product is 15. Follow the row the 3 is in until you come to 15.

×	0	1	2	3	4	5
0	0	0	0	0	0	0
1	0	1	2	3	4	5
2	0	2	4	6	8	10
3	0	3	6	9	12	**15**

D Step 3

Look straight up to the top of that column of the table. The number on the top of the column is 5. The missing factor is 5.

$3 \times 5 = 15$ $15 \div 3 = 5$

×	0	1	2	3	4	**5**
0	0	0	0	0	0	0
1	0	1	2	3	4	5
2	0	2	4	6	8	10
3	0	3	6	9	12	**15**

Convince Me! **Reasoning** Write a missing factor equation and use the multiplication table above to solve each division problem.

$6 \div 3 = ?$ $12 \div 3 = ?$ $9 \div 3 = ?$

Name_____

Another Example!

How can you find the missing numbers in the table?

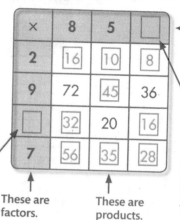

← These are factors.

36 ÷ 9 = 4, so 9 × 4 = 36.

You can think multiplication or division to find missing factors.

4 × 5 = 20, so
20 ÷ 5 = 4.

These are factors.

These are products.

2 × 8 = 16	2 × 5 = 10	2 × 4 = 8
9 × 5 = 45	4 × 8 = 32	4 × 4 = 16
7 × 8 = 56	7 × 5 = 35	7 × 4 = 28

☆ Guided Practice

Do You Understand?

1. Explain how to use a multiplication table to solve a missing factor equation.

Do You Know How?

In **2–5**, find the value that makes the equation correct. Use a multiplication table to help.

2. 24 ÷ 6 = _____

   24 = 6 × _____

3. 63 ÷ 9 = _____

   9 × _____ = 63

4. 25 ÷ 5 = _____

   5 × _____ = 25

5. 42 ÷ 7 = _____

   42 = 7 × _____

☆ Independent Practice ☆

In **6** and **7**, find the missing factors and products.

6.

×	☐	5	☐
2			
☐		25	
6	48		42
☐		45	

7.

×	☐	☐	9
4	12		
☐			54
3		6	
☐			72

Problem Solving

8. Some members of the Bird Club used a tally chart to record how many different birds they each saw one day. Fill in the blanks below to make the sentence correct. _____

saw 4 more birds than _____.

9. Complete the chart to show that Mr. Molina saw 5 fewer birds than Mr. Dobbs and Miss Simmons combined.

Number of Different Birds Seen	
Ms. Chester	𝍢𝍢 //
Mr. Dobbs	////
Miss Simmons	𝍢𝍢 𝍢𝍢 /
Mr. Molina	_____

---

10. Critique Reasoning Bill used a multiplication table to find the value of 12 ÷ 6. His answer was 3. Do you agree? Why or why not?

11. Write the fact family for each fact: 5 × 0, 5 × 1, 5 × 2, 5 × 3, 5 × 4, 5 × 5, 5 × 6, 5 × 7, 5 × 8, 5 × 9, and 5 × 10.

---

12. Higher Order Thinking Brit uses a multiplication table to multiply 2 different factors. She notices that the product is in the same column as the number 35. What is one of the factors in Brit's multiplication problem? Explain your answer.

Think about what you know and what you need to find.

---

13. Use the relationship between multiplication and division to find the missing number in 21 ÷ ☐ = 7.

Ⓐ 1

Ⓑ 3

Ⓒ 7

Ⓓ 9

×	0	1	2	3	4	5	6	7
0	0	0	0	0	0	0	0	0
1	0	1	2	3	4	5	6	7
2	0	2	4	6	8	10	12	14
3	0	3	6	9	12	15	18	21
4	0	4	8	12	16	20	24	28
5	0	5	10	15	20	25	30	35
6	0	6	12	18	24	30	36	42
7	0	7	14	21	28	35	42	49
8	0	8	16	24	32	40	48	56
9	0	9	18	27	36	45	54	63

Name_____

Activity

Solve & Share

Alfredo has 6 bags of oranges. Each bag contains 7 oranges. How many oranges does Alfredo have? Show 2 ways to find this answer.

I can ...
use different strategies to solve multiplication problems.

I can also look for patterns to solve problems.

You can use structure. Look for relationships when using counters, drawings, skip counting, arrays, or known facts to help solve the problem.

Look Back! How do strategies such as skip counting, using known facts, and making arrays help you solve multiplication facts?

How Do You Use Strategies to Multiply?

A

A scientist on a boat is studying hammerhead sharks. The length of 6 hammerhead sharks lined up nose to tail without gaps is equal to the length of the boat. How long is the boat?

An adult hammerhead shark is 5 yards long.

Drawings, skip counting, tools, and properties of operations are strategies you can use to multiply equal groups.

B **One Way**

Use a bar diagram to find 6 × 5.

6 × 5 means 6 groups of 5.
Skip count by 5s.

?

5	5	5	5	5	5

5 10 15 20 25 30

So, 6 × 5 = 30.

The boat is 30 yards long.

C **Another Way**

Use counters and properties to find 6 × 5.

The Distributive Property says you can break the problem into smaller parts. Use 2s facts and 4s facts to help.

} 2 × 5 = 10

} 4 × 5 = 20

Then add the two products: 10 + 20 = 30.
The boat is 30 yards long.

Convince Me! **Use Structure** How can knowing the product of 5 × 6 help you solve 6 × 5?

Practice   Tools   Assessment

☆ Guided Practice

Do You Understand?

1. What two known facts can you use to find 3×5?

2. How could knowing $7 \times 5 = 35$ help you find 9×5?

Do You Know How?

In **3-8**, multiply.

3. $6 \times 4 = \underline{\hspace{1cm}}$ **4.** $\underline{\hspace{1cm}} = 4 \times 5$

5. $\underline{\hspace{1cm}} = 9 \times 3$ **6.** $3 \times 2 = \underline{\hspace{1cm}}$

7. $\begin{array}{r} 1 \\ \times\ 4 \\ \hline \end{array}$ **8.** $\begin{array}{r} 9 \\ \times\ 8 \\ \hline \end{array}$

Independent Practice ☆

In **9-25**, use strategies to find the product.

9. $\underline{\hspace{1cm}} = 5 \times 5$

10. $9 \times 2 = \underline{\hspace{1cm}}$

11. $\underline{\hspace{1cm}} = 5 \times 9$

12. $8 \times 7 = \underline{\hspace{1cm}}$

13. $\underline{\hspace{1cm}} = 3 \times 6$

14. $8 \times 4 = \underline{\hspace{1cm}}$

15. $\begin{array}{r} 10 \\ \times\ 4 \\ \hline \end{array}$

16. $\begin{array}{r} 7 \\ \times\ 6 \\ \hline \end{array}$

17. $\begin{array}{r} 6 \\ \times\ 5 \\ \hline \end{array}$

18. $\begin{array}{r} 2 \\ \times\ 8 \\ \hline \end{array}$

19. $\begin{array}{r} 9 \\ \times\ 0 \\ \hline \end{array}$

20. $\begin{array}{r} 10 \\ \times\ 6 \\ \hline \end{array}$

21. $\begin{array}{r} 4 \\ \times\ 9 \\ \hline \end{array}$

22. $\begin{array}{r} 9 \\ \times\ 7 \\ \hline \end{array}$

23. What is 4×6? $\underline{\hspace{1cm}}$

24. What is 5×8? $\underline{\hspace{1cm}}$

25. What is 10×1? $\underline{\hspace{1cm}}$

Problem Solving

In **26** and **27**, use the pictures below.

26. Dr. Marks is studying 3 blacktip sharks and 4 tiger sharks. What is the total length of the 7 sharks? Show your strategy.

27. Critique Reasoning Kent reasons that the total length of 4 blacktip sharks can be found using addition. Is his reasoning correct? Explain.

Blacktip Shark
2 yards long

Tiger Shark
4 yards long

28. Write the fact family for each fact: 3×0, 3×1, 3×2, 3×3, 3×4, 3×5, 3×6, 3×7, 3×8, 3×9, and 3×10.

29. Higher Order Thinking Show how you can use known facts to find 11×9. Explain how you chose the known facts.

✓ Assessment Practice

30. Which shows one way you could use properties of operations to find 7×2?

   Ⓐ $(5 \times 2) + (2 \times 2)$

   Ⓑ $(7 + 2) + (7 + 2)$

   Ⓒ $(7 \times 2) \times 2$

   Ⓓ $7 \times (2 \times 2)$

31. Which multiplication equation could you use to help find $40 \div 8 = \boxed{}$?

   Ⓐ $5 \times 5 = 25$

   Ⓑ $8 \times 8 = 64$

   Ⓒ $1 \times 8 = 8$

   Ⓓ $8 \times 5 = 40$

Name _____

☆ ☆
Solve & Share

At the Fall Fest parade, members of the Cat Lovers Club and the Dog Lovers Club will march in equal rows. There will be 6 members in each row. How many rows of dog lovers will march in the parade? How many total cat lovers will march in the parade? Complete the table.

Lesson 5-4
Solve Word Problems: Multiplication and Division Facts

I can ...
use strategies to solve word problems that involve multiplication and division.

I can also choose and use a math tool to help solve problems.

Think about how you can use appropriate tools to help solve the problem.

Pet Club	Number of Members at the Parade	Number of Rows at the Parade
Dog Lovers	24	
Cat Lovers		5

Look Back! What operations did you use to solve the problem? Explain your reasoning.

A

Gina has 45 hats. She is packing them by putting 9 hats in each of several boxes. How many boxes will she fill?

Drawing pictures and writing equations can help you when solving multiplication and division problems.

B

45 hats

? boxes

9

9 hats in a box

You can use a bar diagram to show how the numbers are related.

C **One Way**

Think: 45 divided by what number equals 9?

$45 \div 5 = 9$

There are 5 groups of 9 in 45.

Gina can divide 45 hats into 5 boxes of 9 hats each.

D **Another Way**

You can use a related fact.

Think: 9 times what number equals 45?

$9 \times 5 = 45$

So, $45 \div 9 = 5$.

Gina can divide 45 hats into 5 boxes of 9 hats each.

Convince Me! **Generalize** Krys has 42 hats. She puts 6 hats in each of several boxes. Can you find how many boxes she needs using the same strategies as in the example above? Explain.

☆ Guided Practice

Do You Understand?

1. Why can you use division to model the problem on the previous page?

2. Casey gives 27 stickers to 3 friends. She writes the equation $27 \div 3 = 9$. What does the 9 represent in this problem?

Do You Know How?

In **3**, represent the problem with an equation or a bar diagram. Then solve.

3. A checkerboard has 64 squares. It has 8 rows. How many columns does it have?

Independent Practice ☆

In **4** and **5**, draw a bar diagram to represent the problem. Then solve.

4. There are 5 pancakes in a stack. Elise makes 40 pancakes. How many stacks does Elise make?

5. A park has 4 swing sets. Each of the sets has 7 swings. How many swings are in the park?

In **6** and **7**, write an equation with an unknown to represent the problem. Then solve.

6. Mrs. Jameson plants 30 tulips in rows. Each row has 6 tulips. How many rows did Mrs. Jameson plant?

7. Bonnie buys 6 paperback books every month. She buys 2 hardcover books every month. How many books does she buy in 4 months?

Problem Solving

8. Jodie has 24 flowers in her garden. She wants to give an equal number of flowers to 4 families in her neighborhood. How many flowers will each family get? Complete the bar diagram and write an equation to help solve this problem.

_____ flowers

← _____ families

9. Model with Math Casey has 2 sisters. He gave each sister 2 pages of stickers. Each page had 9 stickers on it. How many stickers did Casey give in all? Explain what math you used to solve.

10. Write the fact family for each fact: 6×0, 6×1, 6×2, 6×3, 6×4, 6×5, 6×6, 6×7, 6×8, 6×9, and 6×10.

11. Higher Order Thinking Twenty-five students are working in groups on a science project. Each group can have either 2 or 3 students in it. What is the fewest number of groups there could be?

A picture can help you solve a problem!

✓ Assessment Practice

12. Eight vans are going to the zoo. There are 6 children in each van. How many children are going to the zoo?

Select numbers and an operation from the box to complete an equation that could be used to answer the problem. Then solve the equation.

2	4	6	8	+
48	68	86	88	×

? = ☐☐☐

? = ☐ children

13. Ninety children are going to a museum. Nine children can ride in each minibus. How many minibuses are needed?

Select numbers and an operation from the box to complete an equation that could be used to answer the problem. Then solve the equation.

3	6	9	10	÷
19	90	91	100	×

? = ☐☐☐

? = ☐ minibuses

Name _____

Activity

Lesson 5-5
Write Multiplication
and Division Math
Stories

I can ...
write and solve math stories
for multiplication and division
equations.

I can also generalize from
examples.

☆ ☆
Solve & Share

Write a real-world division story for
28 ÷ 4. Then write another real-world story that
shows a different way to think about 28 ÷ 4.

You can generalize.
What is the same in both of
your stories?

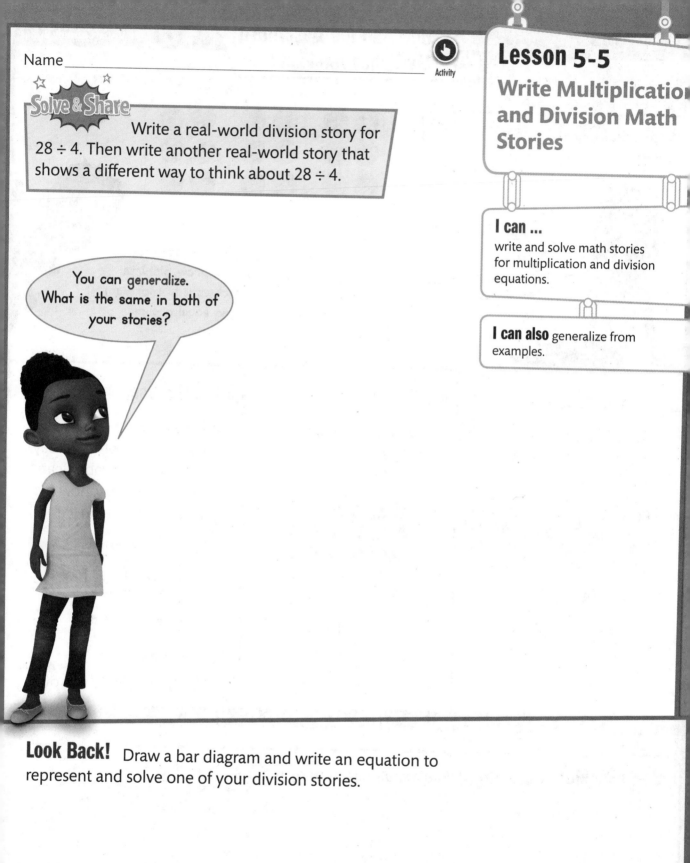

Look Back! Draw a bar diagram and write an equation to
represent and solve one of your division stories.

How Can You Describe a Multiplication Fact?

A

Write a multiplication story for 3 × 6.

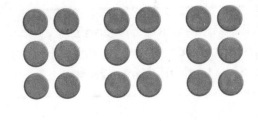

Stories can be written to describe multiplication facts.

You can draw pictures and use objects to represent joining equal groups.

B **Equal Groups**

Randy has 3 packs of 6 buttons. How many buttons does he have?

3 × 6 = 18

Randy has 18 buttons.

C **An Array**

Eliza planted 6 lilies in each of 3 rows. How many lilies did she plant?

3 × 6 = 18

Eliza planted 18 lilies.

D **Bar Diagram**

A rabbit eats an equal amount of carrots each day for 3 days. If the rabbit eats 6 carrots each day, how many carrots does it eat in all?

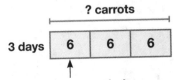

? carrots

| 3 days | 6 | 6 | 6 |

Carrots eaten each day

3 × 6 = 18

The rabbit eats 18 carrots.

Convince Me! **Reasoning** Write a multiplication story for 3 × 10 = ☐.

Another Example!

Seth has 15 fluid ounces of juice. Write and solve division stories about Seth and his juice. Use the equation $15 \div 3 = ?$.

You can write a division story about "How many are in each group?" or a story about "How many groups are there?"

How many in each group?

Seth has 15 fluid ounces of juice. He pours an equal amount of juice into 3 containers. How many fluid ounces of juice are in each container?

$15 \div 3 = 5$ fluid ounces

How many groups are there?

Seth has 15 fluid ounces of juice. He wants to pour 3 fluid ounces of juice into each container. How many containers does Seth need?

$15 \div 3 = 5$ containers

☆ Guided Practice

Do You Understand?

1. When you write a division story, what two pieces of information do you need to include?

Do You Know How?

In **2** and **3**, write a story for the equation. Then solve.

2. $3 \times 5 =$ _____

3. $8 \div 4 =$ _____

Independent Practice ☆

In **4–7**, write a story for each equation. Then solve.

4. $7 \times 3 =$ _____

5. $5 \times 5 =$ _____

6. $18 \div 3 =$ _____

I will write about 18 _____ .

I will put them in 3 equal groups.

7. $14 \div$ _____ $= 2$

I will write about 14 _____ .

I will put them in groups of 2.

Problem Solving

8. Reasoning Write a multiplication story about these pencils. Write an equation for your story.

Think about how many equal groups will be in your story.

9. Write the fact family for each fact: 8×0, 8×1, 8×2, 8×3, 8×4, 8×5, 8×6, 8×7, 8×8, 8×9, and 8×10.

10. A soccer team traveled to a game in 4 vans. Each van held 6 players. Two of the players are goalkeepers. How many of the players are not goalkeepers?

11. Higher Order Thinking A group of 9 monarch butterflies is getting ready to migrate. Write a multiplication story involving this group. Explain what fact you are using and find the product.

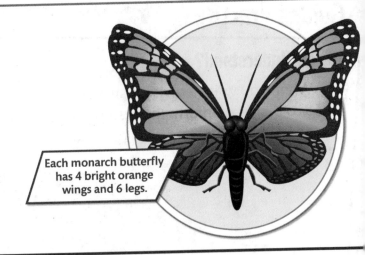

Each monarch butterfly has 4 bright orange wings and 6 legs.

✓ **Assessment Practice**

12. Mary writes the following story for $72 \div 9 = ?$.

There are 72 marbles separated into 9 equal groups. How many marbles are in each group? Select the correct answer for Mary's story.

- Ⓐ 7 marbles
- Ⓑ 8 marbles
- Ⓒ 9 marbles
- Ⓓ 10 marbles

13. Chris writes the following story for $4 \times 10 = ?$.

There are 4 pieces of wood set end to end to make a ramp. Each piece is 10 inches long. How long is the ramp? Select the correct answer for Chris's story.

- Ⓐ 4 inches
- Ⓑ 10 inches
- Ⓒ 20 inches
- Ⓓ 40 inches

Name _____

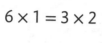

Jacob has started the pattern below. Fill in the blanks to make correct equations and continue the pattern. Explain your thinking.

$$6 \times 1 = 3 \times 2$$

$$6 \times 2 = 3 \times 4$$

$$6 \times 3 = 3 \times \square$$

$$6 \times \square = 3 \times \square$$

$$\square \times \square = \square \times \square$$

I can ...

use the structure of multiplication and division to compare expressions.

I can also compare without computing.

Thinking Habits

Be a good thinker! These questions can help you.

- What patterns can I see and describe?

- How can I use the patterns to solve the problem?

- Can I see expressions and objects in different ways?

Look Back! **Use Structure** Jacob starts this new pattern. Fill in the blank to make the equation true. What do you notice about this pattern compared to the pattern above?

$$3 \times 2 = 6 \times 1$$

$$3 \times 4 = 6 \times 2$$

$$3 \times \square = 6 \times 3$$

How Can You Use the Structure of Mathematics?

A

How can you tell without computing whether the symbol >, <, or = should be placed in each circle below?

1. $4 \times 5 \times 2 \bigcirc 4 \times 3 \times 5$
2. $6 \times 7 \bigcirc 7 \times 6$

You do not have to compute. You can use the structure of the number system to compare.

What do I need to do to complete the task?

I need to compare the expressions. Instead of doing any calculations, I will look at the values of the factors in each expression.

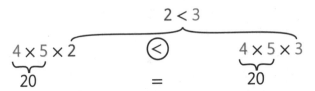

Here's my thinking ...

B **How can I make use of structure to solve this problem?**

I can

- think about properties I know.

- look for patterns and use them as needed.

C Some factors in the expressions are the same and some are different. I will use this to help me compare.

1. I know that I can group factors in any way, so I can rewrite one expression.

$$2 < 3$$

$$\underbrace{4 \times 5} \times 2 \qquad \bigcirc< \qquad \underbrace{4 \times 5} \times 3$$
$$20 \qquad\qquad = \qquad\qquad 20$$

2. I see the factors are the same on both sides. I know this means the products are the same.

$$6 \times 7 \bigcirc= 7 \times 6$$

Convince Me! **Use Structure** Dario says, "I can find $9 \times 0 < 3 \times 1$ without computing. I can think about properties that I know." What could he mean?

Name_____

☆ Guided Practice

Use Structure

Hakeem and Nicole each have 48 stickers. Hakeem shared his stickers among 8 friends. Nicole shared her stickers among 6 friends. These expressions show how Hakeem and Nicole shared their stickers.

$48 \div 8$ ◯ $48 \div 6$

Use structure to compare the values on each side of the circle.

1. Look at the expressions. Explain how you can use what you see to compare without computing.

2. Whose friends each received more stickers? Write the correct symbol >, <, or = in the circle above.

Independent Practice ☆

Use Structure

Dan has saved $10 each week for 7 weeks. Misha has saved $7 each week for 9 weeks. These expressions show how they saved.

$7 \times \$10$ ◯ $9 \times \$7$

3. Look at the expressions. Explain how you can use what you see to compare without computing.

4. Who saved more money? Write the correct symbol >, <, or = in the circle above.

5. Can you use the same symbol you wrote in Exercise **4** to compare $\$10 \times 7$ and $\$7 \times 9$? Explain.

Selling Necklaces

Trina wants to find the least expensive way to buy 24 necklaces. She wants to buy only the same type of packages. She has $48. The table shows the number of necklaces in a package and the cost of each package.

Number of Necklaces in a Package	Number of Packages Trina Should Buy	Cost per Package
3	$24 \div 3 = 8$	$4
4	___ ÷ ___ = ___	$5
6	___ ÷ ___ = ___	$6

6. **Model with Math** Complete the table to find the number of packages Trina would need to buy.

7. **Use Structure** Trina can use 8 × $4 to find the cost of enough $4 packages. Write a similar expression that shows a way to find how much it costs Trina to buy enough $5 packages.

Write a similar expression that shows a way to find how much it costs Trina to buy enough $6 packages.

8. **Make Sense and Persevere** Compare the cost of buying the $5 packages to the $6 packages. Which package type costs less if Trina wants to buy 24 necklaces? Explain how to solve without computing.

> When you use structure, you can look for things in common.

9. **Construct Arguments** Compare the costs of buying the $4 packages to the $6 packages. Which package type costs less if Trina wants to buy 24 necklaces? Explain how to solve without computing.

Name_____

Point & Tally

Find a partner. Get paper and a pencil. Each partner chooses a different color: light blue or dark blue.

Partner 1 and Partner 2 each point to a black number at the same time. Both partners multiply those numbers.

If the answer is on your color, you get a tally mark. Partners then write the remaining facts in the fact family. Work until one partner has seven tally marks.

I can ...
multiply and divide within 100

I can also make math arguments

Partner 1

| 9 |
| 5 |
| 6 |
| 8 |
| 4 |

63	24	40
42	81	28
36	35	56
16	72	30
54	20	48
25	45	32

Partner 2

| 7 |
| 4 |
| 5 |
| 6 |
| 9 |

Tally Marks for Partner 1

Tally Marks for Partner 2

Vocabulary Review

Glossary

A-Z

Word List

- column
- equation
- even
- fact family
- odd
- row

Understand Vocabulary

For each of these terms, give an example and a non-example.

	Example	Non-example
1. equation	_____	_____
2. odd number	_____	_____
3. even number	_____	_____
4. fact family	_____	_____
	_____	_____

Write *always*, *sometimes*, or *never*.

5. An *even* number can _____ be divided by 2 with none left over.

6. A *fact family* _____ has *odd* numbers.

7. An array _____ has the same number of *rows* and *columns*.

8. The product of an *odd* number times an *odd* number is _____ an *even* number.

Use Vocabulary in Writing

9. Explain the pattern in the green squares. Use at least 2 terms from the Word List in your explanation.

×	0	1	2	3	4	5
0	0	0	0	0	0	0
1	0	1	2	3	4	5
2	0	2	4	6	8	10
3	0	3	6	9	12	15
4	0	4	8	12	16	20
5	0	5	10	15	20	25

Name_____

Set A pages 169–172 _____

Reteaching

You can see patterns in a multiplication table.

×	0	1	2	3	4	5	6	7
0	0	0	0	0	0	0	0	0
1	0	1	2	3	4	5	6	7
2	0	2	4	6	8	10	12	14
3	0	3	6	9	12	15	18	21
4	0	4	8	12	16	20	24	28
5	0	5	10	15	20	25	30	35
6	0	6	12	18	24	30	36	42
7	0	7	14	21	28	35	42	49
8	0	8	16	24	32	40	48	56

In each row, the sum of the green numbers equals the purple number.

$0 + 0 = 0$ $1 + 6 = 7$

$2 + 12 = 14$ $3 + 18 = 21$

This is because of the Distributive Property.

A 1s fact plus a 6s fact equals a 7s fact.

Example: $(1 \times 5) + (6 \times 5) = (7 \times 5)$

Remember that properties can help to explain patterns.

In **1** and **2**, use the multiplication table to answer the questions.

×	0	1	2	3	4	5	6	7	8
0	0	0	0	0	0	0	0	0	0
1	0	1	2	3	4	5	6	7	8
2	0	2	4	6	8	10	12	14	16
3	0	3	6	9	12	15	18	21	24
4	0	4	8	12	16	20	24	28	32
5	0	5	10	15	20	25	30	35	40
6	0	6	12	18	24	30	36	42	48
7	0	7	14	21	28	35	42	49	56
8	0	8	16	24	32	40	48	56	64

1. Find the column that has products that are the sum of the green shaded numbers in each row. Shade this column.

2. Explain why this pattern is true.

Set B pages 173–176 _____

Use a multiplication table to find $20 \div 4$.

×	0	1	2	3	4	5	6	7
0	0	0	0	0	0	0	0	0
1	0	1	2	3	4	5	6	7
2	0	2	4	6	8	10	12	14
3	0	3	6	9	12	15	18	21
4	0	4	8	12	16	20	24	28
5	0	5	10	15	20	25	30	35
6	0	6	12	18	24	30	36	42
7	0	7	14	21	28	35	42	49
8	0	8	16	24	32	40	48	56
9	0	9	18	27	36	45	54	63

Find 4 in the first column of the table.

Follow the 4s row until you come to 20.

Then look to the top of that column to find the missing factor: 5. $20 \div 4 = 5$

Remember how multiplication and division are related.

In **1–12**, use the multiplication table to find each product or quotient.

1. $2 \times 7 =$ _____   2. $5 \times 8 =$ _____

3. $2 \times 10 =$ _____   4. $5 \times 4 =$ _____

5. $3 \times 5 =$ _____   6. $6 \times 5 =$ _____

7. $63 \div 9 =$ _____   8. $56 \div 8 =$ _____

9. $45 \div 9 =$ _____   10. $40 \div 8 =$ _____

11. $35 \div 7 =$ _____   12. $36 \div 6 =$ _____

Set B, continued pages 173–176

You can use basic facts and properties to find missing numbers in a multiplication table.

×	4	5	☐	7
3	12	15	18	21
4	16	20	24	28
5	20	25	30	35
6	24	30	36	42
7	28		42	49
8	32	40	48	56

Use multiplication or division to find missing factors.

$42 \div 7 = 6$, so $7 \times 6 = 42$

Use strategies to find products.

$3 \times 5 = 15 \quad 4 \times 5 = 20$

$5 \times 5 = 25 \quad 6 \times 5 = 30$

So, $7 \times 5 = 35$

Remember that you can use strategies and reasoning to find missing numbers.

Use multiplication and division strategies to complete the multiplication table. Show your work.

×	☐	5	6	☐
☐	12	15	18	
☐	16	20		28
5	20	25	30	35
6	24	30		42
7		35	42	49
8	32	40	48	

Set C pages 177–180

Find 4×7.

There are different strategies you can use when multiplying.

You can use skip counting:
7, 14, 21, 28

You can use known facts:

$2 \times 7 = 14$

$4 \times 7 = (2 \times 7) + (2 \times 7)$

$4 \times 7 = 14 + 14 = 28$

Remember that you can use patterns, known facts, or skip counting to find products.

In **1–8**, use strategies to find the product.

1. $5 \times 9 = $ ____

2. $8 \times 10 = $ ____

3. $4 \times 10 = $ ____

4. $9 \times 8 = $ ____

5. $6 \times 9 = $ ____

6. $7 \times 3 = $ ____

7. $6 \times 5 = $ ____

8. $4 \times 9 = $ ____

Name _____

Set D pages 181–184

You can solve word problems using multiplication and division.

Aaron has 49 books. His bookcase has 7 shelves. He wants to display an equal number of books on each shelf. How many books can Aaron put on each shelf?

Think: 49 ÷ 7 = ?

You can use a related multiplication fact:

$7 \times 7 = 49$

$49 \div 7 = 7$

Aaron can put 7 books on each shelf.

Reteaching
Continued

Remember that multiplication and division use equal groups.

Solve each problem. Show your work.

1. Oksana's dad has 36 batteries in his desk drawer. The batteries come in packs of 4. How many packs of batteries does he have?

2. Every time Lee wins the ring toss at the carnival, he gets 3 prize tickets. Lee needs to win the ring toss 9 times to have enough prize tickets for 1 toy. How many prize tickets does Lee need for 2 toys?

Set E pages 185–188

Write a multiplication story for 4 × 7.

You can think of multiplication as equal groups.

Tim has 4 bunches of flowers. Each bunch has 7 flowers. How many flowers does Tim have?

Tim has 28 flowers.

Remember that rows and columns can also represent multiplication.

Write a multiplication story for each equation. Then solve.

1. $3 \times 9 =$ _____

2. $5 \times 6 =$ _____

Write a division story for 20 ÷ 5.

If 20 children form 5 equal teams, how many children are on each team?

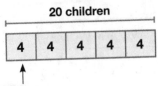

20 children

| 4 | 4 | 4 | 4 | 4 |

↑
**Children on
each team**

20 ÷ 5 = 4

There are 4 children on each team.

Remember that division stories can ask for the number in each group, or the number of equal groups.

Write a division story for each equation. Then solve.

1. 60 ÷ 10 = _____

2. 32 ÷ 4 = _____

Think about these questions to help you **look for and make use of structure**.

Thinking Habits

- What patterns can I see and describe?

- How can I use the patterns to solve the problem?

- Can I see expressions and objects in different ways?

Remember that properties can help you understand patterns.

Leroy earns $7 each hour that he works. He works for 8 hours. Rebecca earns $8 each hour that she works. She works for 7 hours. These expressions show the money they earned.

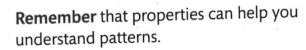

8 × $7 ◯ 7 × $8

1. Look at the expressions. Explain how you can use what you see to compare without computing.

2. Who earned more money? Write the correct symbol >, <, or = in the circle above.

1. Find $48 \div 6$.

2. A. Fill in the missing factors and products in the multiplication table below.

×			8
0			
		7	8
2			16
3	18		
		28	

B. What pattern do you see in the first row of products in the table? Explain why this pattern is true.

3. Find $45 \div 5$. Draw a bar diagram to represent the problem.

4. Find the product.

5×7

Ⓐ 28

Ⓑ 30

Ⓒ 35

Ⓓ 42

5. Find the product.

$6 \times 3 = \square$

6. Which of the following strategies can help you solve 4×6? Select all that apply.

☐ $(6 \times 6) + (6 \times 6)$

☐ $(4 \times 3) + (4 \times 3)$

☐ $(5 \times 5) + (4 \times 1)$

☐ $(5 \times 4) + (1 \times 4)$

☐ $(2 \times 4) + (2 \times 6)$

7. What number is missing from this multiplication table?

×	5	6
2	10	?
3	15	18

Ⓐ 8

Ⓑ 9

Ⓒ 11

Ⓓ 12

---

8. Select the correct product or quotient for each equation.

	56	7	36	9
54 ÷ 6 = ?	❑	❑	❑	❑
8 × 7 = ?	❑	❑	❑	❑
49 ÷ 7 = ?	❑	❑	❑	❑
6 × 6 = ?	❑	❑	❑	❑

9. Some squares are shaded orange to show a pattern in the multiplication table.

×	4	5	6	7
4	16	20	24	28
5	20	25	30	35
6	24	30	36	42
7	28	35	42	49
8	32	40	48	56

A. Identify a pattern shown in the multiplication table.

B. Explain why this pattern is true.

---

10. Divide.

70 ÷ 7

11. Which division equation could be used to solve $8 \times ? = 32$?

Ⓐ $32 \div 7 = ?$

Ⓑ $32 \div 2 = ?$

Ⓒ $32 \div 8 = ?$

Ⓓ $8 \div ? = 32$

12. Twelve can be evenly divided by which of the following numbers? Select all that apply.

☐ 9

☐ 3

☐ 5

☐ 4

☐ 7

13. What is the product of 9 and 3? Write an equation to solve the problem.

14. Look at these two expressions.

$40 \div 4 \qquad 40 \div 8$

A. Explain how you can compare the expressions without computing.

B. Check your answer by computing both quotients.

15. Which shows a way to solve 5×5?

Ⓐ Skip count 5 times by numbers that end in 5: 5, 15, 25, 35, 45

Ⓑ Use the Distributive Property: $(4 \times 5) + (1 \times 5)$

Ⓒ Look at a multiplication table: Find the 5s row. Go across until you find 5. The product is the number at the top of that column, 1.

Ⓓ Use repeated addition: $5 + 5 + 5 + 5$

16. Roberta is planting flowers in her garden. She plants 9 rows of flowers. There are 7 flowers in each row. How many flowers does does she plant in all? Write an equation to solve the problem.

17. Multiply.

7×2

18. Look at the multiplication table below.

×	4	5	6	7
3	12	15	18	21
4	16	20	24	28
5	20	25	30	35
6	24	30	36	42
7	28	35	42	49
8	32	40	48	56

A. Shade the products in the 5s column of the table. What pattern do you see there?

B. Explain the pattern you found.

Name_____

Photograph Gallery

Riley is setting up a display. She is hanging photographs on two walls. The photographs are hung in arrays. Riley has to decide how to arrange the photographs. She makes tables to decide which arrangement to use.

TOPIC 5

Performance Task

1. Use the **Left Wall** table to answer the questions.

   Part A

   Which arrangement on the left wall has the most photographs?

   Left Wall

Arrangement	A	B	C	D
Rows	3	3	7	8
Columns	7	9	2	3

   Part B

   Explain how Riley could find the answer to Part A without calculating the size of each arrangement.

   Right Wall

×	□	□	6	7	□
4					36
□		30		42	
□	28		42		
□				63	

   ← Rows

   ↑ Columns

Use the **Right Wall** table to answer Exercises **2** and **3**.

2. Fill in the missing columns, rows, and numbers of photographs so that Riley's table is complete.

3. Riley has 42 on her table twice. Is this reasonable? Explain why or why not.

Use the **Right Wall** table to answer Exercises **4–6**.

4. Some of the photographers were men, and some were women. Riley wants the number of photographs taken by men to be equal to the number of photographs taken by women. Shade the squares in the table to show the arrangements that let Riley do this. Explain what pattern you find.

5. Riley shares this table with her friend Leo. Leo is working on a different project. He is **NOT** hanging photographs. For what project could Leo use the table? Explain what 7×4 means for Leo's project.

6. Riley also shares this table with her mother. Riley's mother is working on a different project. She is also **NOT** hanging photographs. For what project could Riley's mother use the table? Explain what $30 \div 6$ means for Riley's mother's project.

Connect Area to Multiplication and Addition

Essential Question: How does area connect to multiplication and addition?

Digital Resources

 Interactive Student Edition
 Activity
 Visual Learning
 Video
Practic

 Assessment
 Games
Tools
A-Z Glossary

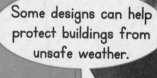
Some designs can help protect buildings from unsafe weather.

This lightning rod on top of the building is connected to the ground. It can direct the electrical current from a lightning strike safely to the ground.

This helps protect the building from being damaged by lightning! Here's a project on building designs and area.

enVision STEM Project: Design Solutions

Do Research There are different designs that help protect against weather, such as as lightning rods, flood-defense barriers, and wind-resistant roofs. Use the Internet or another source to gather information about these kinds of designs and how they work.

Journal: Write a Report Include what you found. Also in your report:

- Tell how some window or door designs can help protect against weather.

- Use a grid to draw one of the window or door designs. Count the number of unit squares your design measures. Label your drawing to show how the design works to protect against weather.

Name_____

Review What You Know

Division as Sharing

4. Chen has 16 model cars. He puts them in 4 rows. Each row has an equal number of cars. How many columns are there?

5. Julie has 24 glass beads to give to 4 friends. Each friend gets an equal share. How many glass beads does each friend get?

Arrays

6. Write an addition equation and a multiplication equation for the array shown at the right.

Relating Multiplication and Division

7. There are 12 team members. They line up in 3 equal rows. Which multiplication equation helps you find how many are in each row?

    Ⓐ $2 \times 6 = 12$ Ⓑ $1 \times 12 = 12$ Ⓒ $3 \times 4 = 12$ Ⓓ $3 \times 12 = 36$

8. There are 20 bottles of juice lined up in 4 equal rows. Explain how you can use a multiplication equation to find out how many bottles of juice are in each row.

Name_____

PROJECT 6A

How are cities built?

Project: Plan a Dog Park

PROJECT 6B

What are community gardens?

Project: Design a Community Garden

What are carpenters?

Project: Draw a School
Floor Plan

How do you play the game?

Project: Make an Area Game

Name_____

☆ ☆
Solve & Share

Look at Shapes A–C on Area of Shapes Teaching Tool. How many square tiles do you need to cover each shape? Show your answers below. Explain how you decided.

I can ...
count unit squares to find the area of a shape.

I can also choose and use a math tool to help solve problems.

Shape	Number of Square Tiles
Shape A	
Shape B	
Shape C	

Use appropriate tools. Think about how to place your tiles to cover each shape with no gaps or overlaps.

Look Back! Can you be sure you have an accurate answer if there are gaps between the tiles you used? Explain.

Essential Question **How Do You Measure Area?**

A

Emily made a collage in art class. She cut shapes to make her design. What is the area of this shape?

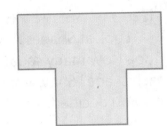

Area is the number of unit squares needed to cover a region with no gaps or overlaps.

A unit square is a square with sides that are each 1 unit long. It has an area of 1 square unit.

This is the unit square for this lesson.

B Count the unit squares that cover Emily's shape. The count is the area of the shape.

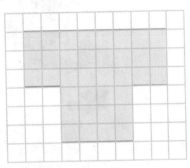

36 unit squares cover the shape. The area of the shape is 36 square units.

C

Sometimes you can estimate the area. You can combine partially filled squares to estimate full squares.

Count the unit squares that cover this shape.

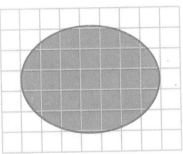

About 27 unit squares cover the shape.

The area of the shape is about 27 square units.

Convince Me! **Construct Arguments** Karen says these shapes each have an area of 12 square units. Do you agree with Karen? Explain.

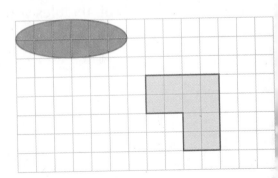

Name _____

Another Example!

Emily wants to cover this octagon.

If she tries to cover it using unit squares, there will be gaps or overlaps.

Emily can break the square into two same-size triangles. She can cover the shape completely using this triangle:

Fourteen triangles cover the octagon. The area of the octagon is 7 square units.

☆ Guided Practice

Do You Understand?

1. How do you know the area of the octagon is 7 square units?

2. Explain how finding the area of a shape is different from finding the length of a shape.

Do You Know How?

In **3** and **4**, count to find the area. Tell if the area is an estimate.

3.

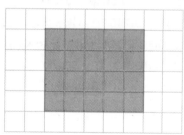

4.

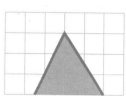

Independent Practice ☆

In **5–7**, count to find the area. Tell if the area is an estimate.

5.

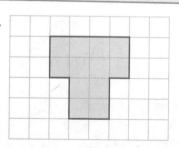

6.

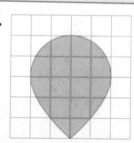

7.

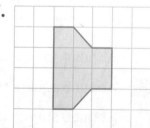

8. Maggie buys 4 sketch pads. She pays with a 20-dollar bill. How much change does Maggie get back?

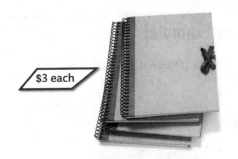

$3 each

9. Critique Reasoning Janet covers the red square with square tiles. She says, "I covered this shape with 12 unit squares, so I know it has an area of 12 square units." Do you agree with Janet? Explain.

10. Higher Order Thinking Chester drew this picture of a circle inside a square. What would be a good estimate of the green-shaded area of the square? How did you calculate your answer?

11. Number Sense Arthur puts 18 erasers into equal groups. He says there are more erasers in each group when he puts the erasers in 2 equal groups than when he puts the erasers in 3 equal groups. Is Arthur correct? Explain.

12. Daryl draws this shape on grid paper. Estimate the area of the shape Daryl draws.

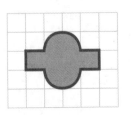

Ⓐ About 4 square units

Ⓑ About 5 square units

Ⓒ About 6 square units

Ⓓ About 7 square units

Name_____

☆ Solve & Share ☆

Find the area of the postcard on each grid. What do you notice about the size of the postcard on each grid? What do you notice about the area of the postcard on each grid? Explain.

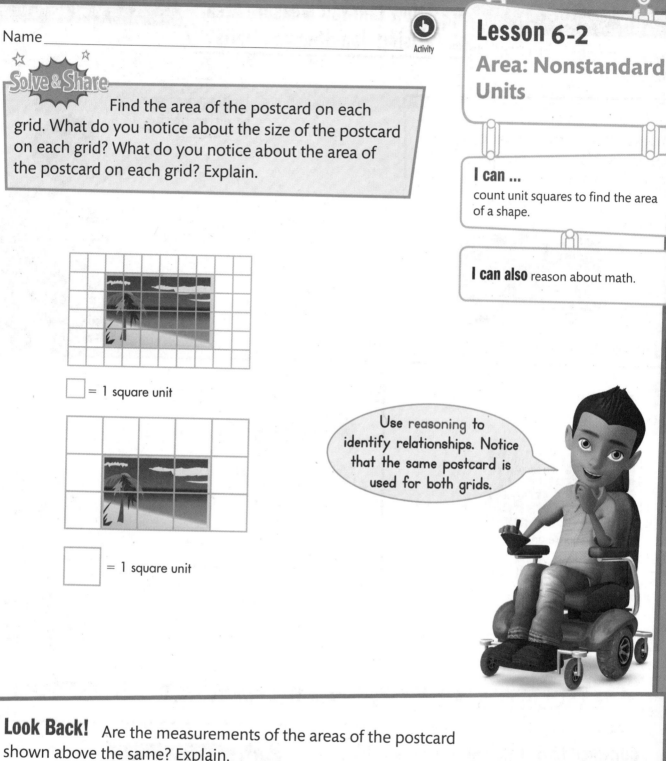

☐ = 1 square unit

☐ = 1 square unit

Use reasoning to identify relationships. Notice that the same postcard is used for both grids.

Look Back! Are the measurements of the areas of the postcard shown above the same? Explain.

A

Tran designs a bookmark for a book. How can he use unit squares to find the area of the bookmark?

Unit squares can be different sizes.

B You can count the number of unit squares.

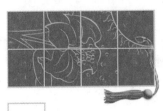

□ = 1 square unit

There are 32 unit squares.

Area = 32 square units

C You can use a different unit square.

□ = 1 square unit

There are 8 unit squares.

Area = 8 square units

The size of the unit square determines the measurement of the area.

Convince Me! Reasoning How are the areas of these two squares alike and how are they different?

Name _____

☆ Guided Practice

Do You Understand?

1. Which of these shapes has an area of 5 square units? How do you know?

Do You Know How?

2. Draw unit squares to cover the figures and then find the area. Use the unit squares shown.

☐ = 1 square unit   ☐ = 1 square unit

Independent Practice ☆

In **3–5**, draw unit squares to cover the figures and find the area. Use the unit squares shown.

3.

☐ = 1 square unit   ☐ = 1 square unit

4.

☐ = 1 square unit   ☐ = 1 square unit

5.

☐ = 1 square unit   ☐ = 1 square unit

Problem Solving

6. Ben finds that the area of this figure is 14 square units. Draw unit squares to cover this figure.

Think about the size of the unit squares you need to use.

7. Luke eats 6 grapes from the bowl. Then Juan and Luke equally share the grapes that are left. How many grapes does Juan eat? Show how you used reasoning to solve the problem.

24 grapes

8. Construct Arguments Riaz estimates that the area of this figure is 45 square units. Martin estimates the area is 48 square units. Whose estimate is closer to the actual measure? Explain.

 = 1 square unit

9. Higher Order Thinking Theo wants to cover the top of a small table with square tiles. The table is 12 square tiles long and 8 square tiles wide. How many tiles will Theo need to cover the table?

10. Rick used the smaller unit square and found that the area of this shape is 18 square units. If he used the larger unit square, what would the area of the shape be?

Ⓐ   1 square unit

Ⓑ   2 square units

Ⓒ   3 square units

Ⓓ   4 square units

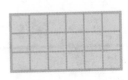

▢ = 1 square unit

▢ = 1 square unit

Name_____

Activity

☆ ☆
Solve & Share

Draw a square to represent 1 unit square. Use your unit square to draw a rectangle that has an area of 8 square units. Compare your shape with a partner's shape. What is the same? What is different?

I can ...
measure the area of a shape using standard units.

I can also be precise in my work.

Be precise. Check your shape to make sure you used the correct number of unit squares.

Look Back! Are the sizes of your and your partner's shapes something that is the same or something that is different? Explain.

Essential Question **How Can You Measure Area Using Standard Units of Length?**

A

Meg bought this sticker. What is the area of the sticker in square centimeters?

You can measure area in standard units. A square centimeter is a standard unit of area.

B

Here are some standard units of length and area.

DATA

Unit	Square Unit
inch (in.)	square inch
foot (ft)	square foot
centimeter (cm)	square centimeter
meter (m)	square meter

C Count the unit squares.

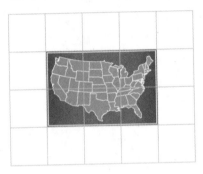

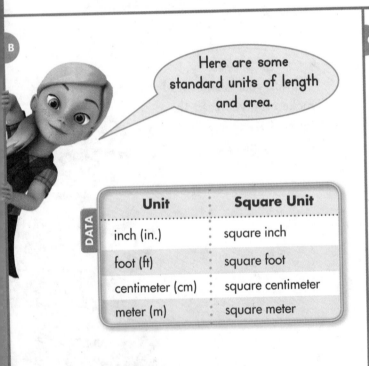

☐ = 1 square centimeter

6 unit squares cover the sticker. The sticker is measured in square centimeters.

So, the area of the sticker is 6 square centimeters.

Convince Me! **Be Precise** If square inches rather than square centimeters were used for the problem above, would more unit squares or fewer unit squares be needed to cover the shape? Explain.

Practice Tools Assessment

☆ Guided Practice

Do You Understand?

1. If Meg's sticker on the previous page measured 2 inches by 3 inches, what would its area be?

2. Zoey paints a wall that measures 8 feet by 10 feet. What units should Zoey use for the area of the wall? Explain.

Do You Know How?

In **3** and **4**, each unit square represents a standard unit. Count the shaded unit squares. Then write the area.

3.

□ = 1 square ft

4.
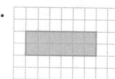
□ = 1 square m

☆ Independent Practice ☆

In **5–10**, each unit square represents a standard unit. Count the shaded unit squares. Then write the area.

5.

□ = 1 square in.

6.

□ = 1 square ft

7.
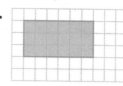
□ = 1 square in.

8.
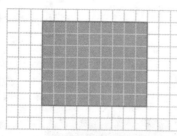
□ = 1 square m

9.
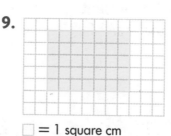
□ = 1 square cm

10.
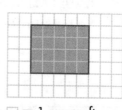
□ = 1 square ft

Problem Solving

11. Reasoning Mr. Sanchez grows three types of vegetables in his garden. What is the area of the garden that Mr. Sanchez uses to grow lettuce and cucumbers? Explain how to use the units in this problem.

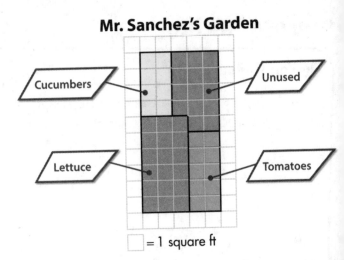

Mr. Sanchez's Garden

Cucumbers

Unused

Lettuce

Tomatoes

☐ = 1 square ft

---

12. Lisa received 34 text messages on Monday and 43 text messages on Tuesday. She received 98 text messages on Wednesday. How many more text messages did Lisa receive on Wednesday than on Monday and Tuesday combined?

13. Monica buys a postage stamp. Is the area of the stamp more likely to be 1 square inch or 1 square meter? Explain.

---

14. Algebra Which operation can you use to complete the equation below?

$8 = 56 \;\square\; 7$

15. Higher Order Thinking Brad says a square that has a length of 9 feet has an area of 18 square feet. Is Brad correct? Why or why not?

☑ **Assessment Practice**

16. Each of the unit squares in Shapes A–C represent 1 square foot. Select numbers to tell the area of each shape.

| 0 | 1 | 2 | 4 | 6 | 7 |

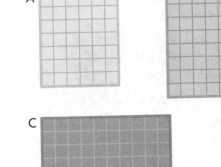

A

B

C

Shape A ☐☐ square feet

Shape B ☐☐ square feet

Shape C ☐☐ square feet

Name_____

☆ **Solve & Share** ☆

Jorge is carpeting two rooms. One room is a square with a side that measures 6 meters. The other room is a rectangle with sides that measure 3 meters and 12 meters. How many square meters of carpet does Jorge need?

I can ...
find the area of squares and rectangles by multiplying.

I can also generalize from examples.

You can *generalize*. What do you know about squares that can help you find the number of square meters of carpet Jorge will need?

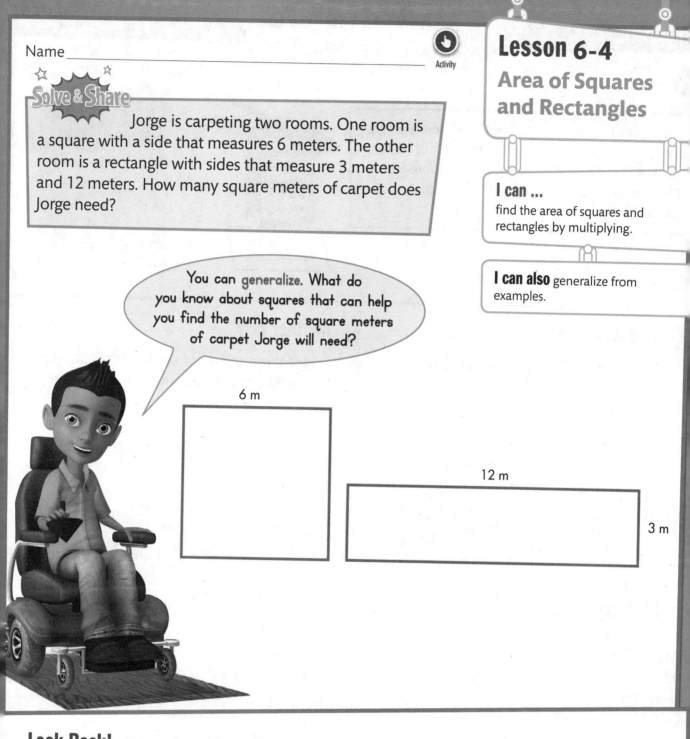

6 m

12 m

3 m

Look Back! What do you notice about the lengths of the sides and the areas of the two rooms Jorge is carpeting?

How Can You Find the Area of a Figure?

A

Mike paints a rectangular wall in his room green. The picture shows the length and width of Mike's wall. A small can of paint covers 40 square feet. Does Mike need more than one small can to paint the wall of his room?

1 can covers 40 square feet

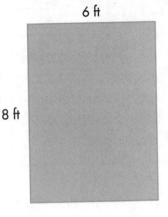

6 ft

8 ft

B **One Way**

Count the unit squares to find area.

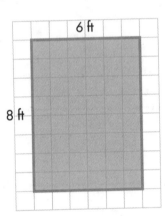

6 ft

8 ft

That's a lot of squares to count!

There are 48 unit squares. The area of Mike's wall is 48 square feet.

C **Another Way**

Count the number of rows and multiply by the number of squares in each row. There are 8 rows and 6 squares in each row.

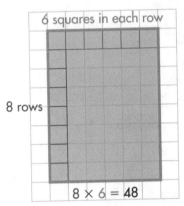

6 squares in each row

8 rows

$8 \times 6 = 48$

The area of Mike's wall is 48 square feet. He will need more than one small can of paint.

Convince Me! **Model with Math** Mike plans to paint a wall in his living room blue. That wall measures 10 feet tall and 8 feet wide. What is the area of the wall Mike plans to paint blue? How many cans of paint will he need?

Another Example!

The area of another wall in Mike's room is 56 square feet. The wall is 8 feet high. How wide is the wall?

$56 = 8 \times ?$

You can use division: $56 \div 8 = ?$

$56 \div 8 = 7$

The wall is 7 feet wide.

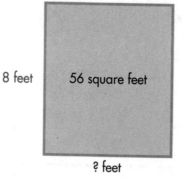

8 feet   56 square feet

? feet

☆ Guided Practice

Do You Understand?

1. Suji's garden is 4 yards long and 4 yards wide. What is the area of Suji's garden?

2. The area of Michi's garden is 32 square feet. The garden is 8 feet long. How wide is Michi's garden?

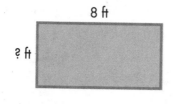

8 ft

? ft

Do You Know How?

In **3** and **4**, find the area of each figure. Use grid paper to help.

3.
7 in.

3 in.

4.
9 ft

6 ft

Independent Practice ☆

In **5** and **6**, find the area. In **7**, find the missing length. Use grid paper to help.

5.
3 cm

1 cm

6.
4 ft

9 ft

7.
7 in.

? in.   35 square in.

Problem Solving

8. Jen's garden is 4 feet wide and has an area of 28 square feet. What is the length of Jen's garden? How do you know?

9. Make Sense and Persevere Briana has 2 grandmothers. She mailed 2 cards to each of them. In each card she put 6 photographs. How many photographs did Briana mail in all?

10. Kevin thinks he found a shortcut. He says he can find the area of a square by multiplying the length of one side by itself. Is Kevin correct? Why or why not?

11. Higher Order Thinking Ryan measures a rectangle that is 9 feet long and 5 feet wide. Teo measures a rectangle that has an area of 36 square feet. Which rectangle has the greater area? Explain how you found the answer.

Assessment Practice

12. Marla makes maps of state preserves. Two of her maps of the same preserve are shown. Select all the true statements about Marla's maps.

☐ You can find the area of Map A by counting the unit squares.

☐ You can find the area of Map B by multiplying the side lengths.

☐ The area of Map A is 18 square feet.

☐ The area of Map B is 18 square feet.

☐ The areas of Maps A and B are **NOT** equivalent.

Map A

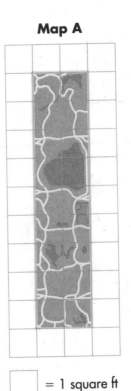

Map B

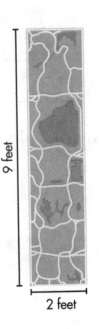

9 feet

2 feet

☐ = 1 square ft

Name_____

☆ ☆
Solve & Share

The new reading room floor is a rectangle that is 8 feet wide by 9 feet long. Mrs. Wallace has a rectangular rug that is 8 feet wide by 5 feet long. What area of the reading room floor will not be covered by the rug?

Activity

I can ...
use properties when multiplying to find the area of squares and rectangles.

I can also model with math.

You can draw rectangles on the grid or use square tiles to model with math.

Look Back! Does your strategy change if the rug is in the corner of the room or in the center? Explain why or why not.

Visual Learning   A-Z Glossary   Essential Question

How Can the Area of Rectangles Represent the Distributive Property?

Visual Learning Bridge

A

Gina wants to separate this rectangle into two smaller rectangles. Will the area of the large rectangle equal the sum of the areas of the two small rectangles?

Area = 7 × 8

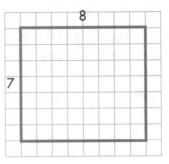

You can use the Distributive Property to break apart facts to find the product.

B Separate the 8-unit side into two parts.

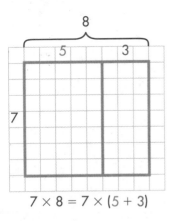

7 × 8 = 7 × (5 + 3)

C 7 × 8 = 7 × (5 + 3) = (7 × 5) + (7 × 3)

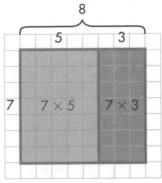

So, the area of the large rectangle is equal to the sum of the areas of the two small rectangles.

Convince Me! Generalize Find another way to separate this rectangle into two smaller parts. Write an equation you can use to find the areas of the two smaller rectangles. Is the area of the large rectangle still the same? What can you generalize?

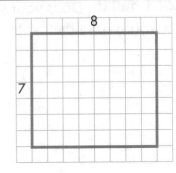

Name_____

☆ Guided Practice

Do You Understand?

1. Describe a way to separate a 6 × 6 square into two smaller rectangles.

2. What multiplication facts describe the areas of the two smaller rectangles you identified in Exercise 1?

Do You Know How?

Complete the equation that represents the picture.

3.

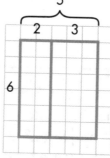

$6 \times \square = 6 \times (2 + \square) =$
$(\square \times 2) + (6 \times \square)$

Independent Practice ☆

In **4** and **5**, complete the equation that represents the picture.

4.

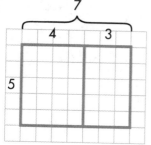

$5 \times \square = 5 \times (4 + \square) =$
$(\square \times 4) + (5 \times \square)$

5.

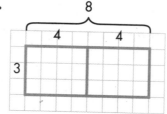

$3 \times \square = \square \times (4 + \square) =$
$(\square \times 4) + (\square \times \square)$

In **6**, write the equation that represents the picture.

6.

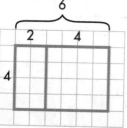

You can use the Distributive Property to help find areas of rectangles when you do not know the product of the initial length and width.

Problem Solving

7. Amit sold 3 shells last week for $5 each and 2 more shells this week for $5 each. Show two ways to determine how much money Amit made in the two weeks.

8. enVision® STEM Claudia wants to replace the roof of a dog house with a new wind-resistant material. The roof has two rectangular sides that are 6 feet by 4 feet. What is the total area of the roof?

9. Use Structure Chiya has an 8 × 6 sheet of tiles. Can she separate the sheet into two smaller sheets that are 8 × 4 and 8 × 2? Do the two smaller sheets have the same total area as her original sheet? Explain.

10. Higher Order Thinking List all possible ways to divide the rectangle at the right into 2 smaller rectangles.

11. Which equation represents the total area of the green shapes?

Ⓐ $4 \times 8 = 4 \times (6 + 2) = (4 \times 6) + (4 \times 2)$

Ⓑ $4 \times 7 = 4 \times (3 + 4) = (4 \times 3) + (4 \times 4)$

Ⓒ $4 \times 7 = 4 \times (4 + 3) = (4 \times 4) + (4 \times 3)$

Ⓓ $4 \times 7 = 4 \times (5 + 2) = (4 \times 5) + (4 \times 2)$

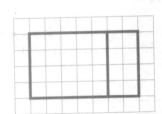

Name_____

☆ ☆
Solve & Share

Mrs. Marcum's desk is shaped like the picture below. The length of each side is shown in feet. Find the area of Mrs. Marcum's desk.

I can ...
use properties to find the area of irregular shapes by breaking the shape into smaller parts.

I can also look for patterns to solve problems.

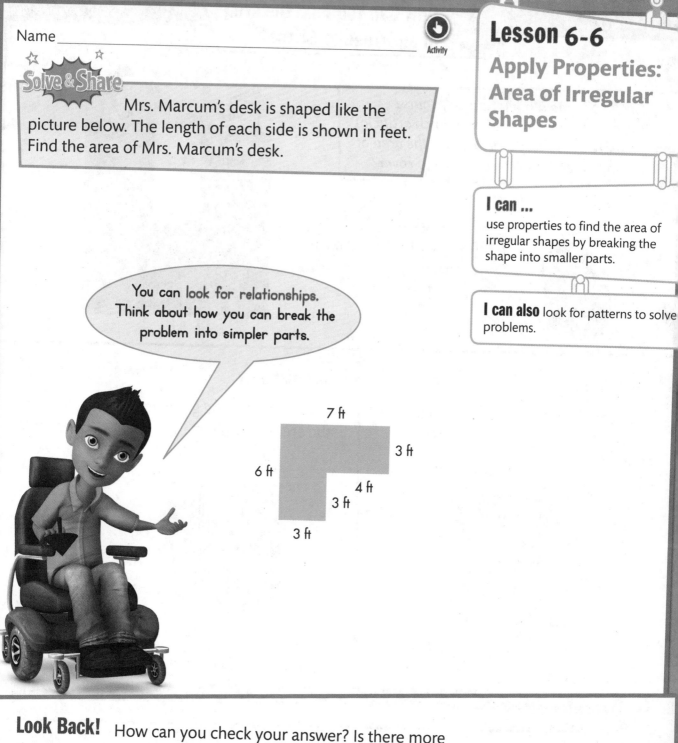

You can look for relationships. Think about how you can break the problem into simpler parts.

7 ft

3 ft

6 ft

4 ft

3 ft

3 ft

Look Back! How can you check your answer? Is there more than one way to solve this problem? Explain.

How Can You Find the Area of an Irregular Shape?

A

Mr. Fox is covering a miniature golf course putting green with artificial grass. Each artificial grass square is 1 square foot. What is the area of the putting green that Mr. Fox needs to cover?

Look for relationships. Think about smaller shapes that are part of the larger shape.

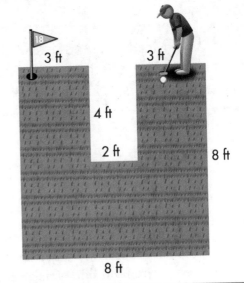

3 ft   3 ft
4 ft
2 ft   8 ft
8 ft

B One Way

You can draw the figure on grid paper. Then count the unit squares to find the area.

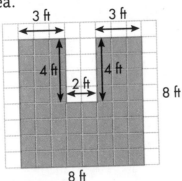

3 ft   3 ft
4 ft   4 ft
2 ft
8 ft
8 ft

The area of the putting green is 56 square feet.

C Another Way

Divide the putting green into rectangles. Find the area of each rectangle. Then add the areas.

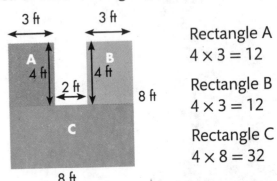

3 ft   3 ft
A   4 ft   4 ft   B
2 ft
8 ft
C
8 ft

Rectangle A
$4 \times 3 = 12$

Rectangle B
$4 \times 3 = 12$

Rectangle C
$4 \times 8 = 32$

$12 + 12 + 32 = 56$. The area of the putting green is 56 square feet.

Convince Me! Use Structure Find another way to divide the putting green into smaller rectangles. Explain how you can find the area of the putting green using your smaller rectangles.

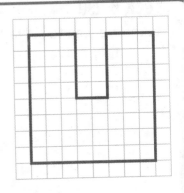

Name_____

☆ Guided Practice

Do You Understand?

1. Explain why you can find the area of the putting green on the previous page using different rectangles.

2. Explain what operation you use to find the total area of the smaller rectangles.

Do You Know How?

In **3** and **4**, find the area of each figure. Use grid paper to help.

3.

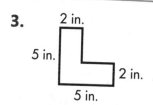

2 in.
5 in.
2 in.
5 in.

4.

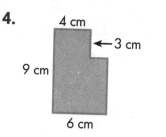

4 cm
3 cm
9 cm
6 cm

Independent Practice ☆

In **5–8**, find the area of each figure. Use grid paper to help.

5.

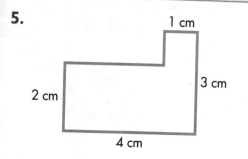

1 cm
3 cm
2 cm
4 cm

6.

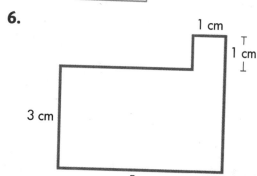

1 cm
1 cm
3 cm
5 cm

7.

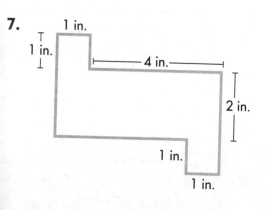

1 in.
1 in.
4 in.
2 in.
1 in.
1 in.

8.

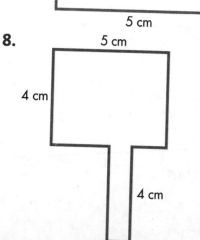

5 cm
4 cm
4 cm

Problem Solving

9. Reasoning Mrs. Kendel is making a model house. The footprint for the house is shown at the right. What is the total area? Explain your reasoning.

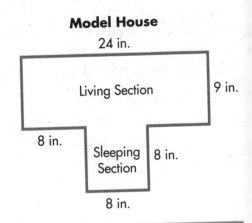

Model House

24 in.

Living Section

9 in.

8 in.

Sleeping Section

8 in.

8 in.

---

10. (A-Z) **Vocabulary** Fill in the blanks. Mandy finds the _____ of this shape by dividing it into rectangles. Phil gets the same answer by counting

_____.

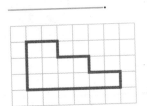

11. Algebra Write an equation. Use a question mark to represent the unknown quantity for the phrase "six times a number is 24." Solve your equation.

---

12. Higher Order Thinking Mr. Delancy used 3-inch square tiles to make the design at the right. What is the area of the design he made? Explain how you found it.

3 in.

✓ **Assessment Practice**

13. Jared drew the figure at the right. Draw lines to show how you can divide the shape to find the area. Then select the correct area for the figure at the right.

Ⓐ 6 square inches

Ⓑ 24 square inches

Ⓒ 30 square inches

Ⓓ 33 square inches

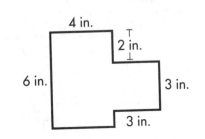

4 in.

2 in.

6 in.

3 in.

3 in.

Name_____

☆ ☆
Solve & Share

Mr. Anderson is tiling his kitchen floor. He will not need tiles for the areas covered by the kitchen island or the counter. How many square meters of tiles does Mr. Anderson need?

I can ...
use the relationships between quantities to break a problem into simpler parts.

I can also solve area problems.

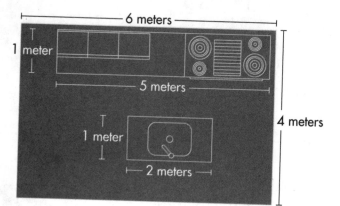

Thinking Habits

*Be a good thinker!
These questions can help you.*

- What patterns can I see and describe?

- How can I use the patterns to solve the problem?

- Can I see expressions and objects in different ways?

Look Back! **Use Structure** Is the tiled area greater than or less than the total area of the kitchen? Explain.

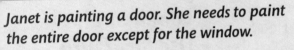

Essential Question: How Can You Use Structure to Solve Problems?

A

Janet is painting a door. She needs to paint the entire door except for the window.

What is the area of the part of the door that needs paint?

You can use the picture to help see the structure.

What do I need to do to solve this problem?

I need to find the area of the door without the window.

B

How can I make use of structure to solve this problem?

I can

- break the problem into simpler parts.

- find equivalent expressions.

C

I will subtract the area of the window from the total area.

Here's my thinking...

Find the area of the whole door.
4 feet × 9 feet = 36 square feet

Find the area of the window.
2 feet × 2 feet = 4 square feet

Subtract to find the area that needs paint.
36 − 4 = 32 square feet

The area of the part of the door that needs paint is 32 square feet.

Convince Me! **Use Structure** Janet thinks of a different way to solve the problem. She says, "I can divide the area I need to paint into 4 smaller rectangles. Then I will find the area of each smaller rectangle and add the 4 areas." Does Janet's strategy make sense? Explain.

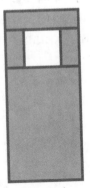

☆ Guided Practice

Use Structure

Lil glued beads on the border of the frame. What is the area of the part she decorated with beads?

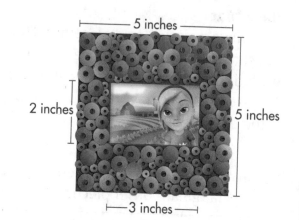

1. How can you think about the total area of the frame?

2. Use what you know to solve the problem.

A picture can help you see equivalent expressions. Think about the structure.

Independent Practice ☆

Use Structure

A keypad has 10 rubber buttons. Each button is 1 centimeter by 2 centimeters. The rest is made out of plastic. Is the area of the plastic greater than the area of the rubber buttons?

3. How can you break the problem into simpler parts? What is the hidden question?

4. How can you find the area of all the rubber buttons?

5. Use what you know to solve the problem.

Problem Solving

Place Mat

Genevieve is designing a placemat. The center measures 8 inches by 10 inches. A 2-inch border goes around the center. Genevieve cuts the corners to make the placemat an octagon. She wants to find the area of the placemat.

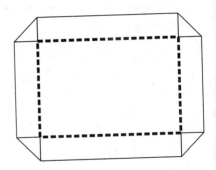

6. **Use Structure** What are the lengths and widths of each rectangular border piece?

7. **Use Appropriate Tools** How can Genevieve find the area of the 4 corner pieces using grid paper?

☐ = 1 square in.

8. **Model with Math** What equation can Genevieve use to find the area of the center? Find the area of the center using your equation.

Use structure to simplify a problem.

9. **Reasoning** How are the quantities in this problem related?

10. **Be Precise** Solve the problem. Explain what unit you used for your answer.

Name_____

Follow the Path

TOPIC 6

Fluency Practice Activity

I can ...
multiply and divide within 100.

I can also be precise in my work

Shade a path from **START** to **FINISH**.
Follow the quotients that are odd numbers.
You can only move up, down, right, or left.
Once you complete the path, write the fact
families for each of the squares you shaded.

Start				
15 ÷ 5	45 ÷ 5	40 ÷ 8	36 ÷ 4	6 ÷ 3
28 ÷ 7	12 ÷ 2	90 ÷ 9	63 ÷ 9	0 ÷ 8
48 ÷ 8	50 ÷ 5	81 ÷ 9	9 ÷ 3	56 ÷ 7
20 ÷ 5	48 ÷ 6	42 ÷ 6	10 ÷ 5	6 ÷ 1
30 ÷ 3	16 ÷ 8	35 ÷ 7	45 ÷ 9	56 ÷ 8
				Finish

Vocabulary Review

TOPIC 6

 Glossary

Word List

- area
- column
- Distributive Property
- estimate
- multiplication
- product
- row
- square unit
- unit square

Understand Vocabulary

Choose the best term from the Word List. Write it on the blank.

1. A(n) _____ has sides that are each 1 unit long.

2. _____ is the number of unit squares that cover a region or shape.

3. You can use the _____ to break apart facts and find the _____.

4. A unit square has an area of 1 _____.

5. When you _____, you give an approximate answer.

Write *always*, *sometimes*, or *never*.

6. Area is _____ measured in square meters.

7. Multiplication _____ involves joining equal groups.

8. The area of a shape can _____ be represented as the sum of the areas of smaller rectangles.

Use Vocabulary in Writing

9. What is the area of this rectangle? Explain how you solved the problem. Use at least 3 terms from the Word List in your answer.

Name_____

Set A | pages 209–212

A unit square has sides that are 1 unit long.

Count the unit squares that cover the shape. The count is the area of the shape.

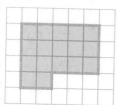

☐ = 1 unit square

Seventeen unit squares cover the shape. The area of the shape is 17 square units.

Sometimes you need to estimate to find the area. First count the full squares. Then estimate the number of partially filled squares.

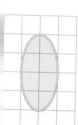

About 6 unit squares cover this shape.

Remember that area is the number of unit squares needed to cover a region with no gaps or overlaps.

In **1** and **2**, count to find the area. Tell if the area is an estimate.

1.

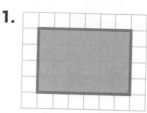

2.

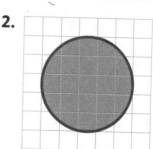

Set B | pages 213–216

Unit squares can be different sizes. The size of a unit square determines the area.

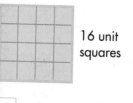

16 unit squares

4 unit squares

☐ = 1 square unit   ☐ = 1 square unit

Area = 16 square units   Area = 4 square units

The measurements are different because different sizes of unit squares were used.

Remember that you can use unit squares to measure area.

Draw unit squares to cover the figures and find the area. Use the unit squares shown.

1.   **2.**

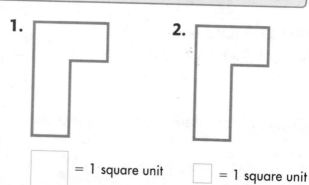

☐ = 1 square unit   ☐ = 1 square unit

The unit squares below represent square inches.

What is the area of the figure below?

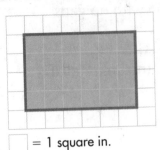

= 1 square in.

Twenty-four unit squares cover the figure. The area of the figure is measured in square inches.

So, the area of the figure is 24 square inches.

Remember that you can measure using standard or metric units of area for unit squares.

In **1** and **2**, each unit square represents a standard unit. Count the unit squares. Then write the area.

1.

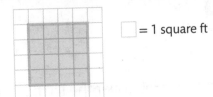

= 1 square ft

2.

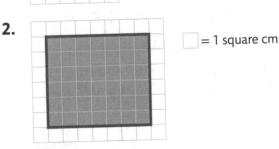

= 1 square cm

You can find area by counting the number of rows and multiplying by the number of squares in each row.

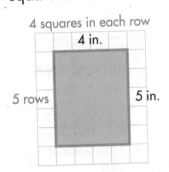

4 squares in each row
4 in.
5 rows   5 in.

There are 5 rows.
There are 4 squares in each row.

$5 \times 4 = 20$

The area of the figure is 20 square inches.

Remember that you can multiply the number of rows by the number of squares in each row to find the area.

In **1–3**, find the area of each figure. Use grid paper to help.

1.

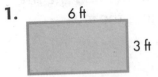

6 ft
3 ft

2.

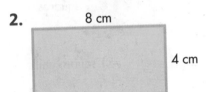

8 cm
4 cm

3.

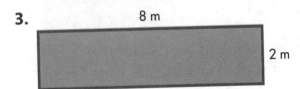

8 m
2 m

Name_____

Set E pages 225–228 _____

You can use the Distributive Property to break apart facts to find the product.

Separate the 5 unit side into two parts.

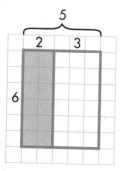

Area of the large rectangle: $6 \times 5 = 30$

Areas of the small rectangles:

$6 \times 2 = 12$

$6 \times 3 = 18$

Add the two areas: $12 + 18 = 30$

You can write an equation to show that the area of the large rectangle is equal to the sum of the areas of the two small rectangles.

$6 \times 5 = 6 \times (2 + 3) = (6 \times 2) + (6 \times 3)$

When you divide a rectangle into two smaller rectangles, the total area does not change!

Remember that you can separate a rectangle into two smaller rectangles with the same total area.

In **1–3**, write the equations that represent the total area of the red shapes. Find the area.

1.
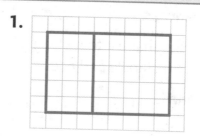

2.
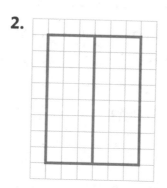

3.
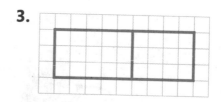

Find the area of this irregular shape.

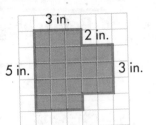

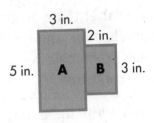

You can place the shape on grid paper and count the unit squares. The area of the shape is 21 square inches.

You also can divide the shape into rectangles. Find the area of each rectangle and add.

$5 \times 3 = 15$ square inches

$3 \times 2 = 6$ square inches

$15 + 6 = 21$ square inches

Remember that you can add smaller areas to find a total area.

In **1** and **2**, find the area of each shape.

1.

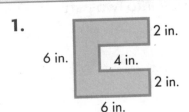

2.

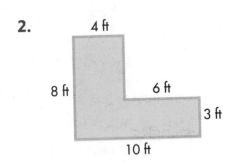

Think about these questions to help you **use structure** in solving problems.

Thinking Habits

- What patterns can I see and describe?

- How can I use the patterns to solve the problem?

- Can I see expressions and objects in different ways?

Remember to look for simpler ways of representing an area.

Debra made this design from 1-inch square tiles. What is the area of the blue tiles?

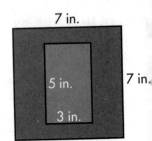

1. How can you express the area of the blue tiles?

2. Solve the problem. Explain how you solved.

Name_____

1. Count to find the area of the shape. Tell if the area is exact or an estimate.

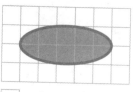

☐ = 1 unit square

2. Use the Distributive Property to write the equation that represents the picture. Then give the area of each smaller rectangle and the large rectangle.

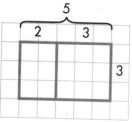

3. Lewis says that the figure below has an area of 4 square meters. Is he correct? Explain.

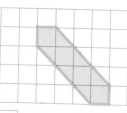

☐ = 1 square cm

4. Select all of the ways to break apart the area of the large rectangle into the sum of the areas of two smaller rectangles. Then give the area of the large rectangle.

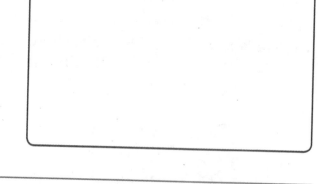

☐ $5 \times 7 = 5 \times (1 + 5) = (5 \times 1) + (5 \times 5)$

☐ $5 \times 7 = 5 \times (3 + 4) = (5 \times 3) + (5 \times 4)$

☐ $5 \times 7 = 5 \times (2 + 3) = (5 \times 2) + (5 \times 3)$

☐ $5 \times 7 = 5 \times (1 + 6) = (5 \times 1) + (5 \times 6)$

☐ $5 \times 7 = 5 \times (2 + 5) = (5 \times 2) + (5 \times 5)$

Area = ☐ square inches

5. What is the total area of the design below?

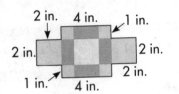

2 in. 4 in. 1 in.

2 in. 2 in.

1 in. 4 in. 2 in.

(A) $4 \times 4 = 16$ square inches

(B) $(4 \times 4) + (2 \times 2) =$ 20 square inches

(C) $(4 \times 4) + (2 \times 2) + (2 \times 2) =$ 24 square inches

(D) $8 \times 4 = 32$ square inches

6. Jared draws a rectangle. Explain how to find the area using the Distributive Property.

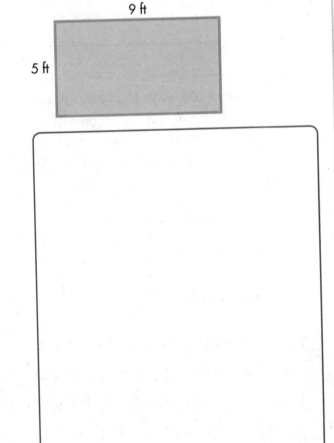

9 ft

5 ft

7. Fran has a square flower bed. One side of the flower bed is 3 feet long. How can you find the area of the flower bed?

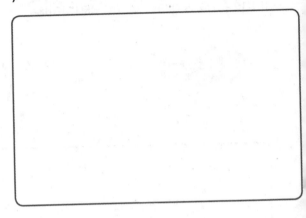

8. Find the missing side length. Then find the area and explain how to find it.

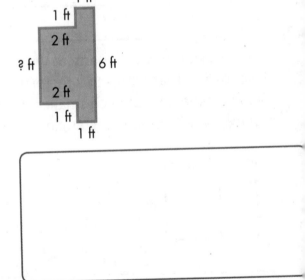

1 ft

1 ft

2 ft

? ft   6 ft

2 ft

1 ft

1 ft

9. This rectangle has an area of 56 square centimeters. What is the missing length? Use an equation to explain.

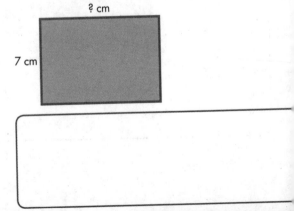

? cm

7 cm

Name_____

10. What is the area of Ron's figure? Explain.

1 ft   1 ft   1 ft   1 ft

3 ft

1 ft

2 ft

9 ft

11. Maddie makes a mosaic with 1-inch glass squares, as shown below. Which color of glass has the greatest area in Maddie's mosaic?

12. Select the correct side length for each square given its area.

	6 ft	9 ft	7 ft	4 ft
16 square feet	❑	❑	❑	❑
49 square feet	❑	❑	❑	❑
81 square feet	❑	❑	❑	❑
36 square feet	❑	❑	❑	❑

13. Explain how to find the area of each rectangle and the total area of the rectangles.

Jodie

Ryan

❑ = 1 square centimeter

14. Some students in Springfield make a parade float with the letter S on it. Draw lines to divide the shape into rectangles. Then find how many square feet the letter is.

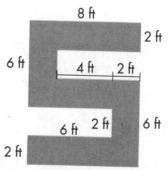

8 ft

2 ft

6 ft

4 ft   2 ft

6 ft   2 ft   6 ft

2 ft

Ⓐ 28 square ft   Ⓒ 56 square ft

Ⓑ 54 square ft   Ⓓ 90 square ft

15. Max draws 2 rectangles, each with an area of 24 square centimeters. What could be the side lengths of Max's rectangles? Show how he could use the Distributive Property to represent the area in each case.

16. A community center builds a new activity room in the shape shown below. Explain how to find the area of the room, and solve.

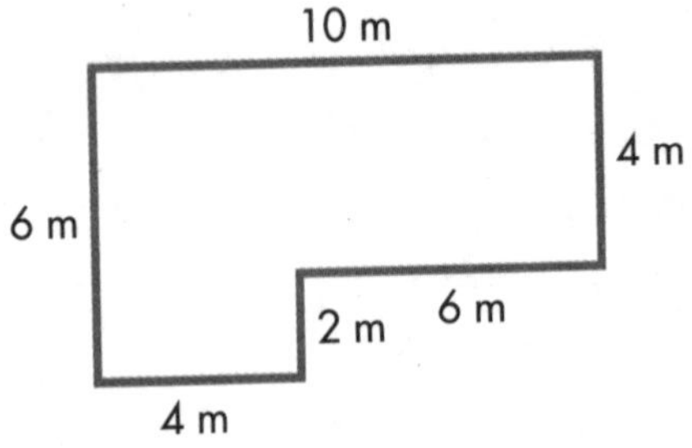

10 m

4 m

6 m

2 m   6 m

4 m

17. Show 2 different unit squares that you can use to measure the area of these rectangles. Find the area with your unit squares.

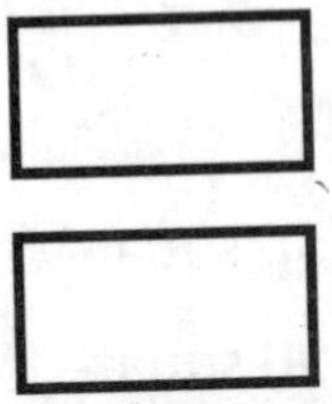

18. Ethan wants to know the area of the yellow part of this design.

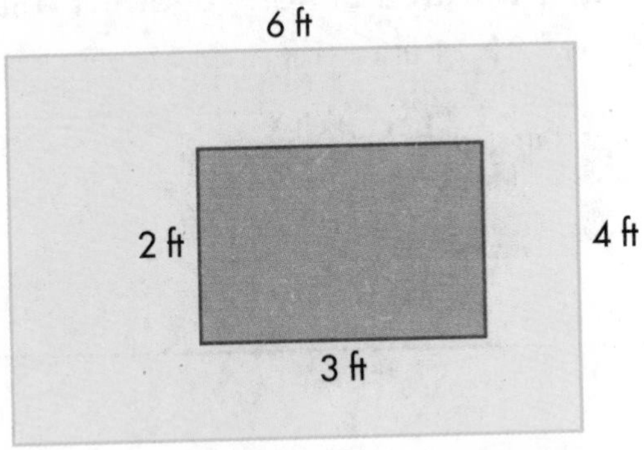

6 ft

2 ft   4 ft

3 ft

A. Explain how you can break this problem into simpler problems.

B. Find the yellow area. Show your work.

Banner Design

Jessie is designing a banner that has red, blue, and white sections.
The **Banner Details** list shows the rules for each color.
The **Jessie's Banner** diagram shows the different sections of the banner.

Banner Details

• Red sections must have a total area greater than 40 square inches.

• Blue sections must have a total area greater than 30 square inches.

• The white section must have an area less than 40 square inches.

Use the **Jessie's Banner** diagram to answer Question **1**.

1. To check if his banner fits the rules, Jessie started this table. Complete the table. Use multiplication and addition as needed.

Jessie's Banner

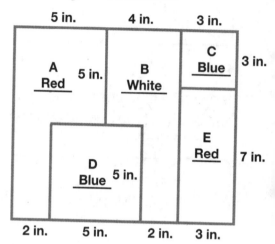

Section	Color	Show How to Find the Area	Area
A	Red		
B	White		
C	Blue		9 square inches
D	Blue		
E	Red	7×3	

Use the table above and the **Banner Details** list to answer Question **2**.

2. Is Jessie's banner within the totals in the **Banner Details** list? Explain.

3. Jessie makes a square patch to go on top of the banner.

Part A

Draw unit squares to cover the patch. How many unit squares cover the patch?

Jessie's Patch

[ ] = 1 square cm

Part B

Jessie says if he checks the area by multiplying, the area will be the same as if he counts each unit square. Is he correct? Explain.

4. Jessie uses two colors to make the patch. The colors have different areas.

Part A

Explain how to separate the square into two smaller rectangles with different areas. Use multiplication to find the areas of each of the smaller rectangles.

Part B

Is the area of the square equal to the total area of the two smaller rectangles? Use an equation to explain.

Represent and Interpret Data

Essential Question: How can data be represented, analyzed, and interpreted?

Digital Resources

 Interactive Student Edition
 Activity
 Visual Learning
 Video
Practic

 Assessment
 Games
 Tools
A-Z Glossary

The weather and temperature can change a lot during different seasons.

The seasons can have a huge impact on how we lead our daily lives.

I better prepare for the upcoming season! Here's a project on seasons and data.

enVision STEM Project: Seasons

Do Research Use the Internet or other sources to find information about patterns of temperature in the different seasons where you live. Include information about the average monthly temperatures and the record low and high temperatures.

Journal: Write a Report Include what you found. Also in your report:

- For one week, record the daily high and low temperatures in the area where you live. Make a graph displaying this information.

- Find the difference between the highest and lowest daily temperatures from your graph.

Name_____

Review What You Know

A-Z Vocabulary

Choose the best term from the box.
Write it on the blank.

- equal groups
- multiples
- multiplication
- number line

1. _____ have the same number of items.

2. A _____ can be used to help compare numbers.

3. _____ is used to find a total when joining equal groups.

Multiplication

In **4** and **5**, complete the equation.

4. $5 \times 3 =$ ____

5. $3 \times$ ____ $= 21$

6. Make a bar diagram to represent 4×6.

Multiplication on the Number Line

7. Ed bought 2 bags of grapefruit. There are 6 grapefruit in each bag. How many grapefruit did he buy? Draw jumps on the number line to find the answer.

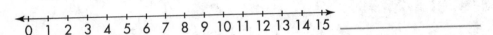

0 1 2 3 4 5 6 7 8 9 10 11 12 13 14 15 _____

8. Show the multiplication fact 3×4 on the number line. Write the product.

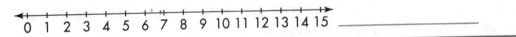

0 1 2 3 4 5 6 7 8 9 10 11 12 13 14 15 _____

Finding Area

9. Find the area of the rectangle.

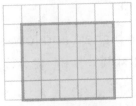

☐ = 1 square inch   _____

Name_____

PROJECT 7A

How is a book printed?

Project: Collect Data and Create Picture Graphs

PROJECT 7B

Would you like to live in a city?

Project: Make a Bar Graph About Cities and Towns

PROJECT 7C

What is your favorite animal?

Project: Develop a Picture Graph About Animals

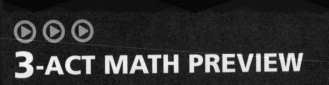

Before watching the video, think:

Playgrounds have many different spaces and objects. A playground space built for toddlers looks different from a playground space built for older children.

I can ...
model with math to solve a problem that involves anayzing data to make decisions.

Name_____

☆ ☆
Solve & Share

Students in Jorge's class took a survey of their favorite cereals and made this graph to show the results. Name at least three facts about the information in the graph.

I can ...
use picture graphs and bar graphs to answer questions about data sets.

I can also look for patterns to solve problems.

You can use structure. How can you find the number of votes for each type of cereal?

Favorite Cereals

Berry Crunch	✕ ✕ ✕ ✕ ╲
Honey Granola	✕ ✕
Corn Puffs	✕ ✕ ✕ ╲
Nuts and Wheat	✕ ✕ ✕ ✕ ✕

Each ✕ = 2 votes. Each ╲ = 1 vote.

Look Back! What do the two different symbols on the graph stand for?

A

How many teams are in the East Falls League?

Information you collect is called data. A scaled picture graph uses pictures or symbols to show data.

The scale is the value each picture or symbol represents.

Number of Hockey Teams in Each League	
East Falls	✕ ✕ ✕ ╱
North Falls	✕ ✕ ╱
South Falls	✕ ✕
West Falls	✕ ✕ ✕ ✕ ✕ ╱

Each ✕ = 2 teams.
Each ╱ = 1 team.

The key explains the scale used in the graph.

B

Use the key.

Look at the data for East Falls League.

There are 3 ✕ and 1 ╱.

The 3 ✕ represent 3 × 2 = 6 teams.

The 1 ╱ represents 1 × 1 = 1 team.

6 + 1 = 7

There are 7 teams in the East Falls League.

C

How many more teams does the East Falls League have than the South Falls League?

Use the picture graph to write equations and compare the two rows.

East Falls   ✕ ✕ ✕ ╱
3 × 2 + 1 = 7

South Falls   ✕ ✕
2 × 2 = 4

Subtract: 7 − 4 = 3

The East Falls League has 3 more teams than the South Falls League.

Convince Me! **Be Precise** Tell something about each league you can find out from the picture graph.

Name_____

Another Example!

A scaled bar graph uses bars to represent and compare information. This bar graph shows the number of goals scored by different players on a hockey team. The scale shows the units used.

On this bar graph, each horizontal grid line represents two units. Every other grid line is labeled: 0, 4, 8, and so on. For example, the line halfway between 4 and 8 represents 6 goals.

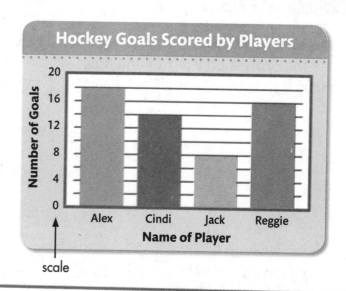

Hockey Goals Scored by Players

Number of Goals — Name of Player

scale

☆ Guided Practice

Do You Understand?

In **1** and **2**, use the bar graph above.

1. How many goals in all did Alex and Reggie score?

Do You Know How?

2. Explain how to find how many fewer goals Cindi scored than Alex.

Independent Practice ☆

In **3–5**, use the picture graph.

3. Which area has lights on for exactly 50 hours each week?

4. What does the half bulb in the data for the exercise room represent?

5. In one week, how many more hours are lights on in the exercise room than at the swimming pool?

Hours of Light Usage at Sports Center
Number of Hours Lights Are on Each Week

Exercise Room	💡💡💡💡💡💡💡🔆
Locker Room	💡💡💡💡💡💡💡💡
Swimming Pool	💡💡💡💡💡🔆
Tennis Court	💡💡💡💡💡

Each 💡 = 10 hours. Each 🔆 = 5 hours.

Problem Solving

In **6-8**, use the picture graph.

6. Reasoning For which days can you use the expression 9×7 to find how many points were scored?

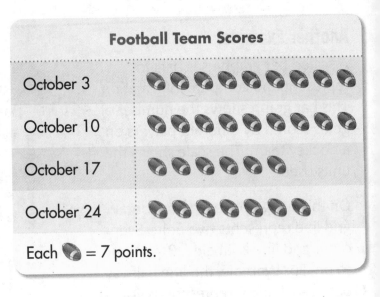

Football Team Scores

October 3	🏈🏈🏈🏈🏈🏈🏈🏈🏈
October 10	🏈🏈🏈🏈🏈🏈🏈🏈🏈
October 17	🏈🏈🏈🏈🏈🏈
October 24	🏈🏈🏈🏈🏈🏈🏈

Each 🏈 = 7 points.

7. On which days did the football team score fewer than 50 points?

8. Higher Order Thinking How many more points were scored on October 10 and 24 combined than on October 3 and 17?

✓ Assessment Practice

In **9** and **10**, use the bar graph at the right.

9. How many more miles per hour is the top running speed of the cheetah than of the Cape hunting dog?

Ⓐ 25 miles per hour

Ⓑ 30 miles per hour

Ⓒ 35 miles per hour

Ⓓ 40 miles per hour

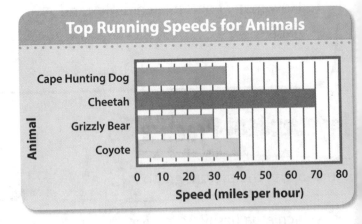

Top Running Speeds for Animals

Animal: Cape Hunting Dog, Cheetah, Grizzly Bear, Coyote

Speed (miles per hour): 0 10 20 30 40 50 60 70 80

10. How many fewer miles per hour is the top running speed of the grizzly bear than of the coyote and the Cape hunting dog combined?

Ⓐ 40 miles per hour

Ⓑ 45 miles per hour

Ⓒ 50 miles per hour

Ⓓ 55 miles per hour

You need to look at the scale when reading information in bar graphs.

Name _____

Solve & Share

Mary is helping her teacher count school playground equipment. She records the data in a frequency table. Use the data in the table to complete the picture graph. Write two statements about your completed graph.

I can ...
make a picture graph to record information and answer questions about a data set.

I can also make sense of problems.

DATA

School Playground Equipment		
Equipment	Tally	Number
Basketballs	卌 卌	10
Jump Ropes	卌 卌	10
Bats	卌	5
Soccer Balls	卌 卌 卌	15

_____

Basketballs

Jump Ropes

Bats

Soccer Balls

Each 🏀 = 2 items.   Each 🏐 = 1 item.

You can make sense and persevere. How can the tally marks and the key help you represent the data in the picture graph?

Look Back! How did you know the number of symbols to draw for jump ropes?

How Do You Make a Picture Graph?

Sam recorded the number of each kind of bicycle a store sold during one month. He made a frequency table. Use the table to make a picture graph.

> You can also collect data with a survey by asking people questions.

DATA

Kinds of Bicycles Sold

Kind of Bicycle	Tally	Number
Road	丗丗	10
Track	丗丗丗丗	20
Training	丗丗丗	15
Racing	丗丗	10

B Write a title for the picture graph.

The title is "Kinds of Bicycles Sold."

Choose a symbol for the key. Decide what each whole symbol and half-symbol will represent.

Each ▲ means 10 bicycles.

Each ◢ means 5 bicycles.

> A half-symbol is used to represent 5 bicycles because 5 is half of 10.

C Set up the graph and list the kinds of bicycles. Decide how many symbols you need for each number of bicycles sold. Draw the symbols.

Kinds of Bicycles Sold

Road	▲
Track	▲ ▲
Training	▲ ◢
Racing	▲

Each ▲ = 10 bicycles.
Each ◢ = 5 bicycles.

Convince Me! **Model with Math** Suppose 25 mountain bicycles were also sold. Draw symbols to show a row in the picture graph for mountain bicycles. Explain how you decided.

Name_____

☆Guided Practice

Do You Understand?

In **1** and **2**, use the picture graph on the previous page.

1. Explain the symbols that were used for the number of training bicycles sold.

2. If the scale used in the key were ▲ = 2 bicycles, how many symbols would be used for the number of road bicycles sold? For the number of track bicycles sold?

Do You Know How?

3. Use the table to complete the picture graph.

DATA

Favorite School Lunch		
Lunch	**Tally**	**Number**
Taco	//	2
Pizza	THL ///	8
Salad	///	3

Favorite School Lunch	
Taco	
Pizza	
Salad	

Each 🥛 = 2 votes.
Each ☕ = 1 vote.

Independent Practice ☆

In **4-6**, use the data in the chart.

4. Complete the picture graph.

_____	
Cubs	
Hawks	
Lions	
Roadrunners	

Each ⬤ = ___ goals. Each ◖ = ___ goals.

5. Which two teams scored more goals, the Cubs and the Lions or the Hawks and the Roadrunners?

DATA

Goals Each Team Has Scored		
Team Name	**Tally**	**Number**
Cubs	THL THL	10
Hawks	THL THL THL THL	20
Lions	THL THL THL THL THL THL	30
Roadrunners	THL THL THL	15

6. Explain how you decided the number of each symbol to draw to show the goals for the Roadrunners.

Problem Solving

In **7-9**, use the frequency table at the right.

7. **Use Appropriate Tools** Select and use appropriate tools to help make a picture graph to show the data in the table.

DATA

Favorite Vegetables

Kind	Tally	Number
Corn	////	4
Green Beans	//	2
Tomatoes	₩₩	5

8. What is the difference between the odd number and the sum of the even numbers in the table?

9. Ask six students in your class which of the three vegetables is their favorite. Record the answers in your picture graph.

10. **Higher Order Thinking** Suppose you are going to make a picture graph to show the data in the Simon's Book Shop table. Choose a symbol to stand for 5 books sold. Draw the row for fiction books sold. Justify your drawing.

DATA

Simon's Book Shop

Kind of Book	Number Sold
Fiction	25
Nonfiction	40
Poetry	20
Dictionary	15

Assessment Practice

11. The Garden Shop sold 25 plants in April, 30 plants in May, and 35 plants in June. Complete the picture graph for this data. Choose the symbols you will use.

Plants Sold at Garden Shop

April	
May	
June	

Each ___ = 10 plants.   Each ___ = 5 plants.

Name_____

☆ ☆
Solve & Share

Use the data in the table below to complete the bar graph. What conclusions can you make by analyzing the bar graph?

I can ...
make a bar graph to record information and answer questions about a data set.

I can also reason about math.

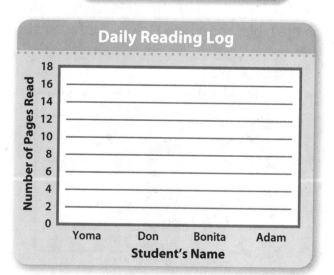

DATA

Daily Reading Log

Student's Name	Number of Pages Read
Yoma	13
Don	10
Bonita	10
Adam	6

Daily Reading Log

Number of Pages Read
18
16
14
12
10
8
6
4
2
0

Yoma   Don   Bonita   Adam

Student's Name

You can use reasoning. You can use the data in the table to help draw the bars on the graph.

Look Back! How can tools such as a ruler help you create a bar graph?

Essential Question How Do You Make a Bar Graph?

Greg made a table to show the amount of money he saved each month from tutoring. Use the data in the table to make a bar graph.

DATA

Amount Greg Saved Each Month	
Month	Amount Saved
January	$25
February	$50
March	$65
April	$40

A bar graph can make it easy to compare data.

B Write a title. Use the same title as in the table.

The title of this bar graph is **Amount Greg Saved Each Month.**

Choose the scale. Decide how many units each grid line will represent.

Each grid line will represent $10.

C Set up the graph with the scale, each month listed in the table, and labels. Draw a bar for each month.

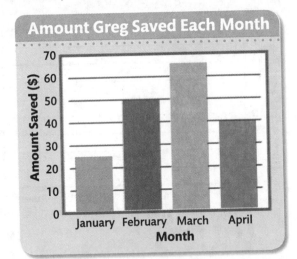

Amount Greg Saved Each Month

Convince Me! Be Precise Write new amounts for how much Greg saved in 4 later months. Consider the scale.

In May, Greg saved _____.

In June, Greg saved _____.

In July, Greg saved _____.

In August, Greg saved _____.

Draw bars on the graph to show your new data.

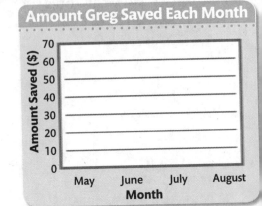

Amount Greg Saved Each Month

Name _____

★ **Guided Practice**

Do You Understand?

In **1–3**, use the bar graph on the previous page.

1. Explain why the bar for January ends between 20 and 30.

2. Suppose Greg saved $35 in May. Between which grid lines would the bar for May end?

3. How can you tell how much more Greg saved in February than in April?

Do You Know How?

4. Use the table to complete the bar graph.

DATA

Number of People Signed Up for Classes

Class	Tally	Number of People
Chess	卌 l	6
Guitar	卌 卌	10
Painting	卌 ll	7
Writing	卌 llll	9

Number of People Signed Up for Classes

★ **Independent Practice** ★

In **5**, use the table at the right.

5. Complete the bar graph to show the data.

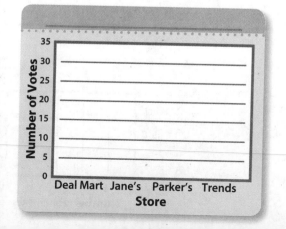

DATA

Favorite Store for Clothes

Store	Tally	Number of Votes
Deal Mart	卌 卌 卌	15
Jane's	卌 卌 卌 卌 卌 卌	30
Parker's	卌 卌 卌 卌	20
Trends	卌	5

Problem Solving

In **6-8**, use the table at the right.

6. Make a bar graph to show the data.

Favorite Kind of Movie

Kind of Movie	Adventure	Cartoon	Comedy	Science Fiction
Number of Votes	16	7	10	6

7. **Construct Arguments** Which two kinds of movies received about the same number of votes? Explain how to use your bar graph to find the answer.

8. Each movie ticket costs $8. Jo buys tickets for the number of people who voted for science fiction. How much change does she get from $50?

9. **Higher Order Thinking** Suppose you are going to make a bar graph to show the data in the table at the right. What scale would you choose? Explain.

Speed of Birds

Kind of Bird	Flying Speed (miles per hour)
Northern Mockingbird	95
Peregrine Falcon	180
Spin-Tailed Swift	105

Assessment Practice

10. Tanji collected data on the colors of his friends' shoes. Eight friends have black shoes. Five friends have blue shoes. Seven friends have white shoes. Use Tanji's data to complete the bar graph.

Friends' Shoes

Name_____

Activity

Lesson 7-4
Solve Word
Problems Using
Information
in Graphs

☆ ☆
Solve & Share

The students in Ms. Seymour's class voted for their favorite kind of sandwich. How many more students voted for peanut butter than cheese? How many fewer students voted for tuna than peanut butter?

I can ...
use graphs and other tools to solve word problems.

I can also make sense of problems.

Think about what you are trying to find out to make sense and persevere in solving this problem.

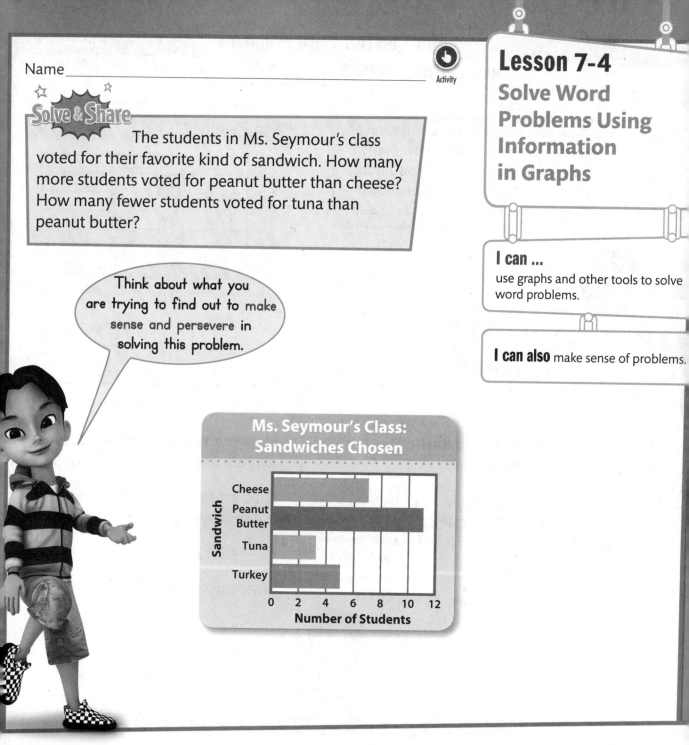

Ms. Seymour's Class: Sandwiches Chosen

Sandwich

Cheese
Peanut Butter
Tuna
Turkey

0   2   4   6   8   10 12
Number of Students

Look Back! What is the scale for this graph? How do you know the number of votes a bar represents when it is between two lines on this graph?

Essential Question

How Can You Solve Problems Using Graphs?

A

Angela wants Karli and Monique to have a total of 60 paper cranes. The bar graph shows how many paper cranes her friends already have. How many more paper cranes does Angela need to make for Karli and Monique to have 60 paper cranes in all?

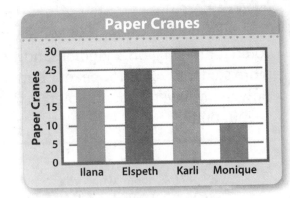

Paper Cranes

This problem has a hidden question!

B Solve the hidden question.

How many paper cranes do Karli and Monique already have?

Use the scale to find how many paper cranes Karli and Monique each have. Then add.

 Remember you still need to answer the main question.

Karli has 30 paper cranes.
Monique has 10 paper cranes.

$30 + 10 = 40$

Together they have 40 paper cranes.

C Solve the main question.

How many paper cranes does Angela need to make?

Subtract the number of cranes the friends already have from the total.

$60 - 40 = 20$

Angela needs to make 20 paper cranes.

Convince Me! **Critique Reasoning** Angela says, "I want Ilana and Elspeth to also have 60 cranes in all. I can subtract two times to find how many more cranes I need to make for them." Is Angela correct? Explain.

☆ Guided Practice

Do You Understand?

1. Look at the graph on the previous page. Explain whether you would add, subtract, multiply, or divide to find how many more paper cranes Karli already has than Monique.

2. How does a bar graph help you compare data?

Do You Know How?

In **3**, use the bar graph.

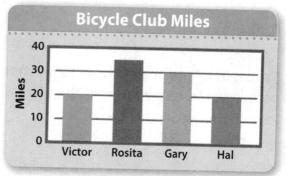

3. How many more miles did Hal and Victor ride together than Rosita?

Independent Practice ☆

In **4–6**, use the picture graph at the right.

4. How many more red T-shirts were sold at Ultimate T than at Jazzy's?

T-Shirt Sales	Jazzy's	Ultimate T
Blue	👕👕🔼	👕
Red	👕👕	👕👕🔼
Green	🔼	👕👕👕

Each 👕 = 10 T-shirts. Each 🔼 = 5 T-shirts.

5. How many fewer green T-shirts were sold at Jazzy's than at Ultimate T?

6. How many more blue and red T-shirts combined were sold at Jazzy's than green T-shirts were sold at Ultimate T?

Using the key, you can see that each half shirt equals 5 T-shirts in the graph.

Problem Solving

In **7-9**, use the bar graph at the right.

7. **Number Sense** How many people voted for their favorite type of exercise? How can you find the answer?

Favorite Type of Exercise

8. **Construct Arguments** How many more people voted for gymnastics than for jogging? How do you know?

9. How many fewer people voted for swimming than for gymnastics and jogging combined?

10. Leslie delivers papers on weekdays and Saturdays. She delivers 6 papers each weekday and 16 papers on Saturday. How many papers does Leslie deliver during the entire week?

11. **Higher Order Thinking** What kinds of comparisons can you make when you look at a bar graph or a picture graph?

Assessment Practice

12. Daryl made a bar graph to record the number of books read by each member of a reading club.

    How many fewer books did Alice read than Sandra and Daryl combined?

    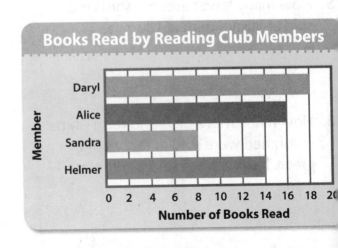

    Books Read by Reading Club Members

    Ⓐ 6 books

    Ⓑ 8 books

    Ⓒ 10 books

    Ⓓ 12 books

Name _____

Activity

☆ ☆
Solve & Share

Action books and mystery books cost $5 each. Biography books cost $10 each. A librarian has $100 to spend on new books. She collected some information about the kinds of books that students checked out to read last month.

How should the librarian spend the money? Use math words and symbols to explain your thinking.

I can ...
be precise when solving math problems.

I can also use data in graphs.

Thinking Habits

Be a good thinker!
These questions can help you.

- Am I using numbers, units, and symbols appropriately?

- Am I using the correct definitions?

- Am I calculating accurately?

- Is my answer clear?

Look Back! **Be Precise** How did you use words and symbols to explain your answer?

How Can You Be Precise When Solving Math Problems?

Bella has a bakery. She will use the bakery items at the right to make a gift basket worth $40. Bella wants the basket to have more than one of each bakery item. Show one way to make a gift basket.

Bakery Items Available

Wheat Loaves ($4 each)

Cinnamon Buns ($2 each)

Muffins ($1 each)

Each 🍞 = 2 items

What do I need to do to make a gift basket?

I need to be precise. I will decide how many of each item to put in a basket so the total is exactly $40.

Here's my thinking...

B How can I be precise in solving this problem?

I can

- correctly use the information given.

- calculate accurately.

- decide if my answer is clear and appropriate.

- use the correct units.

C

I will start with $40.
I know how many of each item is available.

3 wheat loaves × $4 = $12
$40 − $12 = $28

9 cinnamon buns × $2 = $18
$28 − $18 = $10

10 muffins × $1 = $10
$10 − $10 = $0

All calculations are correct. My gift basket has 3 wheat loaves, 9 cinnamon buns, and 10 muffins. The total is exactly $40.

Convince Me! Be Precise Is there another way to make a gift basket that totals exactly $40? Explain.

☆ Guided Practice

Be Precise

Use the graph on the previous page. Suppose Bella wanted to make a gift basket worth $25 instead. The gift basket must also have more wheat loaves than muffins. Show one way Bella can make the gift basket.

To be precise, you need to check that the words, numbers, symbols, and units you use are correct and that your calculations are accurate.

1. What given information will you use to solve?

2. Show and explain one way Bella can make the gift basket.

☆ Independent Practice ☆

Be Precise

Derek is making a tile pattern that will be 30 inches long. The graph shows how many of each length of tile Derek has. He wants to use more than one of each length of tile in his pattern. Show one way to make the pattern.

3. What given information will you use to solve?

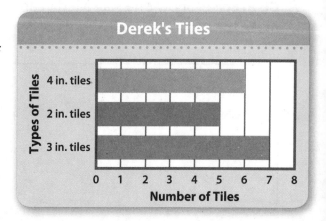

Derek's Tiles

Types of Tiles: 4 in. tiles, 2 in. tiles, 3 in. tiles

Number of Tiles: 0 1 2 3 4 5 6 7 8

4. Show and explain one way Derek can make the pattern.

Problem Solving

Picture Planning

Marta has $50 to spend on sketches. She wants to display them in an array of 3 rows, with 4 sketches in each row. Marta wants to include each type of sketch at least two times in her array.

Sketch Types and Pricing	
Landscape ($2 each)	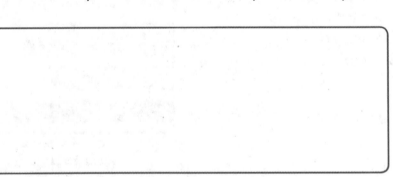
Animal ($4 each)	
Portrait ($10 each)	

Each □ = 2 sketches in stock.
Each ⊏ = 1 sketch in stock.

5. Reasoning How many sketches does Marta want?

6. Make Sense and Persevere What is a good plan for solving the problem?

7. Be Precise Show one way Marta can buy sketches to make the array. Use math words and symbols to explain.

> Be precise when analyzing the symbols, words, and numbers displayed in a picture graph.

8. Generalize Suppose Marta wants to make an array of 4 rows, with 3 sketches in each row. Would your answer still work? Explain.

Point & Tally

Find a partner. Get paper and a pencil. Each partner chooses a different color: light blue or dark blue.

Partner 1 and Partner 2 each point to a black number at the same time. Both partners multiply those numbers.

If the answer is on your color, you get a tally mark. Partners then write the remaining facts in the fact family. Work until one partner has seven tally marks.

I can ...
multiply and divide within 100.

I can also make math argument

Partner 1

| 5 |
| 8 |
| 4 |
| 3 |
| 10 |

48	90	35	20
50	72	27	9
60	30	12	15
45	18	27	25
36	28	21	56
40	56	70	24

Partner 2

| 7 |
| 3 |
| 9 |
| 5 |
| 6 |

Tally Marks for Partner 1

Tally Marks for Partner 2

Vocabulary Review

Word List

- data
- frequency table
- graph
- key
- scale
- scaled bar graph
- scaled picture graph
- survey

Understand Vocabulary

Rainy Days

| April | ☂ ☂ ☂ ☂ ☂ ☂ |
| May | ☂ ☂ ☂ ☂ |

Each ☂ = 2 days.

Graph A

Complete each sentence with *scaled picture graph*, *scaled bar graph*, *key*, or *scale*.

1. The _____ in Graph A shows that each umbrella represents 2 days.

2. Graph A is a _____.

3. The _____ in Graph B increases by 5.

4. Graph B is a _____.

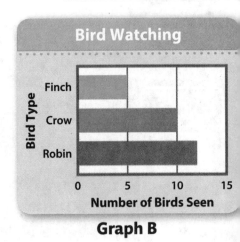

Graph B

Write T for *True* or F for *False*.

_____ **5.** A survey is the only way to collect data.

_____ **6.** A scaled bar graph has a key.

_____ **7.** Data from a frequency table can be used to make a scaled bar graph.

Use Vocabulary in Writing

8. Suppose you found out the number and type of pets your classmates have. Explain how you can display that information. Use at least 3 terms from the Word List in your answer.

Name_____

| Set A | pages 253–256 |

Picture graphs use pictures or parts of pictures to represent data.

The scale is the number each picture represents. The key explains the scale that is used.

Caps on Sale

Baseball	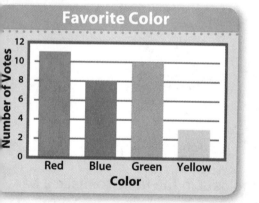
Basketball	
Racing	

Each 🧢 = 10 caps.   Each 🧢 = 5 caps.

Bar graphs use bars to represent data. You can use a scale to find how much a bar represents.

Favorite Color

Number of Votes — scale 0 to 12

Red Blue Green Yellow
Color

Each line in this bar graph represents 2 votes.

Remember to use a key or scale. The number of pictures in picture graphs and the lengths of bars in bar graphs help to compare data.

Reteaching

In **1–3**, use the picture graph on the left.

1. How many more baseball caps are on sale than racing caps?

2. How many more baseball caps are on sale than basketball and racing caps combined?

3. How many fewer basketball caps are on sale than baseball caps?

In **4–7**, use the bar graph on the left.

4. Which color got the most votes? How many votes did that color get?

5. How many fewer votes were for yellow than for green?

6. How many more votes were for red than for blue?

7. What is the difference between the votes for red and the votes for blue and yellow combined?

This frequency table shows data about the number of coins Mark has.

DATA

Mark's Coins		
Coin	Tally	Number of Coins
Penny	ℋℋ ///	8
Nickel	ℋℋ ℋℋ	10
Dime	ℋℋ /	6

You can use the data to make a picture graph. Picture graphs include a title, symbol, and a key to show the scale.

Mark's Coins	
Coin	Number of Coins
Penny	●●●●
Nickel	●●●●●
Dime	●●●

Each ● = 2 coins.

In this picture graph, each symbol equals 2 coins.

You also can use the data to make a bar graph.

1. Label the bottom and side of the graph.

2. Choose a scale.

3. Draw a bar for each type of coin.

4. Include a title.

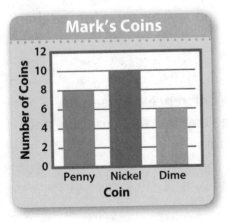

Remember that a frequency table includes tally marks or numbers. A picture graph uses pictures to show data.

In **1** and **2**, use the frequency table below.

Dan's class voted for their favorite pet. The results are shown in this frequency table.

Favorite Pet		
Pet	Tally	Number
Bird	////	
Dog	ℋℋ ℋℋ ////	
Fish	ℋℋ /	
Cat	ℋℋ ///	

1. Complete the frequency table.

2. Use the data in the frequency table to make a picture graph.

3. Use the data in the table to make a bar graph.

Name_____

You can use data from bar graphs or picture graphs to draw conclusions.

In a picture graph, Erica recorded the number of magazines she read. How many more magazines did she read in April and May combined than in June?

Magazines Read

You can solve 2-step data problems.

There are 6 symbols for April and May. There are 3 symbols for June.

$6 - 3 = 3$. There are 3 more symbols for April and May.

Each symbol represents 2 magazines. $3 \times 2 = 6$. Erica read 6 more magazines in April and May than in June.

Remember you can use tables and graphs to make comparisons. Sometimes you need to find and answer hidden questions.

In **1–6**, use the picture graph below.

Trees in Park

Each 🌳 = 6 trees.

1. How many more maple trees than elm trees are there?

2. How many fewer beech trees are there than maple trees?

3. How many trees are **NOT** maple trees?

4. How many more maple and beech trees combined are there than oak trees?

5. How many fewer oak trees are there than beech and elm trees combined?

6. If the city wants to have 24 elm trees, how many more elm trees does it need to plant? Explain how to solve.

Think about these questions to help you **attend to precision**.

Thinking Habits

- Am I using numbers, units, and symbols appropriately?

- Am I using the correct definitions?

- Am I calculating accurately?

- Is my answer clear?

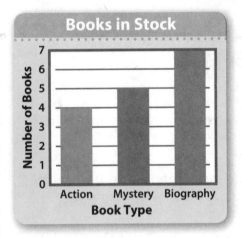

Books in Stock

Remember to use words, numbers, and symbols to show your reasoning.

In **1** and **2**, use the bar graph at the left to solve.

Jackie has $50 to spend on books. She has made a bar graph to show the number of each type of book the store has in stock. Jackie wants to buy at least 2 of each type of book. Show one way Jackie can spend $50 on books.

Action books cost $5.

Biographies cost $10.

Mysteries cost $5.

1. What given information will you use to solve the problem?

2. Show one way Jackie can spend $50 on books. Use math words and symbols to explain your thinking.

Name_____

1. Use the data from the frequency table to make a picture graph.

Favorite Sandwiches		
Sandwich	**Tally**	**Frequency**
Turkey	⑦⑦⑦⑦ ⑦⑦⑦⑦ ////	14
Ham	⑦⑦⑦⑦ /	6
Tuna	//	2
Egg	////	4

A. Circle the key you will use.

 = 1 sandwich   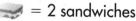 = 2 sandwiches

 = 3 sandwiches   = 4 sandwiches

B. Draw a picture graph.

2. Use the data from the picture graph you made in Question 1. How many students did **NOT** choose turkey as their favorite sandwich?

Ⓐ 10   Ⓒ 13

Ⓑ 12   Ⓓ 14

3. Jamie's class made a picture graph to show how many hours they volunteered each week. In which week or weeks did the class volunteer 9 hours?

Hours Volunteered in October

Week 1
Week 2
Week 3

Each = 2 hours. Each = 1 hour.

Ⓐ Week 1   Ⓒ Week 3

Ⓑ Week 2   Ⓓ Weeks 1 and 3

4. Look at the picture graph above. How many total hours did the class volunteer?

5. How many more hours did the class volunteer in Weeks 2 and 3 combined than in Week 1?

6. Mr. Thomas's class made a bar graph of the number of brothers and sisters each student has. How many students in the class have 1 brother or sister?

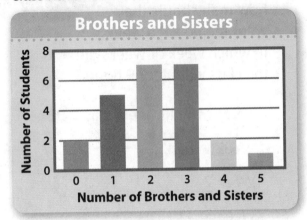

Brothers and Sisters

Number of Students (y-axis: 0, 2, 4, 6, 8)

Number of Brothers and Sisters (x-axis: 0, 1, 2, 3, 4, 5)

Ⓐ 1

Ⓑ 2

Ⓒ 5

Ⓓ 7

7. Compare students with 3 brothers and sisters and students with 0 brothers and sisters. How many more students have 3 brothers and sisters?

☐ more student(s)

8. How many students in the class have 2 or more brothers and sisters?

9. Beth is making a bar graph to compare how many marbles of each color she has. She has 25 blue marbles, 35 red marbles, 5 green marbles, and 15 yellow marbles. Which scale makes the most sense for Beth to use with her graph?

Ⓐ Each grid line equals 1 marble.

Ⓑ Each grid line equals 2 marbles.

Ⓒ Each grid line equals 5 marbles.

Ⓓ Each grid line equals 20 marbles.

10. Use the information in Question 9 to make a bar graph of Beth's marbles.

Beth's Marbles

Number of Marbles (y-axis)

Marble Color (x-axis: Blue, Red, Green, Yellow)

11. Select all the statements that are true. Use the information from Question 9.

☐ Beth has more green and yellow marbles combined than blue ones.

☐ Beth has as many blue and yellow marbles combined as red ones.

☐ Beth has more red marbles than blue and green ones combined.

☐ Beth has fewer yellow marbles than blue and green ones combined.

☐ Beth has fewer red marbles than green and yellow ones combined.

12. The school had a fundraiser in the first part of the school year. In which month did the school make the most money?

Ⓐ September

Ⓑ October

Ⓒ November

Ⓓ December

13. Look at the bar graph above. Suppose $45 was raised in January. Where would the bar end?

14. Did the school earn more money in September and October combined than in November? Explain.

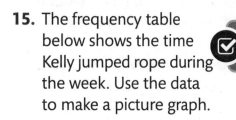
15. The frequency table below shows the time Kelly jumped rope during the week. Use the data to make a picture graph.

Minutes Kelly Jumped Rope		
Day	Tally	Number of Minutes
Monday	𝍷𝍷𝍷 𝍷𝍷𝍷 𝍷𝍷𝍷	15
Tuesday	𝍷𝍷𝍷 𝍷𝍷𝍷 𝍷𝍷𝍷 𝍷𝍷𝍷	20
Wednesday	𝍷𝍷𝍷 𝍷𝍷𝍷	10
Thursday	𝍷𝍷𝍷	5
Friday	𝍷𝍷𝍷 𝍷𝍷𝍷 𝍷𝍷𝍷 𝍷𝍷𝍷	20

A. Circle the key you will use.

⌇ = 2 minutes   ⌇ = 5 minutes

⌇ = 10 minutes   ⌇ = 15 minutes

B. Draw a picture graph.

Minutes Kelly Jumped Rope	
Monday	
Tuesday	
Wednesday	
Thursday	
Friday	

16. Look at the picture graphs below. Which type of book was chosen by the same number of students in each class?

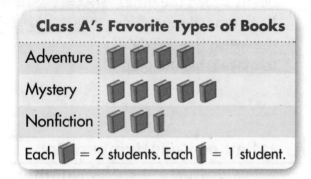

Class A's Favorite Types of Books

Adventure

Mystery

Nonfiction

Each 📙 = 2 students. Each 📗 = 1 student.

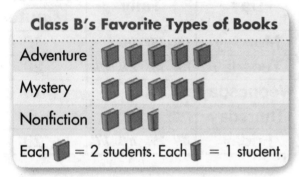

Class B's Favorite Types of Books

Adventure

Mystery

Nonfiction

Each 📙 = 2 students. Each 📗 = 1 student.

Ⓐ Adventure

Ⓑ Mystery

Ⓒ Nonfiction

Ⓓ Not here

---

17. How many students in Classes A and B chose mystery as their favorite type of book?

18. A. Ellie has $22 to spend on art supplies. She wants to buy at least one canvas, one tube of paint, and one brush. Which art supplies can she buy if she spends all of her money?

Art Supplies

Number to Buy

6

4

2

0

Canvas   Tube of   Brush
($4 each)   Paint   ($2 each)
            ($3 each)

Item

B. Describe the given information and solve the problem. Explain your thinking and show the supplies she can buy on the bar graph.

Name_____

Twisting Balloons

Miles twisted balloons into different animals at his daughter's birthday party. The **Balloons Used** picture graph shows the different color balloons he used.

Use the **Balloons Used** picture graph to answer Questions **1** and **2**.

1. How many more green balloons than yellow balloons did Miles use? Explain.

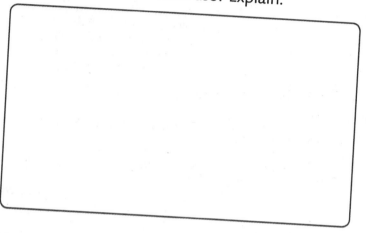

2. How many fewer blue balloons were used than all of the other colors combined? Explain.

e the **Balloons Used** picture graph and the
lloons Bought** bar graph to answer Question **3**.

. How many balloons does Miles have left? Complete the table below.

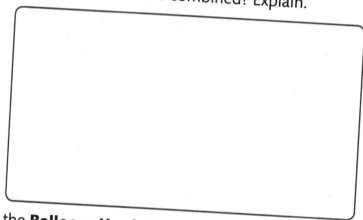

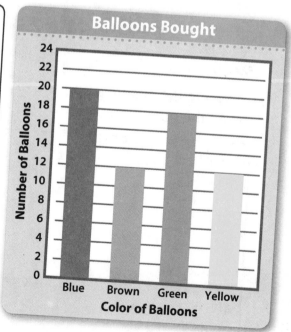

Color	Bought	Used	Left
Blue			
Brown			
Green			
Yellow			

Use your response to Question 3 to answer Question 4.

4. Complete the bar graph to show how many balloons are left.

The **Balloon Shapes and Colors** table shows the number and color of balloons Miles needs to use to make each balloon animal. Use your response to Question 4 and the **Balloon Shapes and Colors** table to answer Question 5.

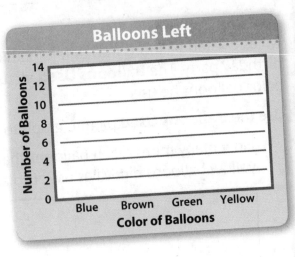

5. Miles plans to use all of the balloons that are left and wants to make at least one of each balloon animal. Make a picture graph to show one way Miles can finish using the balloons.

Part A

Circle the key you will use.

 = 1 balloon animal   = 2 balloon animals

 = 3 balloon animals   = 4 balloon animals

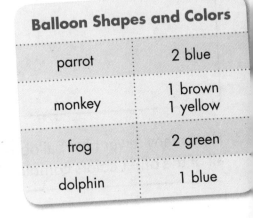

Balloon Shapes and Colors

parrot	2 blue
monkey	1 brown 1 yellow
frog	2 green
dolphin	1 blue

Part B

Complete the picture graph and explain how you solved the problem.

Balloon Animals

Parrot	
Monkey	
Frog	
Dolphin	

Glossary

A

A.M. The time between midnight and noon.

acute angle An angle that is open less than a right angle.

addends Numbers added together to give a sum.
Example: $2 + 7 = 9$

Addend   Addend

angle A figure that is formed where two sides meet.

angle measure The degrees of an angle.

area The number of unit squares needed to cover a region.

array A way of displaying objects in equal rows and columns.

Associative (Grouping) Property of Addition The grouping of addends can be changed and the sum will be the same.

Associative (Grouping) Property of Multiplication The grouping of factors can be changed and the product will be the same.

B

benchmark fraction A commonly used fraction such as $\frac{1}{4}, \frac{1}{3}, \frac{1}{2}, \frac{2}{3}$, and $\frac{3}{4}$.

C

capacity (liquid volume) The amount a container can hold measured in liquid units.

centimeter (cm) A metric unit of length.

column An arrangement of objects or numbers, one above another.

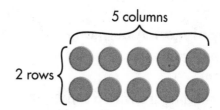

5 columns

2 rows

Commutative (Order) Property of Addition Numbers can be added in any order and the sum will be the same.

Commutative (Order) Property of Multiplication Numbers can be multiplied in any order and the product will be the same.

compare To decide if one number is greater than or less than another number.

compatible numbers Numbers that are easy to add, subtract, multiply, or divide mentally.

compensation Choosing numbers close to the numbers in a problem to make computation easier and then adjusting the answer for the numbers chosen.

compose To combine different parts.

concave polygon A polygon that has 1 or more angles pointing inward.

conjecture A statement that is believed to be true, but it has not been proven.

cone A solid figure with a circle as its base and a curved surface that meets at a point.

convex polygon A polygon in which all angles point outward.

cube A solid figure with 6 same-size squares as its faces.

cylinder A solid figure with 2 circular bases.

D

data Pieces of information.

decompose Breaking a number into parts.
Example: $\frac{2}{5}$ can be broken into $\frac{1}{5} + \frac{1}{5}$.

degrees (°) A unit of measure for angles.

denominator The number below the fraction bar in a fraction, which shows the total number of equal parts.

difference The answer when subtracting one number from another.

digits The symbols 0, 1, 2, 3, 4, 5, 6, 7, 8, and 9 used to write numbers.

Distributive Property A multiplication fact can be broken apart into the sum of two other multiplication facts.
Example: $5 \times 4 = (2 \times 4) + (3 \times 4)$

dividend The number to be divided.
Example: $63 \div 9 = 7$

↑
Dividend

division An operation that tells how many equal groups there are or how many are in each group.

divisor The number by which another number is divided.
Example: $63 \div 9 = 7$

↑
Divisor

dollar sign A symbol ($) used to indicate money.

E

edge A line segment where 2 faces meet in a solid figure.

eighth One of 8 equal parts of a whole.

elapsed time The total amount of time that passes from the starting time to the ending time.

equal (equality) When the two sides of an equation have the same value.

equal groups Groups that have the same number of items.

equation A number sentence that uses an equal sign (=) to show that the value on its left side is the same as the value on its right side.

equilateral triangle A triangle with all sides the same length.

equivalent fractions Fractions that name the same part of a whole or the same location on a number line.

estimate To give an approximate number or answer.

even number A whole number that can be divided by 2 with none left over.

expanded form A number written as the sum of the values of its digits.
Example: $476 = 400 + 70 + 6$

F

face A flat surface of a solid that cannot roll.

fact family A group of related facts using the same numbers.

factors Numbers that are multiplied together to give a product.
Example: $7 \times 3 = 21$

↑ ↑
Factor Factor

foot (ft) A customary unit of length. 1 foot equals 12 inches.

fourth One of 4 equal parts of a whole.

fraction A symbol, such as $\frac{1}{2}$, used to name a part of a whole, a part of a set, or a location on a number line.

frequency table A table used to show the number of times something occurs.

gram (g) A metric unit of mass, the amount of matter in an object.

half (halves) One of 2 equal parts of a whole.

half hour A unit of time equal to 30 minutes.

hexagon A polygon with 6 sides.

hour A unit of time equal to 60 minutes.

I

Identity (Zero) Property of Addition The sum of any number and zero is that same number.

Identity (One) Property of Multiplication The product of any number and 1 is that number.

inch (in.) A customary unit of length.

intersecting lines Lines that cross at one point.

inverse operations Two operations that undo each other.

K

key The explanation for what each symbol represents in a pictograph.

kilogram (kg) A metric unit of mass, the amount of matter in an object. One kilogram equals 1,000 grams.

kilometer (km) A metric unit of length. One kilometer equals 1,000 meters.

L

line A straight path of points that is endless in both directions.

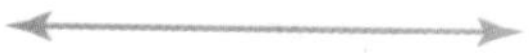

line plot A way to organize data on a number line, where each dot or X represents one number in a set of data.

line segment A part of a line that has 2 endpoints.

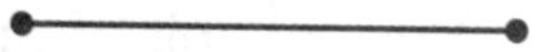

liter (L) A metric unit of capacity. One liter equals 1,000 milliliters.

M

mass A measure of the amount of matter in an object.

meter (m) A metric unit of length. One meter equals 100 centimeters.

mile (mi) A customary unit of length. One mile equals 5,280 feet.

millimeter (mm) A metric unit of length. 1,000 millimeters = 1 meter.

minute A unit of time equal to 60 seconds.

mixed number A number with a whole number part and a fraction part.
Example: $2\frac{3}{4}$

multiple The product of a given whole number and any non-zero whole number.
Example: 4, 8, 12, and 16 are multiples of 4.

multiplication An operation that gives the total number when you join equal groups.

N

nearest fourth inch A measurement that ends with a $\frac{1}{4}$, $\frac{2}{4}$, $\frac{3}{4}$, or full inch.

nearest half inch A measurement that ends with a $\frac{1}{2}$ or full inch.

not equal When two sides of a number sentence do not have the same value.

number line A line that shows numbers in order using a scale.
Example:

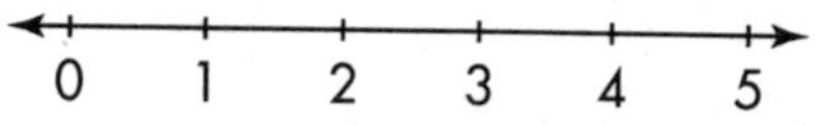

numerator The number above the fraction bar in a fraction, which shows how many equal parts are described.

obtuse angle An angle that is open more than a right angle.

octagon A polygon with 8 sides.

odd number A whole number that cannot be divided by 2 with none left over.

open number line A number line which only displays the numbers being computed.

order To arrange numbers from least to greatest or from greatest to least.

ounce (oz) A customary unit of weight.

P.M. The time between noon and midnight.

parallel lines Lines that never cross each other.

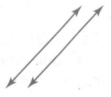

parallel sides Sides of a polygon that go in the exact same direction; if the sides cross when they are made longer, they are not parallel.

parallelogram A quadrilateral with 2 pairs of parallel sides.

pentagon A polygon with 5 sides.

perimeter The distance around a figure.

perpendicular lines Two intersecting lines that form right angles.

pint (pt) A customary unit of capacity. One pint equals 2 cups.

place value The value given to the place a digit has in a number.
Example: In 946, the place value of the digit 9 is *hundreds*.

point An exact position often marked by a dot.

polygon A closed figure made up of straight line segments.

pound (lb) A customary unit of weight. One pound equals 16 ounces.

product The answer to a multiplication problem.

Q

quadrilateral A polygon with 4 sides.

quart (qt) A customary unit of capacity. One quart equals 2 pints.

quarter hour A unit of time equal to 15 minutes.

quotient The answer to a division problem.

R

ray A part of a line that has one endpoint and continues endlessly in one direction.

rectangle A parallelogram with 4 right angles.

rectangular prism A solid figure with 6 rectangular faces.

regroup (regrouping) To name a whole number in a different way.
Example: 28 = 1 ten 18 ones

remainder The number that is left over after dividing.
Example: 31 ÷ 7 = 4 R3

Remainder

rhombus A parallelogram with all sides the same length.

right angle An angle that forms a square corner.

round To replace a number with a number that tells about how much or how many to the nearest ten, hundred, thousand, and so on.
Example: 42 rounded to the nearest 10 is 40.

row An arrangement of objects or numbers, one to the side of another.

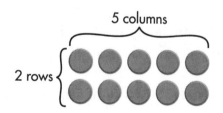

S

scale The numbers that show the units used on a graph.

scaled bar graph a graph that uses bars to show data.

scaled picture graph a graph that uses pictures to show data.

second A unit of time. 60 seconds equal 1 minute.

side A line segment forming part of a polygon.

sixth One of 6 equal parts of a whole.

solid figure A figure that has length, width, and height.

sphere A solid figure in the shape of a ball.

square A parallelogram with 4 right angles and all sides the same length.

square unit A measure of area.

standard form A way to write a number showing only its digits.
Example: 845

straight angle An angle that forms a straight line.

sum The answer to an addition problem.

survey To collect information by asking a number of people the same question and recording their answers.

T

tally mark A mark used to record data on a tally chart.
Example: 𝍷𝍷𝍷𝍷𝍷 = 5

third One of 3 equal parts of a whole.

time interval An amount of time.

trapezoid A quadrilateral with only one pair of parallel sides.

triangle A polygon with 3 sides.

triangular prism A solid figure with two triangular faces.

unit angle An angle with a measurement of 1 degree.

unit fraction A fraction representing one part of a whole that has been divided into equal parts; it always has a numerator of 1.

unit square a square with sides 1 unit long, used to measure area.

unknown A symbol that stands for a number in an equation.

vertex of a polygon The point where two sides of a polygon meet.

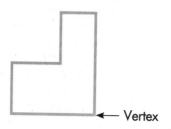

← Vertex

week A unit of time equal to 7 days.

weight A measure of how heavy an object is.

word form A number written in words. *Example:* 325 = three hundred twenty-five

yard (yd) A customary unit of length. One yard equals 3 feet or 36 inches.

Zero Property of Multiplication The product of any number and zero is zero.

⠿enVision® Mathematics

Photographs

Photo locators denoted as follows: Top (T), Center (C), Bottom (B), Left (L), Right (R), Background (Bkgd)

1 Gemenacom/Shutterstock; **3** (T) Pisaphotography/Shutterstock, (C) NASA images/Shutterstock, (B) Tetra Images/Alamy Stock Photo; **4** (Bkgrd) Boris Bulychev/Shutterstock, ArtCookStudio/Shutterstock **37** Jacek Chabraszewski/Fotolia; **39** (T) Harry B. Lamb/Shutterstock, (B) John Green/Cal Sport Media/Alamy Stock Photo; **40** (T) John Green/Cal Sport Media/Alamy Stock Photo, (B) Monkey Business Images/Shutterstock **73** Pk7comcastnet/Fotolia; **75** (T) Monkey Business Images/Shutterstock, (C) David M. Schrader/Shutterstock, (B) Jeff Kinsey/Shutterstock; **76** (Bkgrd) NavinTar/Shutterstock, MO_SES Premium/Shutterstock, MO_SES Premium/Shutterstock **113** Christopher Dodge /Shutterstock; **115** (T) Joe Petro/Icon Sportswire/Getty Images, (B) Olekcii Mach/Alamy Stock Photo; **116** (T) Image Source/REX/Shutterstock, (B) Stockbroker/123RF **165** Ann Worthy/Shutterstock; **167** (T) STLJB/Shutterstock, (C) Bmcent1/iStock/Getty Images, (B) Monkey Business Images/Shutterstock; **168** (Bkgrd) Ewastudio/123RF, Versus Studio/Shutterstock; **180** Ian Scott/Fotolia **205** Marques/Shutterstock; **207** (T) Stephanie Starr/Alamy Stock Photo, (B) Hero Images Inc./Alamy Stock Photo; **208** (T) Compassionate Eye Foundation/DigitalVision/Getty Images, (B) Spass/Shutterstock **249** Barbara Helgason/Fotolia; **251** (T) Africa Studio/Shutterstock, (C) Tonyz20/Shutterstock, (B) Ermolaev Alexander/Shutterstock; **252** (Bkgrd) Oleg Mayorov/Shutterstock, LightSecond/Shutterstock **285** Erni/Shutterstock; **287** (T) Richard Thornton/Shutterstock,

(B) Hxdyl/Shutterstock; **288** (T) The Linke/E+/Getty Images, (B) David Grossman/Alamy Stock Photo; **308** Goodshoot/Getty Images; **310** Keren Su/Corbis/Getty Images; **320** Rabbit75_fot/Fotolia **333** Arnold John Labrentz/ShutterStock; **335** (T) Judy Kennamer/Shutterstock, (C) ESB Professional/Shutterstock, (B) Zuma Press, Inc./Alamy Stock Photo; **336** (Bkgrd) Monkey Business Images/Shutterstock, Faberr Ink/Shutterstock, **346** (L) hotshotsworldwide/Fotolia, (C) Imagebroker/Alamy, (R) Imagebroker/Alamy; **348** John Luke/Index open; **356** David R. Frazier Photolibrary, Inc/Alamy **377** Sam D'Cruz/Fotolia; **379** (T) Stephen Van Horn/Shutterstock, (B) FS11/Shutterstock; **380** (T) Shafera photo/Shutterstock, (B) Impact Photography/Shutterstock; **384** Palou/Fotolia **405** Nancy Gill/ShutterStock; **407** (T) 123RF, (C) Light field studios/123RF, (B) Hurst Photo/Shutterstock; **408** (Bkgrd) Igor Bulgarin/Shutterstock, Bartolomiej Pietrzyk/Shutterstock, Ianinas/Shutterstock **433** B.G. Smith/Shutterstock; **435** (T) Andy Deitsch/Shutterstock, (B) Liunian/Shutterstock; **436** (T) Holbox/Shutterstock, (B) Hannamariah/Shutterstock; **481** Cathy Keifer/ShutterStock **483** (T) Cheryl Ann Quigley/Shutterstock, (C) Niko Nomad/Shutterstock, (B) Mavadee/Shutterstock; **484** (Bkgrd) Photo.ua/Shutterstock, India Picture/Shutterstock **531** (T) Iassedesignen/Shutterstock, (B) Rawpixel/Shutterstock; **532** (T) 581356/Shutterstock, (B) S_oleg/Shutterstock; **547** (T) Photolibrary/Photos to go, (B) Simple Stock Shot; **548** (L) Ecopic/iStock/Getty Images, (R) Simple Stock Shot; **555** (T) Stockdisc/Punch Stock, (C) Jupiter Images, (B) Getty Images **581** Amy Myers/Shutterstock; **583** (T) Rhona Wise/Epa/REX/Shutterstock, (C) Giocalde/Shutterstock, (B) Anmbph/Shutterstock; **584** (Bkgrd) Peter Turner Photography/Shutterstock, (T) Peyker/Shutterstock, (B) Michael Leslie/Shutterstock **609** Photocreo Bednarek/Fotolia; **611** (T) Margouillat Photo/Shutterstock, (B) Ksenia Palimski/Shutterstock; **612** (T) Topten22photo/Shutterstock, (B) Hola Images/Alamy Stock Photo